ZAGAT®

New Jersey Restaurants
2007/08

LOCAL EDITORS
Sharon Gintzler and Robert Strauss
CONSULTING EDITOR
Andrea Clurfeld
STAFF EDITOR
Robert Seixas

Published and distributed by
Zagat Survey, LLC
4 Columbus Circle
New York, NY 10019
T: 212.977.6000
E: newjersey@zagat.com
www.zagat.com

ACKNOWLEDGMENTS

We thank Lizzie Fuerst, Maria Gallagher, Larry Gershon, A.S. Gintzler, Phyllis Gintzler, Craig LaBan, Fran Levine, Shannon and Eileen Mullen, Steven Shukow, Traci Turi and Nolan Willence, as well as the following members of our staff: Emily Parsons (senior associate editor), Rachel McConlogue (assistant editor), Sean Beachell, Maryanne Bertollo, Sandy Cheng, Reni Chin, Larry Cohn, Caitlin Eichelberger, Jeff Freier, Shelley Gallagher, Caroline Hatchett, Roy Jacob, Natalie Lebert, Mike Liao, Dave Makulec, Andre Pilette, Becky Ruthenburg, Thomas Sheehan, Kilolo Strobert, Sharon Yates and Kyle Zolner.

Contents

About This Survey

Here are the results of our 2007/08 New Jersey Restaurants Survey, covering 857 establishments. Like all our guides, it's based on the collective opinions of thousands of savvy consumers. As a companion to this guide, we also publish *New Jersey Shore Restaurants*, along with guides to the next-door cities of New York and Philadelphia.

WHO PARTICIPATED: Input from over 5,797 avid diners forms the basis for the ratings and reviews in this guide (their comments are shown in quotation marks within the reviews). Of these surveyors, 49% are women, 51% men; the breakdown by age is 9% in their 20s; 23%, 30s; 22%, 40s; 25%, 50s; and 21%, 60s or above. Collectively they bring roughly 911,000 meals worth of experience to this Survey. We sincerely thank each of these participants – this book is really "theirs."

HELPFUL LISTS: Whether you're looking for a celebratory meal, a hot scene or a bargain bite, our lists can help you find exactly the right place. See Most Popular (page 7), Key Newcomers (page 7), Top Ratings (pages 9–14) and Best Buys (page 15). We've also provided 48 handy indexes.

OUR EDITORS: We are especially grateful to our local editors, Sharon Gintzler, who writes about food and dining for *The Star-Ledger*; Robert Strauss, feature writer and former TV critic for the *Asbury Park Press*; and our consulting editor, Andrea Clurfeld, restaurant critic and food editor of the *Asbury Park Press*.

ABOUT ZAGAT: This marks our 28th year reporting on the shared experiences of consumers like you. What started in 1979 as a hobby involving 200 of our friends has come a long way. Today we have over 300,000 surveyors and now cover dining, entertaining, golf, hotels, movies, music, nightlife, resorts, shopping, spas, theater and tourist attractions worldwide.

SHARE YOUR OPINION: We invite you to join any of our upcoming surveys – just register at **zagat.com,** where you can rate and review establishments year-round. Each participant will receive a free copy of the resulting guide when published.

AVAILABILITY: Zagat guides are available in all major bookstores, by subscription at **zagat.com** and for use on mobile devices via **Zagat To Go.**

FEEDBACK: There is always room for improvement, thus we invite your comments and suggestions about any aspect of our performance. Just contact us at newjersey@zagat.com.

New York, NY
May 9, 2007

Nina and Tim Zagat

What's New

From high-rolling debuts in Atlantic City to a spate of Eastern-accented newcomers throughout the state, it's been an active year for New Jersey restaurants and their customers. Here's a snapshot of the scene.

SOUTH JERSEY STORY: Where there's gambling, celebrity chefs and owners will follow. Megawatt names are leading Atlantic City out of the culinary Dark Ages of marginal reef 'n' beeferies. Now, slot players can dine at Bobby Flay Steak, SeaBlue (from West Coast's Michael Mina) and Wolfgang Puck American Grille, all within the Borgata Hotel, Casino & Spa. And Philly superstar Stephen Starr has landed Buddakan and Continental (spin-offs of his wildly successful Philadelphia ventures) in the Pier at Caesars.

THE POT KEEPS MELTING: The globalization of the state is in full force given the influx of Eastern-influenced eateries. Two Middle Easterners, Addiwan and Lalezar, have opened in Montclair, one of the toughest proving grounds for restaurants. DabbaWalla, in Summit, and New Brunswick's Piquant Bread Bar are sparking interest in globally inspired Indian cuisine. Pithari Taverna, in Highland Park, brings focus to classic Greek cooking, while Englewood's Akai Lounge is helping sustain the popularity of sushi houses.

SOME LIKE IT HAUTE: Although "casual" is the buzzword of the day, the appetite for fine dining simply won't go away, and haute-inspired restaurants are sprouting faster than truffles in late autumn. Not only has haute gone modern, but the genre is frequently venturing into uncharted territory: cuisines other than French and Continental. Some examples include: Tenafly's Axia Taverna, a stylish Greek designed by Tony Chi; and two spiffy newcomers, Mehndi (Indian) and Ming II (Pan-Asian), both operating under the same Morristown roof.

BYO-LAND: Our state's arcane BYO laws have more twists and turns than Monaco's Grand Prix circuit. Surveyors, though, clearly see a benefit to bringing their own, with 75% saluting the policy. And to be sure, some restaurateurs also see a positive, since BYO is a selling point in itself. While alcohol sales can account for at least a third of a restaurant's profit, buying a license here easily runs in to the six figures (unlike in NYC, where it's less than $1,000). Talk about markup!

BREAKING NEWS: The Ryland Inn has closed due to a water main break. No word yet on its reopening date.

AT THE CHECK-OUT: Yes, you'll have to cough up more than a few coins to cover most meals in Jersey, where the average cost is $36.95 (compared to $33.19 nationally). But even though 68% of surveyors report spending more than they did two years ago, most find eating out here well worth the money.

New Jersey
May 9, 2007

Sharon Gintzler
Robert Strauss
Andrea Clurfeld

MOST POPULAR

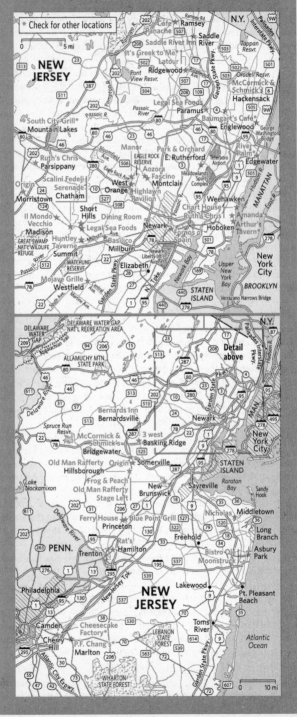

Most Popular

Each surveyor has been asked to name his or her five favorite places. This list reflects their choices.

1	Nicholas	**21**	Huntley Taverne
2	Cheesecake Factory	**22**	3 west
3	Legal Sea Foods	**23**	P.F. Chang's
4	River Palm	**24**	Ferry House
5	Amanda's	**25**	South City Grill
6	Origin	**26**	McCormick/Schmick
7	Scalini Fedeli	**27**	Manor
8	Frog & Peach	**28**	Dining Room
9	Highlawn Pavilion	**29**	Old Man Rafferty
10	Baumgart's Café	**30**	Bistro Olé
11	Serenade	**31**	Il Mondo Vecchio
12	Saddle River Inn	**32**	It's Greek To Me
13	Fascino	**33**	Rat's
14	Bernards Inn	**34**	Park & Orchard
15	Cafe Panache	**35**	Chart House
16	Blue Point Grill	**36**	Arthur's Tavern
17	Basilico	**37**	Aozora
18	Ruth's Chris	**38**	Fornos of Spain
19	Moonstruck	**39**	Mojave Grille
20	Latour	**40**	Stage Left

It's obvious that many of the restaurants on the above list are among New Jersey's most expensive, but if popularity were calibrated to price, we suspect that a number of other restaurants would join the above ranks. Given the fact that both our surveyors and readers love to discover dining bargains, we have added a list of 80 Best Buys on page 15. These are restaurants that give real quality at extremely reasonable prices.

KEY NEWCOMERS

Following is our editors' take on some of the year's most notable arrivals. (For a full list, see page 189.)

Avenue	daddy O
Axia Taverna	David Burke
Blue Bottle Café	Kitchen 233
Bobby Flay Steak	Mehndi
Buddakan	restaurant.mc
Catherine Lombardi	SeaBlue
Continental	Thyme Square
CulinAriane	Wolfgang Puck

Ratings & Symbols

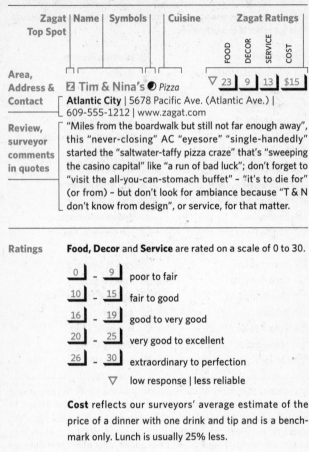

	Zagat Top Spot	Name	Symbols		Cuisine		Zagat Ratings			
							FOOD	DECOR	SERVICE	COST
Area, Address & Contact	**Z** Tim & Nina's ◑ *Pizza*						▽ 23	9	13	$15

Atlantic City | 5678 Pacific Ave. (Atlantic Ave.) | 609-555-1212 | www.zagat.com

Review, surveyor comments in quotes

"Miles from the boardwalk but still not far enough away", this "never-closing" AC "eyesore" "single-handedly" started the "saltwater-taffy pizza craze" that's "sweeping the casino capital" like "a run of bad luck"; don't forget to "visit the all-you-can-stomach buffet" – "it's to die for" (or from) – but don't look for ambiance because "T & N don't know from design", or service, for that matter.

Ratings

Food, Decor and **Service** are rated on a scale of 0 to 30.

0	–	9	poor to fair
10	–	15	fair to good
16	–	19	good to very good
20	–	25	very good to excellent
26	–	30	extraordinary to perfection
▽			low response | less reliable

Cost reflects our surveyors' average estimate of the price of a dinner with one drink and tip and is a benchmark only. Lunch is usually 25% less.

For **newcomers** or survey **write-ins** listed without ratings, the price range is indicated as follows:

I	$25 and below
M	$26 to $40
E	$41 to $65
VE	$66 or more

Symbols

Z	Zagat Top Spot (highest ratings, popularity and importance)
◑	serves after 11 PM
S	closed on Sunday
M	closed on Monday
≠	no credit cards accepted

Top Food Ratings

Ratings are to the left of names. Excludes places with low votes.

29 Nicholas	**26** Washington Inn
28 DeLorenzo's	Le Rendez-Vous
Chef's Table	David Burke
Cafe Panache	Sagami
Bay Ave. Trattoria	Ajihei
27 André's	Perryville Inn
SeaBlue	Black Duck
Saddle River Inn	Gables, The*
Serenade	Dining Room
Whispers	Augustino's
Scalini Fedeli	Fernandes Steak
Latour	Union Park Dining Rm.
Lorena's	La Isla
David Drake	Fascino
CulinAriane	Zoe's
Cafe Matisse	Mélange Cafe
Blue Bottle Café	Peter Shields*
Ebbitt Room	Stage Left
Chez Catherine	Le Fandy
White House	Taka*
410 Bank St.	Origin

BY CUISINE

AMERICAN (NEW)
29 Nicholas
27 André's
Saddle River Inn
Whispers
David Drake

AMERICAN (TRAD.)
28 Bay Ave. Trattoria
26 Washington Inn
Perryville Inn
Ram's Head Inn
25 Doris & Ed's

CARIBBEAN/CUBAN
26 La Isla
24 Casona
Rebecca's
21 Cuba Libre
Martino's

CHINESE
26 Far East Taste
24 Chengdu 46
Lotus Cafe
Meemah
23 Cathay 22

CONTINENTAL
23 Black Forest Inn
Stony Hill Inn
22 Beau Rivage
21 Court Street
Ho-Ho-Kus Inn

ECLECTIC
28 Cafe Panache
27 Cafe Matisse
26 Black Duck
Gables, The*
25 Anthony David's

FRENCH
27 Saddle River Inn
Latour
Lorena's
Chez Catherine
26 Zoe's

FRENCH (BISTRO)
28 Chef's Table
26 Le Rendez-Vous
Le Fandy
Indigo Moon
24 Bienvenue

* Indicates a tie with restaurant above

FRENCH (NEW)

27 Serenade
26 Origin
24 Rat's
23 Stage House
22 Brothers Moon

INDIAN

25 Karma Kafe
24 Moghul
23 Aangan
Passage to India
Saffron

ITALIAN

28 Bay Ave. Trattoria
27 Scalini Fedeli
26 Augustino's
Fascino
Chef Vola's
Mia
Il Capriccio
25 Anthony David's
Lu Nello
Portofino
Girasole
Giumarello's*

JAPANESE

26 Sagami
Ajihei
Taka
Sono Sushi
Yumi

MEDITERRANEAN

25 Varka Fish House
24 Moonstruck
Hamilton's Grill
Frescos
22 Vine

MEXICAN

24 El Meson
Charrito's
23 Los Amigos
Tortilla Press
Juanito's

PIZZA

28 DeLorenzo's
25 Grimaldi's Pizza
23 Il Forno Trattoria

22 Reservoir Tavern
Margherita's

SANDWICHES

27 White House
24 Kibitz Room
21 Sallee Tee's
20 Richard's
19 Jack Cooper's

SEAFOOD

27 SeaBlue
26 Dock's Oyster
25 Varka Fish House
Shipwreck Grill
Doris & Ed's

SOUTH AMERICAN/ PAN-LATIN

26 Cucharamama
25 Casa Solar
24 Zafra
Casona
23 Brasilia Grill

SOUTHERN/CAJUN

23 Silver Oak Bistro
22 Delta's
Indigo Smoke
20 Luchento's
19 Oddfellows

SPANISH/ PORTUGUESE

26 Fernandes Steak
25 Bistro Olé
24 Adega Grill
Tony Da Caneca
Casa Vasca

STEAKHOUSES

26 Fernandes Steak
25 River Palm
Old Homestead
24 Ruth's Chris
Palm

THAI

26 Origin
Far East Taste
25 Thai Thai
Siri's Thai French
Mie Thai

BY SPECIAL FEATURE

BREAKFAST

24 Zafra
23 Meil's
21 Christopher's
Mad Batter
19 Country Pancake

BRUNCH

26 Amanda's
25 Anthony David's
Verjus
24 Rat's
Zafra

BYO

28 Chef's Table
Cafe Panache
Bay Ave. Trattoria
27 Saddle River Inn
Whispers

CHILD-FRIENDLY

27 White House
410 Bank St.
26 Mélange Cafe
Far East Taste
Dock's Oyster

HOTEL DINING

27 SeaBlue
Borgata Hotel
Whispers
Hewitt Wellington
Ebbitt Room
Virginia Hotel
26 Gables, The
Green Gables Inn
Dining Room
Hilton at Short Hills

NEWCOMERS (RATED)

27 SeaBlue
CulinAriane
Blue Bottle Café
26 David Burke
24 Bobby Flay Steak

OFFBEAT

26 La Isla
Taka

Chef Vola's
Yumi
Cucharamama

PEOPLE-WATCHING

27 David Drake
26 Zoe's
Bernards Inn
Cucharamama
Mia

POWER SCENES

28 Cafe Panache
27 SeaBlue
Saddle River Inn
Serenade
Chez Catherine

SINGLES SCENES

26 Cucharamama
Mia
25 Shipwreck Grill
24 Atlantic B&G
Cenzino

TRENDY

28 DeLorenzo's
27 SeaBlue
Scalini Fedeli
Latour
Lorena's

WINNING WINE LISTS

29 Nicholas
27 SeaBlue
Serenade
Scalini Fedeli
David Drake

WORTH A TRIP

28 DeLorenzo's
Trenton
Cafe Panache
Ramsey
27 André's
Newton
SeaBlue
Atlantic City
Saddle River Inn
Saddle River

ATLANTIC CITY

27 SeaBlue
White House
26 Chef Vola's
Mia
Dock's Oyster

CAPE MAY/ WEST CAPE MAY

27 Ebbitt Room
410 Bank St.
26 Washington Inn
Black Duck
Union Park Dining Rm.

CHERRY HILL

26 Mélange Cafe
25 Siri's Thai French
Bobby Chez
24 La Campagne
Kibitz Room

COLLINGSWOOD

26 Sagami
25 Bobby Chez
24 Water Lily
Casona
Word of Mouth

HOBOKEN

26 Augustino's
La Isla
Amanda's
Cucharamama
25 Anthony David's

LAMBERTVILLE

25 Manon
24 Hamilton's Grill
No. 9
23 Ota-Ya
22 Anton's/Swan

MIDDLETOWN

29 Nicholas
26 Sono Sushi
24 Navesink Fishery
22 Crown Palace
Anna's Italian

MONTCLAIR

27 CulinAriane
26 Fascino
25 Osteria Giotto
Aozora
Nouveau Sushi

MORRISTOWN

26 Origin
25 Grand Cafe
Tim Schafer's
Copeland
24 Sushi Lounge

NEWARK

26 Fernandes Steak
24 Adega Grill
Tony Da Caneca
Casa Vasca
23 Brasilia Grill

NEW BRUNSWICK

26 Stage Left
Frog & Peach
24 Panico's
23 Clydz
SoHo on George

PRINCETON

26 Ajihei
25 Blue Point
Ferry House
21 Lahiere's
Teresa's Cafe

RED BANK

24 Bienvenue
23 Sogno
Siam Garden
Juanito's
Teak

RIDGEWOOD

27 Latour
25 Sakura-Bana
Village Green
23 Radicchio
Silver Oak Bistro

SOMERVILLE

26 Origin
25 Shumi
24 Wasabi
da Filippo
23 Chao Phaya

VOORHEES

25 Little Café
Laceno Italian
Bobby Chez
24 Ritz Seafood
Catelli

Top Decor Ratings

Ratings are to the left of names.

28 | Rat's

27 | Highlawn Pavilion
Ombra
Chakra
Peter Shields
Ram's Head Inn

26 | Pluckemin Inn
Taka
Nauvoo Grill
Avenue
Nicholas
Dining Room
CoccoLa
Catherine Lombardi
Washington Inn
Sirena
Serenade

25 | Grand Cafe
Chart House
Il Capriccio

SeaBlue
Molly Pitcher
Lua
Bernards Inn
Saddle River Inn
Manor
Scalini Fedeli
Stony Hill Inn
Specchio
Gables, The
Copeland
Cafe Matisse
Amanda's
Inn at Millrace
Liberty House
Harvest Bistro
Bobby Flay Steak
Raven & Peach
David Burke
Union Park Dining Rm.

OUTDOORS

Anthony David's
Axelsson's
Bernards Inn
Frenchtown Inn
Girasole

Hamilton's Grill
Latour
Lilly's on Canal
Peter Shields
Tisha's

ROMANCE

Cafe Matisse
CulinAriane
Dining Room
Ebbitt Room
Harvest Moon

Le Rendez-Vous
Perryville Inn
Raven & Peach
Sergeantsville Inn
Washington Inn

ROOMS

Chakra
Cucharamama
David Burke
David Drake
Lorena's

Makeda
Nicholas
Ombra
Pluckemin Inn
Rat's

VIEWS

Arthur's Landing
Atlantic B&G
Avenue
Avon Pavilion
Inlet Café

Matisse
McLoone's
Molly Pitcher
Union Park Dining Rm.
Walpack Inn

Top Service Ratings

Ratings are to the left of names.

<u>28</u> Nicholas

<u>26</u> Dining Room
Grand Cafe
André's
Ebbitt Room
Saddle River Inn
David Drake
Serenade
Cafe Panache
Cafe Matisse
Scalini Fedeli
Washington Inn

<u>25</u> Benito's
Union Park Dining Rm.
Il Capriccio
Peter Shields
Capriccio
Whispers
Latour
Amanda's

Lorena's
Ram's Head Inn*
Bernards Inn
SeaBlue
Chef's Table
Stage Left
Chez Catherine
Cenzino
Le Petit Chateau

<u>24</u> Pluckemin Inn
David Burke
Specchio
Il Villaggio
Zoe's*
Manor
Black Duck
Frog & Peach
Rat's
Ristorante Benito
Panico's

Best Buys

In order of Bang for the Buck rating.

1. Amazing Hot Dog
2. Surf Taco
3. Benny Tudino's
4. White House
5. DeLorenzo's
6. Pop Shop
7. Irish Pub
8. Grimaldi's Pizza
9. El Azteca
10. Fedora Cafe
11. Tacconelli's Pizzeria
12. Richard's
13. Aroma Royal Thai
14. Meemah
15. Pad Thai
16. Country Pancake
17. Skylark Diner
18. Far East Taste
19. Brooklyn's Pizza
20. Tick Tock
21. La Isla
22. Sri Thai
23. Thai Kitchen
24. Kibitz Room
25. Karma Kafe
26. Coconut Bay
27. Mie Thai
28. Hunan Chinese
29. El Meson
30. Ali Baba
31. Tortilla Press
32. Chao Phaya
33. P.J. Whelihan's
34. Eurasian Eatery
35. Senorita's
36. Bombay Gardens
37. Charrito's
38. Mr. Chu
39. Joe's Peking
40. Somsak/Taan

OTHER GOOD VALUES

Aby's Mexican
Allen's Clam
Bamboo Leaf
Bistro San Miguel
Brannon's Hurricane
Brickwall Tavern
Champa Laos
China Palace
Conte's
Creole Cafe
Dayi'nin Yeri
Doo Rae Myun Ok
Drew's Bayshore
Espo's
Gagan Bistro
GRUB Hut
Krakus
La Tapatia
Malabar House
Martino's
Mexico Lindo
Moksha
Nazmi's
Nobi
Olde Corner Deli
Passage to India
Pete & Elda's
Pho Thang Long
Pic-Nic
Pithari Taverna
Saffron
Seven Hills
Sister Sue's
Smokey's BBQ
Tashmoo
Thai Thai
Tony Luke's
West Lake
Wondee's Thai
Ya Ya Noodles

ALPHABETICAL
DIRECTORY

		FOOD	DECOR	SERVICE	COST

Aamantran ⓜ *Indian* ▽ 23 | 16 | 21 | $23

Toms River Township | Victoria Plaza | 1594 Rte. 9 S. (Churchill Rd.) | 732-341-5424

The open kitchen at this Toms River Indian BYO dispenses "great" Indian food in a "comfortable" environment; the "hospitable" service, "family"-friendly atmosphere and "value" of a lunch buffet trump the strip-mall surroundings.

Aangan *Indian* 23 | 17 | 19 | $27

Freehold Township | A & M Plaza | 3475 Rte. 9 N. (Three Brooks Rd.) | 732-761-2900

Its lunch buffet is a "deal" and a "good introduction" to "excellent" Indian cooking say fans of this "kid-friendly" BYO "treasure" in a Freehold strip mall; given the "attentive" service, it's hard not to feel accommodated in the "comfortable" dining room.

Aby's Mexican Restaurant *Mexican* ▽ 22 | 14 | 18 | $24

Matawan | 141 Main St. (Ravine Dr.) | 732-583-9119 | www.abysrestaurant.com

"All the basics" taste "good" at this Matawan Mexican BYO storefront whose menu is a "value", the decor "homey" yet "attractive" and the service "friendly", if sometimes "slow"; plus, the weekend guitar brings a touch of the festive.

Acacia ⓜ *American* 25 | 20 | 22 | $47

Lawrenceville | 2637 Main St. (bet. Craven Ln. & Phillips Ave.) | 609-895-9885 | www.acaciacuisine.com

Now in its 15th year, this Lawrenceville BYO still supplies "joy", combining "excellent" New American cuisine, "knowledgeable, friendly" service and a "convivial" vibe; the recently redecorated dining room remains a "tight fit", but fans accede and keep squeezing in.

Acqua ⓢ *Italian* 21 | 21 | 21 | $43

Raritan | 777 Rte. 202 N. (bet. 1st Ave. & Ortho Dr.) | 908-707-1777 | www.acquaristorante.com

"Active" bar fans hit this "noisy" Raritan Italian proffering a "predictably good" menu, weekend entertainment and a staff as "lively" as the setting; the scene's *bellissimo* to everyone – but "bring a big purse" to become part of it.

Acquaviva delle fonti *Italian* 23 | 21 | 21 | $46

Westfield | 115 Elm St. (Broad St.) | 908-301-0700 | www.acquaviva-dellefonti.com

"*Viva!*" to the "consistently good" fare and "classy", "romantic" ambiance say fans who also applaud the "professional" service at this high-ceilinged Westfield Northern Italian in a renovated bank building; yes, it's "pricey", but "wonderful" experiences don't come cheap.

NEW Addiwan ◑ *Mideastern* 18 | 21 | 16 | $27

Montclair | 578 Bloomfield Ave. (Maple Pl.) | 973-744-1300 | www.addiwancafe.com

"You'll feel like you stepped into a scene from *The Arabian Nights*" at this Montclair Middle Eastern BYO that excels at "interesting" mezes

	FOOD	DECOR	SERVICE	COST

and features "lovely" decor, "dimly lit" dining rooms and belly dancing on the weekends; if service splits some ("unpredictable" vs. "excellent"), most agree it's worth a visit since "you won't spend a fortune."

Adega Grill *Portuguese/Spanish* | 24 | 24 | 23 | $37 |

Newark | 130-132 Ferry St. (bet. Madison & Monroe Sts.) | 973-589-8830 | www.adegagrill.com

Smitten surveyors dine on "delicious" "family-style" food at this "romantic" "special-occasion" Iberian in Newark's Ironbound; the "vineyardlike" decor (*adega* means 'wine cellar' in Portuguese) and "comfortable" seating are as pleasing as the "good" service and the bar, where "you'll swear you were in Lisbon" once you sit down.

☑ Ajihei Ⓜ *Japanese* | 26 | 11 | 18 | $30 |

Princeton | 11 Chambers St. (Nassau St.) | 609-252-1158

It's all about the fish at this "little" Princeton Japanese BYO serving "superb" sushi that's "as fresh as can be"; put yourself "on autopilot and let the chef do the flying", and just remember that you're eating "top-flight" fare in "dorm-room" digs.

NEW Akai Lounge *Japanese* | 23 | 20 | 18 | $39 |

Englewood | 11 N. Dean St. (bet. Bergen St. & E. Palisades Ave.) | 201-541-0086

Enthusiasts embrace this "upscale" Englewood Japanese for its "inventive" sushi (some even call it "Nobu"-like) served within a "slick", "modern" space; while the "friendly" "service needs work", "delicious" drinks and a "loungey" vibe help distract.

Akbar *Indian* | 18 | 17 | 17 | $29 |

Edison | 21 Cortland St. (Patrick Ave.) | 732-632-8822 | www.akbarrestaurant.com

This super-sized Edison Indian is "a solid standby in a sea of choices"; though some say the restaurant "could use a little redecorating", the consensus is "you're not there for the wallpaper", just for the "good" food and a buffet that's "one of the best for lunch."

Alan@594 ☒ Ⓜ *Italian* | 20 | 18 | 17 | $34 |

Upper Montclair | 594 Valley Rd. (Bellevue Ave.) | 973-744-4120

Dedicated diners endorse the "good", "reasonably" priced menu at this Upper Montclair Northern Italian BYO whose "pleasant" dining room can be "crowded" on account of "tight" conditions; P.S. fresh-air fans can always opt for the "great" garden.

Alchemist & Barrister *American* | 16 | 16 | 17 | $34 |

Princeton | 28 Witherspoon St. (Nassau St.) | 609-924-5555 | www.alchemistandbarrister.com

"Stick with the pub and you won't be disappointed" aver patrons of this "100 percent old-school" Princeton American where three seating options (in the bar, patio or more formal room) draw preppies of all ages; it's "typical Ivy League", down to "chairs that creak", and correspondents concede if the food "isn't exciting" at least "it serves its purpose well."

Al D'ente Ristorante *Italian*   23 | 20 | 23 | $41

Piscataway | 1665 Stelton Rd. (Ethel Rd.) | 732-985-8220
"Honest", "excellent" homemade pastas and "detailed" service are
the draws of this "pricey" Piscataway Northern Italian "hidden" in a
strip mall; if the decor proves a bit "over-the-top", it still seems to fit
the food and "old-world" mood.

Aldo & Gianni Ⓢ *Italian*   21 | 14 | 19 | $37

Montvale | A&P Shopping Ctr. | 108 Chestnut Ridge Rd. (Grand Ave.) |
201-391-6866
South Hackensack | 268 Huyler St. (bet. Dinallo & Hoffman Sts.) |
201-487-4220
www.aldoandgianni.com
"Good" and "garlicky" "homestyle" Italian is the bill of fare at these
neighborhood storefronts that "cater to businesspeople" at lunch
and a "casual crowd" at dinner; the atmosphere "may not be great",
but "gracious" service compensates; N.B. South Hackensack is BYO.

NEW Alessio 426 Ⓜ *Continental*   ▽ 20 | 17 | 19 | $35

Metuchen | 426 Main St. (New St.) | 732-549-6464 | www.alessio426.com
Expect to "feel at home" in this Metuchen BYO storefront (formerly
Dan's on Main), whose kitchen dishes up a variety of Northern
Italian–influenced Continental specialties; a "generous" lunch buf-
fet reinforces the notion that the food here is "well worth the cost."

Alexander's *French*   ▽ 24 | 26 | 24 | $41

Cape May | Alexander's Inn | 653 Washington St. (bet. Franklin &
Ocean Sts.) | 609-884-2555 | www.alexandersinn.com
Very Victorian in every way – right down to the "attentive", white-
glove service – this longtime B&B restaurant provides a "great" Cape
May experience for patrons who dine on the "wonderful" French
food in "charming" quarters; not even the "pricey" tabs get in the
way of "romantic" rendezvous.

Ali Baba *Mideastern*   20 | 12 | 17 | $20

Hoboken | 912 Washington St. (bet. 9th & 10th Sts.) | 201-653-5319
"Delicious" food is what's kept this "tried-and-true" Middle Eastern
Hoboken BYO a neighborhood eat-in/take-out staple since 1983;
the reasonably priced menu and "friendly" service help smooth the
edges over the "rough", "dour" digs.

Aligado Asian Restaurant *Japanese/Thai*   ▽ 23 | 13 | 18 | $29

Hazlet | 2780 Rte. 35 (Miller Ave.) | 732-888-7568
Japanese and Thai specialties turn up at this Hazlet Asian BYO re-
lied upon for its "well-prepared" fare, but not necessarily for its ambiance, which "it doesn't have much of"; overall, most maintain it's
a "cut above" the pack.

Alisa Cafe Ⓜ *French*   22 | 19 | 21 | $35

Cherry Hill | Barclay Farms Shopping Ctr. | 112 Rte. 70 E. (Kings Hwy.) |
856-354-8807 | www.alisacafe.com
Capitalizing on his base of South Jersey fans, West Philly transplant
Tony Kanjanakorn offers diners this Cherry Hill shopping-center

BYO, where the "excellent" French cuisine is influenced by a "touch of Thai"; given the "good" service, "repeat visits" are no surprise here.

Allendale Bar & Grill ❶ *Pub Food* | 16 | 12 | 16 | $24 |

Allendale | 67 W. Allendale Ave. (bet. Demercurlo Dr. & Maple St.) | 201-327-3197 | www.allendalebarandgrill.com

Trekking to this 70-plus-year-old Bergen County American is "tradition" on account of its "reliable" pub fare (especially the "great" burgers), nice touches (fresh popcorn on the tables) and "friendly" staff; if the "old standby's" decor needs "a shot of Botox", overall, this "quintessential" bar "still holds its own."

Allen's Clam Bar Ⓜ⊘ *Seafood* | – | – | – | M |

New Gretna | 5650 Rte. 9 (Garden State Pkwy.) | 609-296-4106

Take a trip down the Parkway for this seafood BYO destination in New Gretna that may be a half step above a shack in appearance but nevertheless is a sight for sore fresh-fish-seeking eyes; the fried fare here draws both fisher folk and Humvee-driving landlubbers.

NEW Alphabet Soup Ⓢ Ⓜ *American* | – | – | – | E |

Audubon | 34 W. Merchant St. (bet. Atlantic Ave. & White Horse Pike) | 856-310-0605 | www.alphabetsoupnj.com

A is for Audubon, NJ, home to this cute, whimsical New American BYO; everything is to the letter, from helpful service to the French-inspired cuisine; there's a moderately priced à la carte dinner menu Wednesdays–Saturdays, as well as a BYO tasting menu available on Fridays and Saturdays nights.

Z Amanda's *American* | 26 | 25 | 25 | $45 |

Hoboken | 908 Washington St. (bet. 9th & 10th Sts.) | 201-798-0101 | www.amandasrestaurant.com

"After all these years", this "serene", "romantic" Hoboken New American in a "beautiful" brownstone still epitomizes "upscale", "classy" dining with its "impeccably" prepared cuisine, "extensive" wine list, "attentive" service and "lovely" decor; an "amazing" brunch and early-bird special – a "steal" at $14 per person – affirm this winning spot's seemingly everlasting appeal.

Amarone *Italian* | 21 | 16 | 23 | $41 |

Teaneck | 63 Cedar Ln. (bet. Broad St. & Teaneck Rd.) | 201-833-1897 | www.amaroneristorante.net

"Attentive" service ("they treat newcomers like regulars") helps warm this "lovely" "neighborhood" Teaneck Northern Italian distinguished by "quality" home cooking; some say it's "formal", others insist it's "cozy", but just about everyone agrees "it's like eating at your friend's place."

NEW Amazing Hot Dog *Hot Dogs* | 22 | 11 | 19 | $9 |

Verona | 148A Bloomfield Ave. (Pompton Ave.) | 973-433-3073 | www.amazinghotdog.com

"Top dogs" and bargain-basement prices lure aficionados to this Verona BYO (the Survey's No. 1 Bang for the Buck), where fried franks accompanied by a "variety of toppings" and "crisp", "tasty" fries rule; sure, it's safe to say there's "no decor", "but who cares" when the wieners are "the best this side of Coney Island"?

Amici Milano *Italian*
22 | 18 | 21 | $36

Trenton | 600 Chestnut Ave. (Roebling Ave.) | 609-396-6300 | www.amicimilano.com

Northern Italian food followers "keep coming back" to this "crowded" standby in Trenton's Chambersburg section for "delicious" "old-school", "copiously" portioned victuals; the "highlight" of an evening here may be the piano music, which helps sustain the "lively" setting.

Amiya *Indian*
21 | 18 | 18 | $25

Jersey City | Harborside Financial Ctr. | 160 Greene St. (Christopher Columbus Dr.) | 201-433-8000 | www.amiyarestaurant.com

"Subtle twists on the classics" distinguish this contemporary Jersey City Indian in the heart of the Financial District; the lunch buffet is "a cut-above" – and "consistently packed" – so "go on the weekend when the workers are gone" and the restaurant becomes more of "a neighborhood place"; P.S. patio dining is a "treat."

An American Grill 🄱 *American*
21 | 21 | 20 | $44

Randolph | 246 Rte. 10 W. (I-287) | 973-442-9311 | www.anamericangrill.com

"Don't let the strip-mall" locale of this Randolph "treasure" deter you from sampling a "satisfying" selection of American food; aside from the "enjoyable" meals, the "warm" setting also attracts (it's a perfect place for "winding down a work week").

Andaman 🄼 *French/Thai*
23 | 14 | 17 | $28

Morristown | 147 Morris St. (bet. Elm & King Sts.) | 973-538-5624

Still somewhat "undiscovered", this Morristown BYO blends Thai and French in its food, resulting in "oh-so-good" dishes; hence, it's "easy to ignore" the plain decor, even more so when you consider the "great" value of the lunch and dinner prix fixes.

🄩 André's 🄼 *American*
27 | 22 | 26 | $53

Newton | 188 Spring St. (bet. Adams & Jefferson Sts.) | 973-300-4192 | www.andresrestaurant.com

This "friendly" BYO "behind a storefront" in Newton is "always a delight" given the "crafty creations" of "talented" chef-owner André de Waal, the man behind the "sublime" New American menu; if the "pricey" tabs prove a bit daunting, budget-conscious fans go for the "moderately" priced bistro menu on Sundays; N.B. wines may be purchased Wednesdays–Sundays at the on-site boutique.

Angelo's Fairmount Tavern *Italian*
20 | 13 | 19 | $31

Atlantic City | 2300 Fairmount Ave. (Mississippi Ave.) | 609-344-2439 | www.angelosfairmounttavern.com

The "good", "hearty" down-home Italian food (i.e. "nonna"-approved) is perfect for the *famiglia* say fans of this "nothing-fancy", 72-year-old "red-gravy" warhorse in Atlantic City, aka "the best deal in town"; the wine is "homemade" and the joint is filled with "characters", all the more reason to stop by and *mangia.*

	FOOD	DECOR	SERVICE	COST

Anjelica's ☒ Italian
25 | 16 | 21 | $43

Sea Bright | 1070 Ocean Ave. (bet. Peninsula Ave. & River St.) | 732-842-2800 | www.anjelicas.com

While you "shouldn't count on conversation" (it's "loud"), expect "consistently wonderful" food and an "enormous" menu at this Sea Bright Italian BYO also proffering a handful of wines; they "aim to please" here, which more than makes up for the "crowded" conditions in the summer.

Anna's Italian Kitchen ☒ Italian
22 | 14 | 20 | $38

Middletown | Fountain Ridge Shopping Ctr. | 1686 Rte. 35 S. (Old Country Rd.) | 732-275-9142 | www.annasitaliankitchen.com

Anna Perri fills her Middletown BYO by offering a "variety" of "good" Italian food, including "the best gnocchi"; no, it's "not cheap" considering it's located in a shopping center, but the quality of the cooking stamps out any gripes about prices; N.B. students can sign up for one of the restaurant's weekly cooking classes.

Anthony David's Eclectic/Italian
25 | 19 | 21 | $42

Hoboken | 953 Bloomfield St. (10th St.) | 201-222-8399 | www.anthonydavids.com

"Fantastic" fare emerges from the "tiny" kitchen within chef-owner Anthony Pino's pocket-size Hoboken BYO whose Eclectic–Northern Italian menu (along with "amazing" cheeses) is served in "low-key" quarters; what's more, the widely touted brunch is among the "best" in town; N.B. patrons can dine in the more casual, rustic front room, where prepared foods are sold.

NEW Anthony's ☒ Italian
23 | 19 | 20 | $39

Haddon Heights | 512 Station Ave. (White Horse Pike) | 856-310-7766

A part of Downtown Haddon Heights's recent revival, this "quaint" storefront BYO "doesn't strive to be cutting-edge", but does provide "reliably" good Italian food that's a "value"; that you're "never rushed" seems to make the setting even more "inviting."

Anton's at the Swan ☒ American
22 | 22 | 21 | $49

Lambertville | Swan Hotel | 43 S. Main St. (Swan St.) | 609-397-1960 | www.antons-at-the-swan.com

"First-class food in a first-class setting" is a perfect excuse to try this "romantic" New American in a "charming" historic Lambertville hotel; whether you have a "drink by the fireplace with your sweetheart" or on the patio, this "low-key", leisurely dining mainstay is a "true destination for lovers – or for those with expense accounts."

☒ Aozora French/Japanese
25 | 20 | 19 | $40

Montclair | 407 Bloomfield Ave. (Seymour St.) | 973-233-9400

"Eye-pleasing" delights that "look too nice to eat" are proffered at this "stylishly" outfitted Montclair BYO, the showcase for Nelson Yip's "outstanding", "dreamy" Japanese-French handiworks that include "fabulous" sushi; if "somewhat pricey", the quality of the fare is pure "Tiffany's."

	FOOD	DECOR	SERVICE	COST

Aquila Cucina *Italian*
21 | 17 | 20 | $40

New Providence | 30 South St. (Springfield Ave.) | 908-464-8383 |
www.aquilarestaurant.com

For "reliably" good Italian, diners turn to this "steady" (the "menu
never changes") New Providence BYO where a "friendly", "accommodating" staff and "comfortable" atmosphere "don't disappoint";
partisans propose it's perfect for a casual meal or "special occasion."

Aria Ristorante ▣ *Italian*
21 | 22 | 19 | $42

Fairfield | 4 Little Falls Rd. (Passaic Ave.) | 973-227-6066 |
www.ariaristorante.com

This Fairfield Northern Italian stays a "cut-above" the standard
neighborhood restaurant thanks to "wonderfully prepared" cuisine
(the pastas are "great") and weekend pianist; those who long for the
pre-liquor license, "better-value" days are outnumbered.

Aroma Royal Thai ▣▣ *Thai*
22 | 21 | 21 | $24

Franklin Park | 3175 Rte. 27 (Delar Pkwy.) | 732-422-9300

It's "well-named" note patrons of this BYO Thai tucked inside a
Franklin Park strip mall, a sound option on account of "exquisitely
crafted" food proffered by "eager-to-please" servers; the enthused
agree this Asian "diamond" is also "easy on the wallet."

Arthur's Landing *American*
20 | 24 | 20 | $53

Weehawken | 1 Pershing Rd. (Ferry Blvd.) | 201-867-0777 |
www.arthurslanding.com

The "killer" views of Manhattan keep customers enthralled at this
Weehawken waterside New American; a new chef has kicked up the
cuisine quotient (it's "surprisingly good"), the staff "makes you feel
special" and there's always that ever-popular pre-theater $50 per
person "deal" – a three-course meal and round-trip ferry service.

▣ Arthur's Steakhouse & Pub *Steak*
(fka Arthur's Tavern)
18 | 12 | 16 | $28

North Brunswick | 644 Georges Rd. (Milltown Rd.) | 732-828-1117

▣ Arthur's Tavern *Steak*

Emerson | 214 Kinderkamack Rd. (Lincoln Blvd.) | 201-265-5180
Hoboken | 237 Washington St. (3rd St.) | 201-656-5009
Morris Plains | 700 Speedwell Ave. (Littleton Rd.) | 973-455-9705 ▱
www.arthurstavern.com

For a "cholesterol fix that won't bankrupt you", try this chophouse
quartet dishing out "monster"-size slabs of steaks along with "amazing" burgers; the "bare" decor surely doesn't impress, and the service is somewhat "spotty", but they're the best "beef-o-rama" deals
around; N.B. the North Brunswick location, Arthur's Steakhouse &
Pub, is now separately owned.

Arturo's ▣ *Italian*
22 | 19 | 20 | $45

Midland Park | 41 Central Ave. (bet. Godwin & Greenwood Aves.) |
201-444-2466 | www.arturos-restaurant.com

"Nice people, good food" attracts admirers to this "reliable" 25-
year-old Midland Park Southern Italian known for its fare and "stand-

	FOOD	DECOR	SERVICE	COST

up" servers; though now "pricey" thanks to a liquor license, fans can take solace in a "varied" wine list.

NEW Asia Star *Japanese*

| | – | – | – | E |

Tinton Falls | 4060 Asbury Ave. (Greengrove Rd.) | 732-922-1119
Although mostly Japanese and Chinese, the fare at this new Tinton Falls BYO also acknowledges Thailand and Malaysia on its diverse menu; the dark and sleek decor is a draw for locals along with visitors en route to the Shore.

Assembly Steak House *Steak*

| | 16 | 17 | 17 | $50 |

Englewood Cliffs | 495 Sylvan Ave. (Palisades Ave.) | 201-568-2616
Surveyors are split on this "old-standard" Englewood Cliffs chophouse: while fans can't figure out why this "excellent", "pricey-but-worth-it" beef emporium "isn't more popular", contrarians claim it's "disappointing", citing "so-so" steaks while wondering "who goes here?"

A Tavola Ⓜ *Italian*

| | 23 | 14 | 18 | $30 |

Old Bridge | Deep Run Shopping Ctr. | 3345 Rte. 9 S. (Ferry Rd.) | 732-607-1120 | www.atavola1.com
"Fabulous food and friendly folks – what more could you want?" ask fans of this Old Bridge Italian strip-mall BYO distinguished by its "delicious" dishes prepared in an open kitchen; since you can expect a "good value", it's wise to "reserve" before showing up.

Athenian Garden *Greek*

| | 23 | 12 | 20 | $27 |

Galloway Township | 619 S. New York Rd. (bet. Holly Brook Dr. & W. Brook Ln.) | 609-748-1818
The staff's "as nice as can be" at this rustic Greek BYO emphasizing "tasty" seafood and other savories in out-of-the-way Galloway; the open kitchen and fresh fish on display enhance the rustic, if basic digs ("from the look, you'd never expect such great food").

Athens Café Ⓜ *Greek*

| | 19 | 12 | 21 | $24 |

Cherry Hill | Sawmill Vill. | 404 Rte. 70 E. (Brookmead Dr.) | 856-429-1061
True, it's "not much to look at", but fans insist this "longtime" Cherry Hill haven for Greek food does turn out "comfort food" that'll "satisfy"; plus, just about everybody adores the "world's friendliest" staff.

Atlantic Bar & Grill *American/Seafood*

| | 24 | 22 | 22 | $48 |

South Seaside Park | Central & 24th Aves. | 732-854-1588 | www.atlanticbarandgrillnj.com
At this Shore New American, the "awesome" view is a given thanks to floor-to-ceiling windows and the fact that you're dining "as close to the ocean as possible"; but aside from the sight of "waves crashing against the shoreline", expect "well-prepared" seafood and a "terrific" bar, the latter enhanced by live jazz on some nights.

Ⓩ Augustino's Ⓢ⊘ *Italian*

| | 26 | 17 | 23 | $43 |

Hoboken | 1104 Washington St. (bet. 11th & 12th Sts.) | 201-420-0104 | www.augustinosrestaurant.com
"As good as it gets" for NJ homestyle Southern Italian say surveyors about this "small" cash-only Hoboken storefront that's "stuffed like

a manicotti every night"; the staff will "charmingly bust your chops", and "good luck" trying to get a reservation on any night.

🅉 NEW Avenue French

FOOD	DECOR	SERVICE	COST
22	26	20	$59

Long Branch | 23 Ocean Ave. (Laird Ave.) | 732-759-2900 | www.leclubavenue.com

Think "South Beach" – not Long Branch – before arriving at this "pricey" French brasserie/lounge whose "spectacular" ocean views coupled with famed London architect David Collins' "beautiful", "modern" design (featuring marble-tiled floors and floor-to-ceiling windows) are more than a match for the "chic" crowd; despite "spotty" service, most seem sated by Antonio Mora's "tasty" fare and "delicious" drinks at the "sexy" bar.

Avon Pavilion American

FOOD	DECOR	SERVICE	COST
18	16	18	$33

Avon-by-the-Sea | 600 Ocean Ave. (bet. Norwood & Woodland Aves.) | 732-775-1043 | www.avonpavilion.com

Although dinner is the time for "terrific" people-watching, "breakfast is the real star" at this Boardwalk BYO American in Avon where eating is a "fantastic way to enjoy food" since the backdrop is the beach and the water ("just being by the ocean makes anything taste great"); N.B. breakfasts and lunches are cash only.

Axelsson's Blue Claw Seafood

FOOD	DECOR	SERVICE	COST
22	20	20	$43

Cape May | 991 Ocean Dr. (Rte. 109) | 609-884-5878 | www.blueclawrestaurant.com

You "can't go wrong" at this "old-time" Cape May docksider delivering "tasty" preparations of "fresh" seafood; the bar is "beautiful" to boot, though it's important to note the "pricey" fare speaks to the place's "classy" ambiance (there's "no slurping clams out of the shell here").

NEW Axia Taverna Greek

FOOD	DECOR	SERVICE	COST
21	22	19	$46

Tenafly | 18 Piermont Rd. (Central Ave.) | 201-569-5999 | www.axiataverna.com

This "upscale" bi-level Greek is "already popular" and a "welcome addition" to the Tenafly dining scene thanks to its "sophisticated" menu full of "winners", "beautiful" modern design (by famed architect Tony Chi) and mostly Hellenic wine list; given its virtues, this newcomer is easily "worth the detour."

Azúcar Cuban

FOOD	DECOR	SERVICE	COST
19	21	19	$36

Jersey City | 495 Washington Blvd. (Pavonia Ave.) | 201-222-0090 | www.azucarcubancuisine.com

When "looking for Cuban", it can't hurt to hit this Jersey Cityite whose "cool" decor and "lively" ambiance go hand in hand with the fare; P.S. they offer free salsa lessons, and some insist there's nothing like "relaxing with your pals over great cigars" in the lounge.

Bacari Grill 🅜 American

FOOD	DECOR	SERVICE	COST
21	21	20	$44

Washington Township | 800 Ridgewood Rd. (Pascack Rd.) | 201-358-6330 | www.bacarigrill.com

"Reliably good" food and a country-inn setting folks "love" help explain the popularity and longevity of this "consistent" Washington

Township New American; true, you may not find it a bargain outing, but the "sharp" staff, "spirited" ambiance and bar scene keep the "crowds" happy.

Bahama Breeze *Caribbean*

| 17 | 20 | 16 | $26 |

Cherry Hill | Cherry Hill Mall | 2000 Rte. 38 (Haddonfield Rd.) | 856-317-8317 | www.bahamabreeze.com

"If you can't make it to the islands", you can always "pretend you're there" – especially after imbibing one of the "great" tropical drinks – at this "friendly" suburban Caribbean Cherry Hill chainlet known for "long lines"; no, the fare's "nothing amazing", but it's still "better than average", plus, the live music is "good."

Bahrs Landing *Seafood*

| 15 | 14 | 16 | $37 |

Highlands | 2 Bay Ave. (bet. Hillside Ave. & South St.) | 732-872-1245 | www.bahrs.com

This very "New England" 90-year-old Highlands seafooder offers some "excellent" scenery, in this case a "great" view of Sandy Hook Bay thanks to its location right on the water; the "typical", "fried-and-broiled" fare may not win awards, and though the place "looks like it's about to fall into the water", some say "that's part of its charm."

Baja *Mexican*

| 20 | 16 | 18 | $27 |

Hoboken | 104 14th St. (Washington St.) | 201-653-0610
Jersey City | 117 Montgomery St. (bet. Marin Blvd. & Warren St.) | 201-915-0062
www.bajamexicancuisine.com

The "impressive" selection of tequilas fuels the "fun" at this Mexican chips 'n' salsa twosome in Hoboken and Jersey City issuing the "best" margaritas and "solid" "south-of-the-border" fare; it's best to come with patience, since the "staff is fighting the crowds" too.

Bamboo Leaf *Thai/Vietnamese*

| 24 | 19 | 19 | $28 |

Bradley Beach | 724 Main St. (bet. Lareine & McCabe Aves.) | 732-774-1661
Howell | Howell Ctr. | 2450 Rte. 9 S. (White Rd.) | 732-761-3939
Transport yourself into "another land" via these Thai–Vietnamese BYOs that guarantee "delightful" dining thanks to "delicious" dishes, "none of which disappoint"; the "pleasing" bamboo-accented decor provides another reason why diners never want to leaf.

Bangkok Garden *Thai*

| 24 | 15 | 21 | $26 |

Hackensack | 261 Main St. (bet. Camden & Salem Sts.) | 201-487-2620 | www.bangkokgarden-nj.com

"Excellent" – if not "outstanding" – Thai cooking is guaranteed at this "no-frills" Hackensack "hit", Bergen County's "best bet for a taste of Bangkok", especially in light of "can't-be-beat" tabs; "helpful" service rounds out this overall "superb" operation.

Bareli's ⊠ *Italian*

| 23 | 20 | 23 | $56 |

Secaucus | 219 Rte. 3 E. (Plaza Ct.) | 201-865-0473

"Big spenders" show up at this Secaucus Italian turning out "fine" food, "fabulous" wines, "top-notch" service and lots of folks, whether it's those "on business" at lunch or others in the evening; it's all "boy's club" inside, and some marvel that the place is as "consistent as the expensive cars that are always parked in the lot."

Barnacle Ben's *Seafood*
FOOD	DECOR	SERVICE	COST
19	17	19	$30

Moorestown | Acme Shopping Ctr. | 300 Young Ave. (bet. Marne Hwy. & Marter Ave.) | 856-235-5808

"Generously" doled out portions of "fresh", "reliable" seafood helps explain why this Moorestown BYO has stayed in business for over a quarter century; the "friendly" service can be "uneven", but "reasonable" tabs means you'll pay far less than a Franklin.

Barnacle Bill's ◑ *Hamburgers*
FOOD	DECOR	SERVICE	COST
21	16	18	$27

Rumson | 1 First St. (River Rd.) | 732-747-8396

"Eat some peanuts, throw the shells on the floor, then grab a burger and beer" say sage vets of this "nautically" appointed 25-year-old Rumson American still slinging and serving patties that "can't be beat"; "beautiful" views of the Navesink River top it all off.

Barone's *Italian*
FOOD	DECOR	SERVICE	COST
20	18	19	$30

Cherry Hill | Barclay Farms Shopping Ctr. | 210 Rte. 70 E. (Kings Hwy.) | 856-354-1888
Moorestown | 280 Young Ave. (Main St.) | 856-234-7900

Villa Barone *Italian*

Collingswood | 753 Haddon Ave. (bet. Frazer & Washington Aves.) | 856-858-2999
www.baronerestaurants.com

"Don't change a thing!" plead backers of this South Jersey BYO trio whose setting feels "like mom's" and where the "reliably good", "red-gravy" cooking and "friendly" service are hits; overall, it's easy to see how they've "become a favorite" for many.

Barrel's *Italian*
FOOD	DECOR	SERVICE	COST
19	11	17	$27

Linwood | 199 New Rd. (Central Ave.) | 609-926-9900 Ⓢ
Margate | 9 S. Granville Ave. (Ventnor Ave.) | 609-823-4400

"Families" who frequent these Shore Italian BYOs come back for their "affordable" menus of "solid" fare, namely the "great" soups; fans also tout takeout as a "good" option.

☲ Basilico *Italian*
FOOD	DECOR	SERVICE	COST
23	21	21	$44

Millburn | 324 Millburn Ave. (Main St.) | 973-379-7020 | www.basilicomillburn.com

An "impressive array" of "top-quality" Northern Italian dishes greet guests at this "chic" Millburn BYO, a "good bet for tasty pre-theater" supping near the Paper Mill Playhouse; enthusiasts enjoy a "warm" atmosphere and indoor and outdoor dining options, adding it's "never a disappointment – unless you forget to make a reservation."

Basil T's ◑ *American/Italian*
FOOD	DECOR	SERVICE	COST
20	18	19	$34

Red Bank | 183 Riverside Ave. (Maple Ave.) | 732-842-5990 | www.basilt.com

The "crowds" converge on this American-Italian "fixture" in Red Bank, a quintessential "meeting place" known as much for its "excellent" microbrews (crafted on-site) as its "lively", "boisterous" bar scene abetted by TVs all around; otherwise, expect "good" pastas and pizzas and "pricey" checks.

☑ Baumgart's Café *American/Pan-Asian* | 19 | 14 | 18 | $26 |

Edgewater | City Pl. | 59 The Promenade (River Rd.) | 201-313-3889
Englewood | 45 E. Palisade Ave. (bet. Dean St. & Grand Ave.) | 201-569-6267
Ridgewood | 158 Franklin Ave. (N. Walnut St.) | 201-612-5688
www.baumgartscafe.com

For a "diverse" slate of Traditional American (by day) and Pan-Asian (by night), these "kid-friendly" BYOs are counted on for "super-fast" service and "solid" eats, from Chinese and sushi to chicken salad, burgers and "yummy" old-fashioned ice cream; if partisans argue the merits of each location, most report, overall, that these "split-personality" standbys are a winning trio.

☑ Bay Avenue Trattoria 🅜 *American/Italian* | 28 | 11 | 21 | $38 |

Highlands | 122 Bay Ave. (Jackson St.) | 732-872-9800 | www.bayavetrattoria.com

"Back with a bang" are Joe Romanowski and Maggie Lubcke and their "friendly" Highlands BYO, where the "fantastic" American-Italian preparations are a cause for "rejoicing"; true, you "don't have to get dressed up" given the somewhat "lacking" ambiance, but the "top-quality" cooking trumps any decor issues.

NEW Bay Head Bistro & Café *American* | ▽ 21 | 17 | 18 | $46 |

Bay Head | 530 Main Ave. (bet. Howe & Mount Sts.) | 732-714-8881
Go see "the sunsets" while dining at this addition to Bay Head, a BYO American near the beach offering a "comfortable", "under-stated" atmosphere "conducive to entertaining" and a staff that's "friendly"; all agree the "good" food plays well in these parts.

Bayou Cafe 🅜 *Cajun/Creole* | ▽ 23 | 17 | 22 | $26 |

Manasquan | 209 First Ave. (bet. Brielle Rd. & Main St.) | 732-223-6678 | www.bayoucafe.net

This Manasquan BYO is still the go-to for "wonderfully" spicy Cajun-Creole cookery, the kind that "makes you feel like you're in the heart of the Big Easy"; N.B. the new chef, Robert Lumley, may eventually transform the restaurant into a Caribbean destination.

BayPoint Prime *Steak* | ▽ 24 | 12 | 17 | $50 |

Point Pleasant Beach | 1805 Ocean Ave. (Rte. 35) | 732-295-5400
Dennis Foy, one of Jersey's "best" chefs, oversees this seasonal Point Pleasant Beach BYO for "excellent" steaks supplemented by seafood; overall, the cooking "lives up to the toque's standards" – just visit between Memorial Day and Labor Day to experience it.

Bazzarelli *Italian* | 22 | 14 | 18 | $30 |

Moonachie | 117 Moonachie Rd. (Maple St.) | 201-641-4010
"Making Meadowlands events much more enjoyable" for over 35 years, this Moonachie mainstay stays "busy" given "fair" pricing and

"good-all-around" Italian offerings, even when it's just for a "slice and a coke"; perhaps better yet, the family-owned operation does its best to make you "feel at home."

Bazzini at 28 Oak Street Ⓩ *American*   21 | 16 | 19 | $45

Ridgewood | 28 Oak St. (bet. Franklin & Ridgewood Aves.) | 201-689-7313
"Friendly" servers complement the "comfortable" atmosphere at this Ridgewood BYO whose New American preparations generally please; whereas some allow the food is "hit-or-miss", relatively "reasonable" prices – and an early-bird that's a "fantastic" bargain – are pluses.

Beau Rivage Ⓜ *Continental/French*   22 | 22 | 22 | $53

Medford | 128 Taunton Blvd. (Falls Rd.) | 856-983-1999 |
www.beaurivage-restaurant.com
Lobster bisque, beef Wellington and a 500-label wine list help enhance many a "special occasion" at this "expensive" French-Continental Medford stalwart entering its 30th year; the rural scenery outside is a perfect foil for the "lovely", Louis XVI–style decor.

Bella Sogno *Italian*   ▽ 21 | 16 | 17 | $37

Bradley Beach | 600 Main St. (Brinley Ave.) | 732-869-0700
Look forward to a "good" Italian meal in a "nice, quiet" setting at this under-the-radar, wood-appointed Bradley Beach BYO providing a sound "alternative" to the crowded Shore scene; relatively "inexpensive" tabs are just *bella*.

Bellissimo's *Italian*   24 | 20 | 22 | $51

Little Falls | 1 Rte. 23 S. (Rte. 46) | 973-785-4225
"Don't even look at the regular menu" advise those in-the-know at this "high-end" Little Falls Italian where "tuxedo-clad" waiters "recite a very long list" of "amazing" specials; better ask for the prices, though, or "be prepared for sticker shock", but the good news: "you'll have a meal to remember."

Bell's ⊟ *American/Italian*   19 | 11 | 18 | $26

Lambertville | 183 N. Union St. (bet. Buttonwood & Elm Sts.) |
609-397-2226 | www.bellstavern.com
For a "walk down memory lane" look no farther than this cash-only Lambertville American-Italian and bona fide "neighborhood classic" (since 1939) offering "appealing" food and noteworthy pasta dishes, all at "bargain" prices; "comfortable" quarters draw "longtime regulars" to the "cozy" bar area.

Bell's Mansion Ⓜ *American*   18 | 19 | 16 | $40

Stanhope | 11 Main St. (Rte. 183 S.) | 973-426-9977 |
www.bellsmansion.com
In this "charming" converted 1840 Stanhope home (complete with uneven wooden flooring), a "large", diverse American menu – from "pub grub" to more "gourmet" items – awaits clientele who opt for the taproom or one of the more formal areas; while "ordinary" food keeps the disenchanted at bay, more say the place offers "good all-around dining."

	FOOD	DECOR	SERVICE	COST

Belmont Tavern ⌷ *Italian* `24` `7` `15` `$29`
Belleville | 12 Bloomfield Ave. (Heckel St.) | 973-759-9609
This "ma-and-pa" Belleville Italian has the "best-ever" chicken Savoy and other "fabulous" "homestyle" meals; yes, the digs are "drab" and the waitresses "yell at you" (it's all "part of the charm"), but acolytes agree the "cast of characters" that turn up make it all seem very "*Sopranos.*"

Belvedere Ⓜ *Italian* `19` `18` `21` `$38`
Clifton | 247 Piaget Ave. (Main Ave.) | 973-772-5060
The menu is "massive" and the parking "minimal" at this "consistently good" and "often overlooked" Clifton venue lauded for its hearty Italian cooking; it's "nice and old-fashioned", and true believers attest "once you go here, you'll be back."

Benito's Ⓜ *Italian* `24` `21` `25` `$41`
Chester | 44 Main St. (bet. Hedges Rd. & Warren St.) | 908-879-1887 | www.benitostrattoria.com
This "quaint", "romantic" BYO in Chester is where the "locals go" for "excellent" "homestyle" Northern Italian brought by staffers who make you feel like "family" and ultimately help "guarantee a loyal following"; naturally, it can get "noisy", but that comes with the territory of a "real find."

Benny Tudino's ◑⌷ *Pizza* `21` `7` `14` `$11`
Hoboken | 622 Washington St. (bet. 6th & 7th Sts.) | 201-792-4132
"Bigger is better" they say about the "XL"-size slices doled out at this pizza "institution" that's still the place to go when you've had "too many" at one of Washington Street's bars; true, the digs are "dumpy", but at $2 and change a slice, the Hoboken hordes don't mind.

Berkeley Restaurant & Fish Market *Seafood* `18` `12` `17` `$28`
South Seaside Park | Central & 24th Aves. (J St.) | 732-793-0400
Sure, the "decor is unimpressive", but this ramshackle, 60+-year-old South Seaside Parker is still a "real catch" for its "pretty" views of Island Beach State Park and "affordable" seafood, for some, the "freshest you'll find in the area"; P.S. it's hitched to "as authentic a fish market you can find in Jersey."

ⓩ Bernards Inn, The *American* `26` `25` `25` `$65`
Bernardsville | 27 Mine Brook Rd. (Quimby Ln.) | 908-766-0002 | www.bernardsinn.com
It's "high class all the way" at this "romantic", expense-account Bernardsville New American that keeps delivering "consistent excellence" from the kitchen of chef Corey Heyer, an "incredible" 750-label wine list and "professional" service; while the "well-groomed" interior is "wonderful" now, admirers expect the newly redecorated space (in the works) to be the icing on the cake; N.B. jacket required.

Berta's Chateau *Italian* 22 | 17 | 19 | $48

Wanaque | 7 Grove St. (Prospect St.) | 973-835-0992 |
www.bertaschateau.com

The "faithful" return to this "venerable" site in Wanaque for "plenty"
of "delightful" Northern Italian and "good" wines (from an extensive
Italian list) in a country homestyle setting; "nothing's changed in
years – and that's a compliment" – laud fans of this "old-timer"
that's been "part of the North Jersey fabric" for eight decades.

Beyti Kebab *Turkish* 24 | 10 | 16 | $26

Union City | 4105 Park Ave. (41st St.) | 201-865-6281 |
www.beytikebab.com

For a taste of Istanbul, meat mavens head to this Union City Turk ("a
lamb lover's delight") also esteemed for "excellent" meze and salads; the decor may be "lacking" but the price – "cheap" – is right, the
staff "friendly" and "they bring on the belly dancing" on weekends;
N.B. there's an on-premises halal butcher shop.

Bienvenue ☒ *French* 24 | 19 | 21 | $50
(fka La Petite France)

Red Bank | 7 E. Front St. (Wharf Ave.) | 732-936-0640 |
www.bienvenuerestaurant.com

This "delicious" Red Bank BYO bistro emits French "country charm" in
its convincingly "cozy" quarters, where "wonderful" classics (among
them cassoulet, crème brûlée and foie gras) are served; it all "comes
cheaper than flying to Paris" to taste "Gallic romance at its best."

Big Ed's BBQ *BBQ* 17 | 10 | 16 | $24

Old Bridge | 305 Rte. 34 N. (Amboy Rd.) | 732-583-2626
Burlington | 259 Rte. 130 (bet. Jerome St. & Lincoln Ave.) | 609-387-3611
www.bigedsbbq.com

It's "hog heaven" at this barbecue duo, a "meat-eater's paradise"
where "lots of food for the money" means "the whole family" can
feast on the "best" babyback ribs, chicken and steaks delivered by
"friendly" staffers; "laughable" decor makes takeout sensible.

Bistro at Red Bank, The *Eclectic* 21 | 18 | 18 | $36

Red Bank | 14 Broad St. (bet. Front & Mechanic Sts.) | 732-530-5553 |
www.thebistroatredbank.com

A "casual", "attractive" brick-walled interior syncs up nicely with the
"diverse", "interesting" Eclectic menu at this Red Bank BYO that
seems to be "buzzing" all the time; the outdoor dining is so "perfect",
it may even be able to trump the somewhat "inattentive service."

NEW Bistro En ☒ *French* 22 | 16 | 17 | $34

Teaneck | 252 Degraw Ave. (Queen Anne Rd.) | 201-692-0700 |
www.bistro-en.com

"Japanese meets French bistro" at this Teaneck addition knitting
East and West items (think hanger steak and shrimp tempura) in
its "good" menu; the main selection is "reasonably" priced, but it's
the prix fixe lunch and dinners that really add up to a "bargain" at
this "citified" newcomer.

	FOOD	DECOR	SERVICE	COST

Bistro 44 🗷 Ⓜ *American/French* ▽ 25 | 17 | 23 | $37

Toms River | 44 Washington St. (bet. Hooper Ave. & Main St.) |
732-818-7644 | www.bistro-44.com
Those who've made their way to this Toms River BYO in an unlikely
location (an office building) are "so glad they did", since the French-
American slate is "excellent" and the "attentive" service a delight; up for applause is the twilight menu, a steal of a "superb"
deal at $14.95.

🗷 Bistro Olé Ⓜ *Portuguese/Spanish* 25 | 18 | 23 | $39

Asbury Park | 230 Main St. (bet. Cookman & Mattison Aves.) |
732-897-0048 | www.bistroole.com
"Why go to Newark?" when you can step into this Asbury Park
Iberian and experience "consistently delicious" cooking, not to mention "friendly" service and the "ebullience" of owner Rico Rivera,
who showers diners with his well-known hospitality; BYO red wine,
and watch how it somehow turns into "tasty" sangrias.

Bistro San Miguel 🗷 Ⓜ *Filipino* - | - | - | I

Middletown | 273 Rte. 35 (Iroquois Ave.) | 732-530-8150
Eat to the sounds of karaoke at this inexpensive Middletown Filipino
BYO where the chef-owner specializes in 'palm boxes' (broccoli-
sauced noodles with shrimp) and dishes of pig's knuckles; it's liter-
ally a storefont, since products from the Philippines are sold there.

🗷 Black Duck on Sunset *Eclectic* 26 | 22 | 24 | $45

West Cape May | 1 Sunset Blvd. (Broadway) | 609-898-0100 |
www.blackduckonsunset.com
At the sunset end of the West Cape May dining strip dwells this
"thoroughly enjoyable" Victorian BYO where you're bound to "eat
well" in light of the "excellent" Eclectic fare; black-and-white photos
give the place its "low-key" charm.

Black Forest Ⓜ *German* ▽ 19 | 15 | 19 | $34

Allentown | 42 S. Main St. (Lakeview Dr.) | 609-259-3197
Munich comes to Allentown via this Central Jersey Teutonic, one of
the area's only spots for those looking for "good home-cooked"
German meals and a "homey" ambiance to go with them; N.B. the
restaurant is BYO, so bring your best lager.

🗷 Black Forest Inn *Continental/German* 23 | 21 | 21 | $46

Stanhope | 249 Rte. 206 N. (I-80, exit 25) | 973-347-3344
If you dig "dumplings and spaetzle", this rustic Stanhope Continental-
German with its "stick-to-your-ribs" fare and "excellent" wines fits
the bill; some see the atmosphere as "kitschy", others as "quaint",
but the majority maintains this Bavarian has been a "landmark for
years" for good reason.

Black Horse Tavern & Pub *Pub Food* 19 | 19 | 19 | $36

Mendham | 1 W. Main St. (Hilltop Rd.) | 973-543-7300 |
www.blackhorsenj.com
A real "local haunt", this "perpetually crowded" American (in a converted 1742 farmhouse) in "quaint", horse-country Mendham is per-

fect for a "burger and beer" in the "lively" pub, the scene of "all the action"; P.S. for a "more formal" experience, "eat in the tavern."

Black Trumpet *American*　23 | 17 | 22 | $49

Spring Lake | The Sandpiper Inn | 7 Atlantic Ave. (Ocean Ave.) | 732-449-4700 | www.theblacktrumpet.com

Chefs Mark Mikolajczyk and Dave McCleery (both alums of Whispers) try for the 'inn' crowd with this "romantic" New American BYO whose "unfailingly polite" staff serves "exceptional" dishes just steps from the beach in Spring Lake's Sandpiper Inn; N.B. live piano can be heard every weekend.

Blu ☑ *American*　25 | 17 | 20 | $42

Montclair | 554 Bloomfield Ave. (bet. Maple Pl. & Park St.) | 973-509-2202 | www.restaurantblu.com

The plate is a "palette" in the hands of chef Zod Arifai, whose "inspired", "exciting" preparations of New American fare bring acclaim to his Montclair BYO storefront, a "small", "narrow" space suited to its "low-key" service; as for prices, the consensus is it's "a bargain considering the amazing food."

Blue *American/Eclectic*　23 | 19 | 21 | $46

Surf City | 1016 Long Beach Blvd. (11th St.) | 609-494-7556 | www.bluelbi.com

"Upscale yet comfortable", this seasonal Surf City BYO "oasis" is "not-your-average" LBI restaurant, with a "unique" Eclectic–New American menu that stands "several notches above" its competitors; the "minimalist", albeit "warm" decor seems an ideal partner for the food here.

ⓩ NEW Blue Bottle Café ⓈⓂ *American*　27 | 18 | 22 | $43

Hopewell | 101 E. Broad St. (Elm St.) | 609-333-1710 | www.thebluebottlecafe.com

"Super-talented" husband-and-wife team Aaron and Rory Philipson (chef and pastry chef, respectively) join forces at this "rural" Hopewell BYO "home run" serving "fantastic" New American cuisine in a "nondescript" building decked out in blue bottles; it's a "great addition" to the area claim correspondents who advise go and "see what all the fuss is about."

Blue Danube Ⓜ *E Euro.*　▽ 22 | 14 | 17 | $25

Trenton | 538 Adeline St. (bet. Chestnut & Elm Sts.) | 609-393-6133

"Abundant" helpings of "comforting", "old-world" Eastern European (Polish, Hungarian, German) is this allure at this "sweet" "old-time" Trenton spot; the service is "slow" but "always nice", and locals like the idea of supping on something "different" in this mecca of Italian restaurants.

Blue Eyes *Steak*　20 | 22 | 18 | $42

Sewell | 139 Egg Harbor Rd. (Delsea Dr.) | 856-227-5656 | www.blueeyesrestaurant.com

"Wonderful martinis start things off" for Sinatra-ites who've dined at this paean to the Rat Pack in Sewell selling "good" steaks and such along with a "swanky", loungey ambiance abetted by live singing; some say the alfresco option helps takes the "after-work" edge off.

NEW Blue Fish Grill Ⓜ *Seafood* ▽ 20 | 12 | 13 | $24

Flemington | 9 Central Ave. (Mine St.) | 908-237-4528 | www.thebluefishgrill.com

For a "little bit of New England" in Flemington, this "lively", "no-frills" BYO seafooder is quite the catch for "tasty", "well-prepared fish" cooked on a wood-fire grill; it's family-friendly and ideal" for casual outdoor get-togethers", plus it's so "inexpensive", "you'll have money left over for shopping" at the nearby outlet stores.

Blue Pig Tavern *American* 20 | 19 | 19 | $38

Cape May | Congress Hall Hotel | 251 Beach Ave. (bet. Congress & Perry Sts.) | 609-884-8421 | www.congresshall.com

While you "shouldn't expect anything too inventive", there's still "solidly consistent" cooking that emerges from the kitchen at this Cape May American tavern tucked into the "wonderfully restored" Congress Hall Hotel; "sit outside if you can", though in colder months, "ask for a table near the fireplace" in one of the adjacent rooms.

Ⓩ Blue Point Grill *Seafood* 25 | 16 | 21 | $37

Princeton | 258 Nassau St. (Pine St.) | 609-921-1211 | www.bluepointgrill.com

It's all about the gills – not necessarily the frills – at this Princeton BYO seafooder serving a menu of the "finest", "freshest", "perfectly" cooked fish in a "casual" space; a "knowledgeable" staff is on hand to help you wade through the "multiple" choices.

Blueside Grill *American/Seafood* 18 | 17 | 17 | $43

Englewood | 126 Engle St. (Demarest Ave.) | 201-871-1170 | www.bluesidegrill.com

Whether you think this Englewood New American seafooder "fits the bill when" you're hungry for "better-then-average" sushi and other "creative" fish dishes, or dismiss the vittles as "inconsistent" and the service "slow", the colorful, bi-level space (featuring two bars and dining areas), along with karaoke and jazz, helps at least keep things interesting.

NEW Blue Wave Ⓜ *Seafood* - | - | - | E

Westfield | 235 North Ave. W. (Central Ave.) | 908-233-0052

This nautically attired BYO seafooder in Westfield seems to serve everything that swims, whether it's bouillabaisse or more straightforward offerings, such as simple platters of grilled fish; though set in a storefront, it's still spiffy in its own way.

Bobby Chez Ⓜ *Seafood* 25 | 10 | 16 | $22

Margate | 8007 Ventnor Ave. (S. Gladstone Ave.) | 609-487-1922
Cherry Hill | Village Walk Shopping Ctr. | 1990 Rte. 70 E. (Old Orchard Rd.) | 856-751-7373 Ⓢ
Collingswood | 33 W. Collings Ave. (bet. Cove Rd. & Norwood Ave.) | 856-869-8000 Ⓢ

(continued)

(continued)

Bobby Chez

Mount Laurel | Centerton Sq. | Marter Ave. & Rte. 38 (bet. Centerton Rd. & New Jersey Tpke. N.) | 856-234-4146

Voorhees | Southgate Plaza | 1225 Haddonfield-Berlin Rd. (South Gate Dr.) | 856-768-6660 Ⓢ

www.bobbychezcrabcakes.com

"They have no equal" conclude cognoscenti about the "best" crab cakes "bar none" dispensed from these South Jersey specialists, where followers far and wide "stand in line" for the "legendary" signatures; note that the goods aren't necessarily a bargain, and it's not surprising that the quintet is touted for "takeout" (you can always "cook 'em up at home") given the "basic" decor.

NEW Bobby Flay Steak *Steak* | 24 | 25 | 22 | $66 |

Atlantic City | Borgata Hotel, Casino & Spa | 1 Borgata Way (Atlantic City Expwy., exit 1) | 609-317-1000 | www.theborgata.com

"Even if you don't win at the casino tables", you'll still come out on top at Bobby Flay's "winner" in AC's Borgata serving "so-good" steaks (enhanced by the TV toque's "wonderful" Southwest-influenced rubs) amid a "spectacular" leather, wood and glass David Rockwell design; bring extra cash – "all this flavor and beef doesn't come cheap."

BoBo's 33 Ⓢ *Mideastern* | ▽ 22 | 23 | 21 | $44 |

Atlantic Highlands | 33 First Ave. (Bay Ave.) | 732-872-1311 | www.bobos33.com

"Contemporary takes" on Middle Eastern specialties mark the veggie-friendly menu at this Atlantic Highlands spot that's both a "breath of fresh air" for the area and "maturing nicely"; the contemporary decor has "SoHo" written all over it, which may help explain the "lively" vibe.

NEW Bombay Curry & Grill *Indian* | - | - | - | M |

Basking Ridge | Lyons Mall | 973 S. Finley Ave. (Stonehouse Rd.) | 908-953-9400

Warmth from the setting, service and Indian fare make this Basking Ridge BYO a new favorite among locals looking for something other than the usual edible suspects; the lunch buffet's single-digit tabs are alone cause for celebrating.

Bombay Gardens Ⓜ *Indian* | 22 | 13 | 20 | $23 |

East Brunswick | Center 18 Mall | 1020 Rte. 18 N. (bet. Gunia St. & Hillsdale Rd.) | 732-613-9500 | www.bombaygardens.com

"The most helpful servers" ferry "truly delicious", "reasonably" priced Indian dishes at this East Brunswick strip-mall BYO whose food draws "oohs and aahs"; in a county "bursting with similar" restaurants, some say this one stands out among the "best."

Bosphorus *Turkish* | ▽ 22 | 8 | 17 | $21 |

Lake Hiawatha | 32 N. Beverwyck Rd. (bet. Lakeshore Dr. & Vail Rd.) | 973-335-9690

Ok, "don't look for any atmosphere" here, but if you want "great" food "cooked with love", you can't go wrong at this Lake Hiawatha

Middle Eastern BYO, the place for "authentic" Turkish offerings; portions are "plentiful", and fans tout takeout too.

Boulevard Grille *American*

FOOD	DECOR	SERVICE	COST
18	15	16	$35

Mahwah | 1033 MacArthur Blvd. (bet. Corporate Dr. & Ridge Rd.) | 201-760-9400 | www.boulevardgrille.com

Vending "appealing" lunches and dinners on its "diverse" menu, this BYO New American in a Mahwah strip mall also offers a "pleasant" setting and affordable tabs; though cons criticize "inconsistent service", most prefer to say meals here are "better than you'd expect."

Braddock's Tavern *American*

FOOD	DECOR	SERVICE	COST
22	23	22	$41

Medford | 39 S. Main St. (Coates St.) | 609-654-1604 | www.braddocks.com

The menu's been tweaked slightly (some dishes now have a more modern edge), and most applaud the "surprising" quality of the fare at this Medford Traditional American still supplying a "Colonial", "quaint-Americana" setting; as for the ambiance, some say "it's the only place where grandparents and 20-year-olds can eat in harmony."

Brandl. *American*

FOOD	DECOR	SERVICE	COST
24	17	19	$53

Belmar | 703 Belmar Plaza (bet. Main St. & 9th Ave.) | 732-280-7501 | www.brandlrestaurant.com

"Worthy of Manhattan", this storefront Belmar BYO is viewed as an "incredible find" for the Jersey Shore, staying "on top of things" with its "terrific" New American preparations; for those stung by "sticker shock", there's always the three-course prix fixe.

Brannon's Hurricane House *American*

FOOD	DECOR	SERVICE	COST
∇ 21	19	19	$23

Barnegat | 688 E. Bay Ave. (Rte. 9) | 609-698-4401 | www.barnegathurricanehouse.com

Chef Chris Brannon has put his training to use and transformed this former Barnegat ice cream parlor into a New American BYO with an evolving menu; the space also benefits from a makeover, and overall, this arrival is pumping new life into an area with limited dining options.

Brasilia Grill *Brazilian*

FOOD	DECOR	SERVICE	COST
23	15	21	$32

Newark | 99 Monroe St. (bet. Ferry & Lafayette Sts.) | 973-465-1227

"Come hungry and leave stuffed" " at this "festive", roomy Ironbound Brazilian where "quality and quantity" come together; it's an all-you-can-eat "beef orgy", and the salad bar is worth "checking out", as are the prix fixe lunch and dinner specials; N.B. though the original Ferry Street is still shuttered after a fire, it's set to reopen soon.

Brass Rail, The *American*

FOOD	DECOR	SERVICE	COST
19	19	18	$40

Hoboken | 135 Washington St. (2nd St.) | 201-659-7074 | www.thebrassrailnj.com

Although some wish this New American "mainstay" in Hoboken would "figure out" if it's "a sports bar or a restaurant", most like it for a bi-level setup where you can "casually" chow down in the "terrific" ground-floor bar area or head "away from the noise" to the "upscale", "romantic upstairs dining room."

	FOOD	DECOR	SERVICE	COST

Brennan's Steakhouse *Steak*

`22` `20` `22` `$48`

Neptune City | 62 W. Sylvania Ave. (Morris Ave.) | 732-774-5040
They've got the chops to pull off consistently "solid" steaks at this Neptune City carnivorium that feels like one you'd find in "Midtown Manhattan"; the "plus" of a partition between the bar and dining area is a welcome relief for meat eaters distracted by "noise."

NEW Brickwall Tavern & Dining Room ● *American*

▽ `19` `23` `20` `$25`

Asbury Park | 522 Cookman Ave. (Bangs Ave.) | 732-774-1264 | www.brickwalltavern.com
"Catch up with friends and have a bite" at Asbury Park's latest "hangout" that attracts with "above-average" Americana (think mac 'n' cheese and chicken pot pie) and with its *"Cheers"*-like atmosphere, the latter bolstered by nightly live music.

Brioso *Italian*

`23` `18` `17` `$37`

Marlboro | Willow Pointe Shopping Ctr. | 184 Hwy. 9 (Union Hill Rd.) | 732-617-1700 | www.briosoristorante.com
Fans "love" this Marlboro BYO, and it's easy to see why on account of the "excellent" cooking that seems like what an "Italian grandma" would offer "for Sunday dinner"; alas, a noticeably "cold attitude" from the staff sends a chill through "commoners" ("if you're not a regular, you'll be ignored").

Brix 67 *Eclectic/Japanese*

`18` `20` `16` `$41`

Summit | 67 Union Pl. (Summit Ave.) | 908-273-4448 | www.brix-67.com
This "'in' place in Summit" attracts a "hip crowd" with its "trendy" milieu and an "extensive" Eclectic menu that ranges from "fresh sushi" to pastas to brick-oven pizzas – with "results that are just as eclectic" as the eats; the service can be "hit-or-miss" here, but the "cool", "clubby feel" keeps it "well-trafficked"; P.S. "they serve NJ wines", but you can also BYO.

Brooklyn's Coal-Burning Brick-Oven Pizzeria ⊄ *Pizza*

`22` `11` `15` `$18`

Edgewater | Edgewater Commons Shopping Ctr. | 443 River Rd. (Hudson River Rd.) | 201-945-9096
Hackensack | 161 Hackensack Ave. (Rte. 4) | 201-342-2727
Ridgewood | 15 Oak St. (Ridgewood Ave.) | 201-493-7600 ⊠
"It ain't Brooklyn", but this "no-frills", "cash-only" Bergen County trio turns out some of the "best pies this side of the Hudson": "tasty, crispy", brick-oven rounds topped with "fresh mozzarella" and "flavorful sauce"; there are "no slices", but surveyors insist "you'll want the whole pie anyway"; P.S. "you can BYO" at the Edgewater and Ridgewood locations, but "Hackensack serves beer and wine."

Brothers Moon ⓜ *French*

`22` `18` `20` `$41`

Hopewell | 7 W. Broad St. (Greenwood Ave.) | 609-333-1330 | www.brothersmoon.com
"An oasis in charming Hopewell", this New French BYO "favorite" receives accolades for chef-owner Will Mooney's "always fresh and

interesting menu" that "strives to incorporate local", seasonal and "organic" ingredients; though a few fret it's been "hit-or-miss recently", most focus on the "professional staff" and "comfortable ambiance"; N.B. there's an on-site retail and take-out shop.

NEW Buddakan Pan-Asian
FOOD	DECOR	SERVICE	COST
–	–	–	E

Atlantic City | Pier at Caesars | 1 Atlantic Ocean (Arkansas Ave.) | 609-674-0100 | www.buddakanac.com

The Pier at Caesars hosts version 3.0 of Stephen Starr's chic Pan-Asian, modeled loosely after his original in Philadelphia and the follow-up hit in NYC; eager servers whisk about with plates of dumplings and oversize drinks, and though the locale is nautical, the atmosphere here is dimly lit and anything but tranquil, despite the mammoth Buddha.

Bula World Cuisine M Eclectic
FOOD	DECOR	SERVICE	COST
∇ 23	16	20	$39

Newton | 134 Spring St. (Rte. 206) | 973-579-7338 | www.bularestaurant.com

Thanks to "interesting", "well-executed" Eclectic cooking and a "sweet" staff, if they could, fans "would eat every night" at this "laid-back" Newton BYO whose menu covers the global gamut; live jazz on Friday nights adds to the "funky, college feel."

Busch's Seafood M Seafood
FOOD	DECOR	SERVICE	COST
19	16	17	$38

Sea Isle City | 8700 Landis Ave. (87th St.) | 609-263-8626 | www.buschsseafood.com

In the same family for 124 years, this durable, "old-school" Sea Isle City roadhouse is still "worth the trip for the she-crab soup alone", although the other "classic" fish fare comes up for praise too; crabs consider the seafood "fresher" than the "dark 'n' dingy" digs.

Buttonwood Manor American
FOOD	DECOR	SERVICE	COST
∇ 18	18	18	$36

Matawan | 845 Rte. 34 (Edgewater Dr.) | 732-566-6220 | www.buttonwoodmanor.net

Tablecloths and flowers complete the very Victorian setting at this "stable" Matawan American dishing a "standard" "steak-and-seafood"-oriented slate; there's a "great" view of Lake Lefferts, and a scene that's mostly "senior citizen."

Cabin, The American
FOOD	DECOR	SERVICE	COST
18	17	18	$24

Howell | 984 Rte. 33 E. (Fairfield Rd.) | 732-462-3090 | www.thecabinrestaurant.net

"Big" portions and "real" American food add up to "happy people" at this "popular" Monmouth County "roadhouse" doling out "very good" bar food amid "woodsy" quarters; the "pickup truck" vibe is so authentic here, some dub the place "HowellAlabama."

Cafe Arugula M Italian
FOOD	DECOR	SERVICE	COST
20	16	19	$38

South Orange | 59 S. Orange Ave. (Scotland Rd.) | 973-378-9099 | www.cafearugula.com

For "generous quantities" of "creative, consistent" Italian fare, head to this "comfortable, cozy neighborhood" "standby" in South Orange where the menu is topped off with an extensive list of "nightly specials" and "wonderful" homemade gelato; though a few feel this "bang-for-your-buck" BYO "needs a face-lift", most agree it's a "reliable" "place to take the family."

Cafe at Rosemont, The ⓜ American 22 | 18 | 22 | $32
Rosemont | 88 Kingwood-Stockton Rd. (Rte. 519) | 609-397-4097 | www.cafeatrosemont.com
"Worth the scenic drive" to Rosemont, this "quaint country cafe" "in an old general store" (circa 1865) offers "wonderful" New American fare served by a "warm", "efficient" staff; although there's a "fantastic weekend brunch", your "best bet" is on Wednesday night, when a three-course, $22 prix fixe menu "highlights a different [global] cuisine each week"; P.S. "the BYO policy is a plus."

Cafe Coloré ⓜ Italian 21 | 18 | 21 | $32
Freehold Township | Chadwick Sq. | 3333 Rte. 9 N. (Jackson Mills Rd.) | 732-462-2233 | www.cafecolorefreehold.com
The strip mall is just part of the "disguise" of this Freehold Township BYO, where you're bound to leave "well fed" on a variety of "quality" Italian preparations offered by "friendly" servers; the "comfortable", "inviting" environs are even good for "dates."

Cafe Cucina ⓢ Italian 23 | 18 | 22 | $39
Branchburg | 3366 Rte. 22 W. (bet. County Line & Readington Rds.) | 908-526-4907 | www.cafecucina.com
Supping on "delicious" Italian fare on the dining room's balcony is a "romantic" touch at this "wonderful" Branchburg restaurant that's "a hit" "for special occasions, celebrations" or "executive lunches"; plus, the "fabulous food" and killer martinis are served by a "courteous" staff; N.B. weekend entertainment is in the offing.

Cafe Emilia Italian 22 | 21 | 22 | $42
Bridgewater | 705 Rte. 202 N. (Charlotte Dr.) | 908-429-1410 | www.cafeemilia.com
They turn out the "charm" at this Bridgewater Italian where clients "return" on account of the ambiance (you'll "feel like a part of their family") and "well-prepared" food; P.S. it's "the place to go" when you want to fill up "before a movie at Bridgewater Commons."

Café Gallery Continental 21 | 22 | 22 | $38
Burlington | 219 High St. (Pearl St.) | 609-386-6150 | www.cafegalleryburlington.com
"Peaceful" views of the Delaware River are just one factor in the "lovely" setting at this bi-level Burlington Continental, since the works of local art (displayed in the dining room and upstairs gallery) lend their own "charm"; while the food's "not mind-blowing", it's still "reliably" good, and most tout the "Sunday brunch as your best bet."

Cafe Graziella Italian 22 | 15 | 19 | $31
Hillsborough | Cost Cutters Shopping Ctr. | 390 Rte. 206 (Andria Ave.) | 908-281-0700 | www.cafegraziella.com
"Sshh . . . don't tell anyone" about this "solid" BYO Italian "surprise" that "doesn't look like much from the outside" (it's "hidden" in a Hillsborough strip mall) but offers "delicious", "dependable food"

brought by "a personable staff"; "friendly owners" and a "nice atmosphere" "make for a relaxing evening."

Cafe Italiano *Italian*

| 18 | 16 | 18 | $40 |

Englewood Cliffs | 14 Sylvan Ave. (Irving Ave.) | 201-461-5041

For "old-world style" and an "up-to-date" Italian menu, locals "just love" this "cheery" Englewood Cliffs cafe that's a "solid standby" for "decent food" ferried by an "amicable" staff; it now serves wine and liquor too (it's no longer BYO), which may "up the ante" pricewise, but doesn't diminish the value of the "great early-bird deal" and "relaxing" outside seating.

Cafe Loren Ⓜ *American*

| ▽ 25 | 20 | 26 | $40 |

Avalon | 2288 Dune Dr. (23rd St.) | 609-967-8228 | www.cafeloren.com

This seasonal BYO Avalon American, the doyenne of the local fine-dining scene for nearly 30 years, keeps turning out "first-class" fare accompanied by "attentive" service; once again, the only lament is that fans "wish it were open all year."

Ⓩ Cafe Matisse *Eclectic*

| 27 | 25 | 26 | $66 |

Rutherford | 167 Park Ave. (bet. E. Park Pl. & Highland Cross) | 201-935-2995 | www.cafematisse.com

This "artful find" in Rutherford is "as good as it gets" for "outstanding", "beautifully presented" Eclectic cuisine (with early-bird and prix fixe options) from "creative" chef-owner Peter Loria; though "pricey", this "special-occasion" experience comes complete with "superior service" and an "exceptional ambiance" that includes an "elegant dining room" with hand-blown glass chandeliers and "romantic" garden seating; P.S. it's BYO with a "lovely wine shop up front."

Cafe Metro *Eclectic*

| 21 | 17 | 20 | $27 |

Denville | 60 Diamond Spring Rd. (bet. 1st Ave. & Orchard St.) | 973-625-1055 | www.thecafemetro.com

"Those looking to eat healthy" "have a range of options" at this veggie-centric Eclectic that's a "casual" stop for lunch or "a light meal" with its "interesting menu" of fish, chicken, pasta and "vegan choices too", all "appealingly presented" in a "cute converted house" in Denville; although it remains BYO in the dining room, they've recently added an upstairs wine bar that's expected to serve small plates.

Ⓩ Cafe Panache Ⓢ *Eclectic*

| 28 | 21 | 26 | $55 |

Ramsey | 130 E. Main St. (Rte. 17) | 201-934-0030 | www.cafepanachenj.com

"From the minute you walk in until you leave", expect a "quality dining experience" at chef-owner Kevin Kohler's "gift to the palate", this "first-rate" "shining star" in Ramsey where an "always wonderful", "always changing" Eclectic menu is served by a "friendly", "knowledgeable" staff in a "charming" if "small" space; it's "expensive", but the BYO policy can "bring costs down"; P.S. be sure to make your reservation "well in advance."

Caffe Aldo Lamberti *Italian*

| 23 | 21 | 22 | $41 |

Cherry Hill | 2011 Rte. 70 W. (Haddonfield Rd.) | 856-663-1747 | www.lambertis.com

At the "high end" of a prominent restaurant group (with outposts in Delaware and Pennsylvania), this "special-occasion" Cherry Hill Italian "never disappoints" its fans given the consistently "excellent" cuisine and service, and "very good" wine list; P.S. bring good credit – the tabs are "pricey."

California Grill *Eclectic*

| 20 | 13 | 17 | $26 |

Flemington | Kitchen Expo Plaza | 1 Rte. 31 (US Hwy. 202) | 908-806-7141 | www.californiagrillnj.com

For "the biggest and best salads you've ever seen" "piled high" with "unique" ingredients plus "fabulous" soups and "thin-crust pizzas", hit this strip-mall Eclectic in Flemington that's a "surprisingly good", "veg-friendly" option for a BYO "lunch or dinner"; although a few find the staff "preoccupied" and the ambiance "a turnoff", most consider it to be a "healthy", "easy" stop after shopping the nearby outlets.

NEW Caneel Bay
Caribbean Grill *Caribbean*

| ∇ 17 | 15 | 18 | $37 |

Harvey Cedars | 7601 Long Beach Blvd. (76th St.) | 609-361-6490 | www.caneelbaycaribbeangrill.com

This north-end LBI Caribbean specialist in Harvey Cedars purveys Island food that tastes "authentic" in "small", blue-and-green digs; its fans want it to "stay around", but not before detractors cite cooking that "falls short of the mark."

Capriccio *Italian*

| 25 | 23 | 25 | $58 |

Atlantic City | Resorts Atlantic City Casino & Hotel | 1133 Boardwalk (North Carolina Ave.) | 609-340-6789

"Splendid dining experiences" are not uncommon at this long-running (since 1979) Italian in the Resorts Casino & Hotel whose "elegant" decor pairs nicely with the "top-notch" menu; slot players pronounce it's even "worth spending part of your jackpot here."

Capt'n Ed's Place *Seafood/Steak*

| 19 | 15 | 17 | $33 |

Point Pleasant | 1001 Arnold Ave. (Pine Bluff Ave.) | 732-892-4121 | www.captainedsplace.com

"Sizzling" surf 'n' turf that you cook on "hot stones" is the hook (or "gimmick") at this Point Pleasant BYO, the catalyst for "interesting" conversations, especially if you're on a "first date"; in fact, some are so focused on DIY cooking that they take the "friendly" staff for granite.

Carmine's ● *Italian*

| 20 | 19 | 19 | $38 |

Atlantic City | The Quarter at the Tropicana | 2801 Pacific Ave. (S. Iowa Ave.) | 609-572-9300 | www.carminesnyc.com

"Lotsa pasta" "busts" lotsa guts at this AC Italian in the Quarter (a spin-off of the famed NYC eatery) where bringing "friends and families" is the only way to polish off the "red-sauce" specialties doled out in "daunting" servings amid a "madhouse" of a setting;

P.S. bolstering its "big-portion" bona fides, the restaurant is host to the International Meatball Eating Contest.

	FOOD	DECOR	SERVICE	COST

Casa Dante *Italian* — 22 | 18 | 21 | $46

Jersey City | 737 Newark Ave. (bet. Kennedy Blvd. & Summit Ave.) | 201-795-2750 | www.casadante.com

Despite a 2005 ownership and menu change, this 35-plus-year-old Jersey City "legend" still pulls down praise for "well-prepared" "old-world Italian" "served with care" by a "capable staff" in a "friendly atmosphere"; though regulars are pleased it's been "given a fresh look", those who feel it's "not what it used to be" urge management to "bring back the old menu."

Casa Giuseppe Ⓜ *Italian* — 24 | 18 | 23 | $41

Iselin | 487 Rte. 27/Lincoln Hwy. (Oaktree Rd.) | 732-283-9111 | www.casagiuseppe.com

A "surprise find" that "belies its location" among the offices of Metropark, this Iselin Northern Italian is "a cut above" considering its "varied menu", "friendly", "attentive service" and "homey atmosphere"; it's "a little pricey" "for the area", however, so keep it in mind "for a business lunch" or "to celebrate a special occasion."

Casa Maya *Mexican* — 20 | 16 | 19 | $26

Meyersville | 615 Meyersville Rd. (Hickory Tavern Rd.) | 908-580-0799
High Bridge | 1 Main St. (W. Main St.) | 908-638-4032 Ⓜ
www.casamayamexican.com

For "*delicioso*" Mexican, aficionados affirm these "charming, kitschy" BYO cantinas are just the ticket for "abundant" portions of "reasonably priced" Sonoran-style (i.e. mildly spiced) fare; although they "can get extremely crowded" (there are "no reservations"), "super-friendly" service atones for it.

Casa Solar Ⓜ *Pan-Latin* — 25 | 19 | 16 | $40

Belmar | 1104 Main St. (bet. 11th & 12th Sts.) | 732-556-1144

The kitchen sends out "memorable" meals at this "tightly spaced" and frequently "busy" Pan-Latin Belmar BYO that's open year-round; some stung by "slow service" and "excessive wait times" for food advise you bring "lots of wine" to pass the time.

Casa Vasca *Spanish* — 24 | 14 | 22 | $33

Newark | 141 Elm St. (Prospect St.) | 973-465-1350

This 31-year-old Ironbound institution is "always crowded for a good reason": "huge portions" of "consistently delicious" Basque cuisine that has an equally "big taste" and is served by a "friendly" staff; it may have "tired decor" and "long waits" (even with reservations), but its "free parking lot" and convenient location near the NJPAC make it a "favorite."

NEW Casona Ⓜ *Cuban* — 24 | 22 | 21 | $34

Collingswood | 563 Haddon Ave. (Knight Ave.) | 856-854-2874 | www.mycasona.com

The "modernized" Cuban dishes are "well prepared" and the mojitos are the "best" (bring rum) at this Collingswood BYO operating in an old Victorian; while the "inviting" dining room attracts, some prefer to "hold out for warm weather" to dine on the "great" wraparound porch.

Catelli *Italian* | 24 | 24 | 22 | $50

Voorhees | The Plaza | 1000 Main St. (bet. Evesham & Kresson Rds.) | 856-751-6069 | www.catellirestaurant.com

"Very good" meals are assured at this "elegant" Voorhees Italian, a welcome "oasis in hoagieland" frequented by South Jersey pols and other bigwigs; it's "special-occasion" central, evidenced by the "expense"-account pricing (though "it's money well spent").

Cathay 22 *Chinese* | 23 | 16 | 20 | $33

Springfield | 124 Rte. 22 W. (Hillside Ave.) | 973-467-8688 | www.cathay22.com

"If you like spicy food, this place is for you" aver acolytes of this "terrific, upscale" Szechuan in Springfield, where the "stark interior should not deter you" from ordering one of the "authentic, delicious" dishes that are "nicely presented" and "elegantly served"; though "expensive", its "fully stocked bar" and "friendly faces" make this Asian "worth every penny."

☑ NEW Catherine Lombardi *Italian* | 21 | 26 | 21 | $54

New Brunswick | 3 Livingston Ave. (George St.) | 732-296-9463 | www.catherinelombardi.com

"What a beautiful place!" rave respondents about this dinner-only New Brunswick addition, an "upscale Italian" – complete with "glowing faux fireplaces [to] add to the ambiance" – from the group behind downstairs sibling, Stage Left; it's named after co-owner Mark Pascal's grandmother, so expect "generous portions" of "yummy" dishes; those who find it "pricey" can "head for the bar" to sample from the 1,000-label wine list and "fantastic cocktail menu."

Cenzino ☒ *Italian* | 24 | 21 | 25 | $46

Oakland | 589 Ramapo Valley Rd. (Franklin Ave.) | 201-337-6693 | www.cenzinos.com

The "affable" "owner is there to greet you" at the door and his "extremely professional", "tuxedoed" staff will "see to every detail to make your evening enjoyable" at this classy Oakland Italian offering "consistent", "terrific" entrees and "creative, tasty specials"; pampered patrons should prepare for a "fabulous dining experience" that may be a "little pricey" but is "first-class" all the way.

☑ Chakra *American* | 21 | 27 | 18 | $52

Paramus | 144 Rte. 4 E. (Arcadian Way) | 201-556-1530 | www.chakrarestaurant.com

"Let loose your inner *om*" at this "exotic" "oasis" within "the concrete jungle of Bergen County", an "upscale" New American "scene" where the "amazing atmosphere" ("romantic candles, pillows and drapes" plus a "cascading" water wall) "stimulates the senses as much as" the "fresh, unique" food; all in all, it's "out of this world", but expect the "loud" environs and "expensive" tabs to bring you back to earth.

	FOOD	DECOR	SERVICE	COST

Champa Laos *French/Thai*

▽ 23 | 18 | 22 | $27

Cherry Hill | 219 Haddonfield-Berlin Rd. (Brace Rd.) | 856-795-0188 | www.champalaos.com

It's "worth seeking out" this Cherry Hill BYO strip-maller (with a counterpart in Philly) if you favor "great" Thai-French food at a "great" buy; there's "no other place like it around", plus, the "nicest people" work there.

Chand Palace *Indian*

22 | 12 | 18 | $24

Parsippany | 257 Littleton Rd. (Parsippany Rd.) | 973-334-5444 | www.chandpalace.com

If you like "tingling taste buds", you'll find "the spice is right" at this "strip-mall find" in Paramus where the "fresh, quality" Indian items include a "variety of vegetarian dishes" that ensure "you'll never miss the meat"; it may be lacking in decor, but a "pleasant" staff and "wonderful lunch buffet" make it "a steal."

Chao Phaya *Thai*

23 | 14 | 20 | $24

NEW **Somerset** | Somerset Village Shopping Ctr. | 900 Easton Ave. (Foxwood Dr.) | 732-249-0110

Somerville | 9 Davenport St. (W. Main St.) | 908-231-0655 www.chaophaya.com

Although the decor is "casual" at this "no-frills Thai" in Somerville, the "delicious" food is "prepared with a touch of mystery" that proves "authentically hot" but can be adjusted "to your tolerance level for spice"; "BYO is a plus here", as is a "quick and courteous" staff; P.S. "the owner just opened a second location in Somerset."

Charley's Ocean Grill *American*

19 | 12 | 19 | $34

Long Branch | 29 Avenel Blvd. (Ocean Ave.) | 732-222-4499

This recently renovated Long Branch "hangout" is a "favorite" for those looking for a "quick bite", "good", "standard" American chow and a "great" value; hence, it's no surprise that the joint is "always crowded."

Charrito's *Mexican*

24 | 18 | 18 | $25

Hoboken | 1024 Washington St. (bet. 10th & 11th Sts.) | 201-659-2800

Hoboken | 121 Washington St. (bet. 1st & 2nd Sts.) | 201-418-8600

Union City | 4900 Bergenline Ave. (49th St.) | 201-863-0345 www.loscharritos.com

"They're tight, but the goods are worth every bite" is the word on these popular family-run BYO Mexicans, sources for "excellent" Oaxacan specialties including the "best" tableside guacamole and "accommodating" service; N.B. a fourth location with three floors and a liquor license is set to open in Weehawken in summer 2007.

☒ Chart House *American/Seafood*

20 | 25 | 20 | $49

Weehawken | Lincoln Harbor | Pier D-T (Harbor Blvd.) | 201-348-6628 | www.chart-house.com

With its floor-to-ceiling windows, you can't ignore the "stunning" views of NYC that keep the "all-time-favorite" standing in tact of this roomy Weehawken American seafooder, the perfect ticket for guaranteed "romantic" dining; though it's given second-stage status, most consider the food "first-rate, especially for a chain."

☑ Cheesecake Factory, The *American*   19 | 19 | 17 | $28

Hackensack | Riverside Square Mall | 197 Riverside Sq. (Hackensack Ave.) | 201-488-0330 ●

Wayne | Willowbrook Mall | 1700 Willowbrook Blvd. (Rte. 46) | 973-890-1400

Edison | Menlo Park Mall | 455 Menlo Park Dr. (Rte. 1) | 732-494-7000

NEW Cherry Hill | 931 Haddonfield Rd. (bet. Graham & Severn Aves.) | 856-665-7550

www.thecheesecakefactory.com

"There should be more of these places around" to feed the throngs, marvel fans of these "overcrowded" Traditional American chain outlets famed for their "oversized" portions, "majestically" long menus and "dependably" good fare, not to mention "great" cheesecakes (with over 30 varieties); despite "crazy" waits, most leave these "cholesterol factories" "happy and well fed."

☑ Chef's Table, The Ⓜ *French*   28 | 18 | 25 | $49

Franklin Lakes | Franklin Square Shopping Ctr. | 754 Franklin Ave. (Pulis Ave.) | 201-891-6644

Everything that comes out of the kitchen is *"extraordinaire"* at this "fabulous" Classic French BYO in Franklin Lakes (the bailiwick of "pro" chef Claude Baills), a "little jewel" shoehorned into a "dowdy" strip mall; the setting's warmed by "knowledgeable" service, and regulars advise to just "sit back and let it all enchant you."

Chef Vola's Ⓜ⇱ *Italian*   26 | 10 | 23 | $49

Atlantic City | 111 S. Albion Pl. (Pacific Ave.) | 609-345-2022

Although you "take one look and stare in disbelief" at the decor, when the Italian "food comes out you'll understand" why this cash-only, 86-year-old Atlantic City BYO in a basement is a "cult" classic for so many admirers; true, it may not be the "best-kept secret it once was", but you still have to "know someone" to get a reservation.

Chengdu 46 Ⓜ *Chinese*   24 | 18 | 21 | $42

Clifton | 1105 Rte. 46 E. (Rock Hill Rd.) | 973-777-8855 | www.chengdu46.com

This "consistent" Clifton performer makes for "memorable" Chinese meals presented by "attentive" servers within an "elegant" space that looks like it hasn't changed in years; for fine dining, this "tried-and-true" institution is still "worth getting dressed up for"; P.S. oenophiles appreciate the "great" wine list.

☑ Chez Catherine ⓈⓂ *French*   27 | 21 | 25 | $64

Westfield | 431 North Ave. (E. Broad St.) | 908-654-4011 | www.chezcatherine.com

For a "top-drawer" experience, be sure to visit this "pretty" Provençal Westfield bistro where the bill of fare is "delectably" "expert" French cuisine backed by "excellent" wines and "polished" service, all presided over by proprietors Didier and Edith Jouvenet; try

| | FOOD | DECOR | SERVICE | COST |

to imagine a "slice of France" to effectively shake off any thoughts about "steep prices."

Chez Elena Wu *Asian/French*
| 24 | 19 | 22 | $33 |

Voorhees | Ritz Shopping Ctr. | 910 Haddonfield-Berlin Rd. (Voorhees Dr.) | 856-566-3222

"First-class" dining, namely "terrific", "beautiful" Asian-French cooking, "attentive", "eager-to-please" service and an upscale setting support the well-deserved popularity of this Voorhees BYO under the stewardship of the "gracious" Elena Wu and family; overall, it's a "great alternative" to the neighborhood's other eateries.

Chilangos *Mexican*
| ∇ 21 | 16 | 19 | $24 |

Highlands | 272 Bay Ave. (Sea Drift Ave.) | 732-708-0505 | www.chilangosnj.com

The food "never fails" followers of this "cute" Highlands Mexican whose menu is priced "reasonably" and where the service is "pleasant"; the spot's stature is enhanced by the "best" selection of tequilas, with over 80 varieties to choose from.

China Palace *Taiwanese*
| - | - | - | I |

Middletown | Harmony Bowl | 1815 Rte. 35 (Old Country Rd.) | 732-957-0554

Tucked inside Harmony Bowl, this authentic Taiwanese specialist (known mostly to local Chinese residents) proffers hearty fare in modest digs; the homey plates warm purists' palates, as do the bargain checks.

Chophouse, The *Chophouse/Seafood*
| 23 | 22 | 21 | $54 |

Gibbsboro | 4 Lakeview Dr. S./Rte. 561 (E. Clementon Rd.) | 856-566-7300 | www.thechophouse.us

There's an ambiance that's pure "high-end" (read: mahogany, leather booths and white tablecloths) at this lively steakhouse in out-of-the-way Gibbsboro that "excels" at steak and seafood; from the sight of things, folks are having "fun", since the noise levels are high and the bar is "yuppie-pickup" paradise.

Chowpatty M *Indian*
| - | - | - | I |

Iselin | Little India | 1349 Oak Tree Rd. (Marconi Ave.) | 732-283-9020 | www.chowpattyfoods.com

Serving a massive menu of Indian foods, including Gujarati selections along with items from the southern and northern parts of India, this Iselin BYO landmark is widely known for not only its fare but also for its catering and mail-order business; take-out fans can stop in the adjacent market, which vends sweets, snacks and the like.

Christie's *Italian*
| 24 | 18 | 20 | $37 |

Howell | Howell Ctr. | 2420 Rte. 9 S. (White Rd.) | 732-780-8310 | www.christiesrestaurant.us

The menu is "wonderful" and the setting "charms" at this strip-center Howell BYO made for those with "big appetites" who savor the "large" portions of "excellent" Italian dishes; "good" specials and "attentive" service are part of the package.

	FOOD	DECOR	SERVICE	COST

Christopher's Cafe Ⓜ *American*   21 | 13 | 16 | $26

Colts Neck | 41 Rte. 34 (Rte. 537) | 732-308-3668 |
www.christopherscafe.com

The "best place around for a satisfying breakfast" draws diners to
this Colts Neck American BYO that also offers "interesting" selections for lunch and dinner; the "cozy" setting counterbalances the
occasionally "slow service."

Cinque Figlie Ⓢ *Italian*   21 | 19 | 21 | $46

Morristown | 302 Whippany Rd. (Park Ave.) | Whippany | 973-560-0545 |
www.fivedaughters.com

It's "not unusual" to have one of the owner's eponymous, "eager-to-
please" *cinque figlie* (five daughters) serve you at this "charming",
"family-operated" Morristown Italian where the "delicious" vittles
are "carefully prepared" "in a "quaint restored house"; P.S. the new
bar/seating area is ideal to "grab a drink if you have to wait."

Circa *French*   ▽ 20 | 21 | 20 | $46

High Bridge | 37 Main St. (McDonald St.) | 908-638-5560 |
www.circa-restaurant.com

Bringing some "SoHo" (think Balthazar) to "small-town" High
Bridge, this "hit" of a French brasserie comes equipped with
pressed-tin ceiling, mirrors and banquettes to highlight chef
Michael Coury's (ex Ryland Inn) "good" food, along with wines and
a "top-flight" raw bar; "who'd have thought" this "favorite" would be
in the neighborhood?

City Bistro *American*   19 | 19 | 19 | $34

Hoboken | 56-58 14th St. (bet. Hudson & Washington Sts.) |
201-963-8200

"Young" Hobokenites descend upon this "always-busy" split-level
New American brownstone for its "phenomenal" rooftop views of
NYC and equally phenomenal scene sparked by "great" drink specials; with all the "socializing" going on, it may be "hard to remember what you ate" – namely solidly "good" food – especially once the
venue morphs into a "meat market."

Clark's Landing *American*   17 | 19 | 17 | $35

Point Pleasant | 847 Arnold Ave. (bet. Lincoln & Trenton Aves.) |
732-899-1111 | www.clarksbarandgrill.com

"Watching the sunset" over the Manasquan River is what it's all about
for a "mature" crowd that convenes at this Point Pleasant American
with "great" bars inside and outside on the deck; indeed, the "gorgeous" views help neutralize any negatives about the "ok" vittles.

Claude's *French*   ▽ 25 | 20 | 22 | $48

North Wildwood | 100 Olde New Jersey Ave. (1st Ave.) | 609-522-0400 |
www.claudesrestaurant.com

Gallic to its core, this white-tablecloth BYO bistro offers an alternative to North Wildwood's bars in large part to a "very good" French
roster (bouillabaisse and the like); "quaint" decor completes the
très français picture.

	FOOD	DECOR	SERVICE	COST

Clementine's Café *Creole*
▽ 24 | 21 | 24 | $37

Avon-by-the-Sea | 306 Main Ave. (Lincoln Ave.) | 732-988-7979
The chef at this "small" Avon-by-the-Sea BYO draws on his knowledge of Louisiana cuisine to turn out "delicious" Creole cookery "treasured" by Shore fans; Tiffany lighting and mahogany emit a genuine old-world, New Orleans vibe.

Clydz ● *American*
23 | 19 | 21 | $42

New Brunswick | 55 Paterson St. (Spring St.) | 732-846-6521 | www.clydz.com
Squeeze into the "so-crowded" quarters for the "longest" list of the "best" martinis at this "dark" "speakeasy" of a New Brunswick New American bar/eatery, where the "amazing" cocktail specialties overshadow the "consistently good", "adventurous" kitchen; no doubt, it's a "loud", sometimes "rowdy" scene, but the "fireplace in the bar is a nice homey touch."

🅉 NEW CoccoLa *American/Italian*
22 | 26 | 19 | $46

Hillsborough | 150 Rte. 206 S. (bet. Brooks Blvd. & Camplain Rd.) | 908-704-1160 | www.coccolarestaurant.com
You "won't feel like you're in Hillsborough" when you show up at this roomy New American–Italian rookie, a "refreshing addition" whose "beautiful" "mod" decor (featuring purple, semicircular banquettes and a raw bar) frames the "delicious" food paired with an eclectic list of wines; P.S. try to secure a table "near the open kitchen."

Coconut Bay Asian Cuisine Ⓜ *Asian*
21 | 18 | 20 | $23

Voorhees | Echelon Village Plaza | 1120 White Horse Rd. (Berlin Rd.) | 856-783-8878 | www.coconutbayasiancuisine.com
Red hues and low lighting set an "exotic" mood at this Voorhees BYO whose Asian menu incorporates Chinese, Japanese and Thai influences and yields "dependably good" dishes; fans forget the strip-mall location once they notice "attentive" service and "inexpensive" tabs.

Columbia Inn Ⓜ *Pizza*
20 | 12 | 17 | $34

Montville | 29 Main Rd./Rte. 202 (Morris Ave.) | 973-263-1300
Although this Montville Italian does a "brisk business" with its "thin-crust" brick-oven pizzas, the "honest", "reliable" cooking extends to the other offerings that include "imaginative" daily specials; "bargain" bills ally with the food to help overcome "not-five-star" decor.

Conte's *Pizza*
– | – | – | I

Princeton | 339 Witherspoon St. (Guyot Ave.) | 609-921-8041
For Princetonians, pizza means this congenial Italian spot in the Downtown district where collegians and families convene over the thin-crust pies; though the menu ventures beyond 'zas, most look no further for a slice and a Coke.

NEW Continental *American*
– | – | – | M

Atlantic City | Pier at Caesars | 1 Atlantic Ocean (Arkansas Ave.) | 609-674-8300 | www.continentalac.com
With its menu of upscale comfort food (and seating areas including one modeled after a '60s-style coffee shop), Stephen Starr's swank

diner adds a postmodernist twist to the spanking-new Pier at Caesars; there's something pleasantly retro about digging into a big bowl of lobster mashed potatoes amid all the glitz of Atlantic City.

Copeland Restaurant *American*
25 | 25 | 23 | $58

Morristown | Westin Governor Morris | 2 Whippany Rd. (Lyndsey Dr.) | 973-451-2619 | www.copelandrestaurant.com

For "NY style in NJ", those in-the-know go to this "outstanding" New American tucked inside Morristown's Westin Governor Morris to "marvel" at "talented" chef Thomas Ciszak's "truly distinguished" fare delivered by an "attentive" staff in a "luxurious", "tiered" setting; although it's "pricey", it'll be "the best money you've spent in a while"; P.S. spot cocktail connoisseurs at the "sophisticated" martini bar.

Copper Canyon 🅂 *Southwestern*
25 | 23 | 18 | $45

Atlantic Highlands | Blue Bay Inn | 51 First Ave. (bet. Center Ave. & Ocean Blvd.) | 732-291-8444 | www.bluebayinn.com

"Superlative" margaritas are crafted from the "enormous" (over 150 kinds) tequila list at this "hip" purveyor of "impressive" Southwestern food in Atlantic Highlands featuring a "fun" bar scene; the place is stocked with "beautiful" people, some of whom don't seem too bothered by the "high noise levels" or occasionally "arrogant" service.

Copper Fish Ⓜ *American/Seafood*
▽ 20 | 19 | 19 | $40

Cape May | 1246 Rte. 109 S. (3rd Ave.) | 609-898-0354

Seafood turns up in eclectic ways at this "out-of-the-way" Cape May New American, where patrons can choose from a "good" selection of dishes (e.g. smoked tuna pizza, lobster martinis); the "snazzy" decor and "nice" staff also add appeal; N.B. they offer NJ wines only.

Cork *American*
21 | 21 | 20 | $35

Westmont | 90 Haddon Ave. (bet. Cooper St. & Cuthbert Blvd.) | 856-833-9800 | www.corknj.com

"Urban sophistication" are the buzzwords on restaurateur Kevin Meeker's Westmont New American "lively" destination serving "well-prepared", "upscale" food; "inconsistent" service is all forgotten once you check out the happy hour and "fabulous" bar.

Corky's Ribs & BBQ *BBQ*
16 | 12 | 17 | $25

Atlantic City | Mktpl. at the Tropicana Casino | 2831 Boardwalk (Brighton Ave.) | 609-345-4100

Some "Tennessee" turns up in the Tropicana with this Memphis-based rib chain dishing up "cheap, plentiful" 'cue; it's worth it when "you're hungry" or "with the guys", but foes find it a "tough sell", citing "unimpressive" chow and a setting that "could use some ambiance."

Corso 98 Ⓜ *Italian*
21 | 18 | 21 | $41

Montclair | 98 Walnut St. (Willow St.) | 973-746-0789 | www.corso98.com

"Off the beaten path" in Montclair, this dinner-only Italian "charmer" stays the course with its "inventive menu" of "delicious", "hearty fare served with gusto" by a "friendly, prompt" staff; its "warm, cozy decor" and BYO policy are just two more reasons admirers agree this "hideaway" "doesn't get the raves it deserves."

	FOOD	DECOR	SERVICE	COST

Country Pancake House 🚫 American
19 | 9 | 15 | $17

Ridgewood | 140 E. Ridgewood Ave. (Walnut St.) | 201-444-8395

For "pancakes the size of pizzas" in "every flavor imaginable", Ridgewood residents head to this "kid-friendly" "institution" that dishes out the "best breakfast in Bergen County" as well as "simple" American lunches and dinners; sure, the staff gets "frazzled" and there's a "long wait on weekends", but "it's worth it" – as long as you're "ready to be rolled out of the restaurant"; N.B. cash-only.

Court Street Continental
21 | 18 | 20 | $32

Hoboken | 61 Sixth St. (bet. Hudson & Washington Sts.) | 201-795-4515 | www.courtstreet.com

The cobblestone street nearby lends charm to this Hoboken "hideaway" serving "excellent" wines and "consistent" Continental cuisine that "satisfies any palate"; Casanovas consider it a "romantic" retreat from the town's other offerings, and bargain-hunters tout the "great" early-bird.

Crab's Claw Seafood
17 | 13 | 18 | $32

Lavallette | 601 Grand Central Ave. (President Ave.) | 732-793-4447 | www.thecrabsclaw.com

Claw through the summer crowds for some seafood at this "typical-Shore", Lavallette "fixture" whose goods attract locals and seasonals on the basis of "price and quantity"; the bar, along with "good" live entertainment, please too.

Crab Trap Seafood
21 | 16 | 19 | $34

Somers Point | 2 Broadway (Somers Point Circle) | 609-927-7377 | www.thecrabtrap.com

Offering "nostalgia" and an "old-fashioned" ambiance for its advocates, this Somers Point seafooder is a "landmark" on the Shore thanks to its "consistent, quality" fish dishes, "superb" views of the bay, "fun" bar and seven-days-a-week live music (summers); P.S. some sing the praises of the "value" early-bird.

Cranbury Inn American
17 | 19 | 19 | $33

Cranbury | 21 S. Main St. (Cranbury Station Rd.) | 609-655-5595 | www.thecranburyinn.com

The "fantastic" pre-Revolutionary ambiance is the main attraction of this 250+-year-old Cranbury American that's still riding along; the food elicits little excitement, though, with surveyors citing "ok" if "boring" preparations; N.B. a new high-ceilinged room seats an additional 220.

Creole Cafe 🅼 Cajun/Creole
▽ 27 | 20 | 23 | $31

Sewell | Harbor Pl. | 288 Egg Harbor Rd. (Huffville Grenloch Rd.) | 856-582-7222 | www.creole-cafe.com

Perhaps "South Jersey's best-kept secret", this "authentic" N'Awlins Sewell BYO (complete with Mardi Gras decorations) prepares Cajun-Creole specialties, all of them "superb" and many of them featuring "to-die-for" sauces; in sum, it's a "favorite" in an "out-of-the-way" location that devotees are willing to trek to.

	FOOD	DECOR	SERVICE	COST

Crown Palace *Chinese*

22 | 20 | 19 | $28

Marlboro | 8 N. Main St. (School Rd.) | 732-780-8882
Middletown | 1283 Hwy. 35 (Kings Hwy.) | 732-615-9888

The "extremely popular" weekend dim sum is an "absolute hit" at this duo hosting "capacity crowds" that savor other Chinese offerings, including the "great buy" of a dinner prix fixe; in light of the "upscale" decor, acolytes appreciate that the settings come "without a take-out vibe."

Cuba Libre *Cuban*

21 | 24 | 19 | $41

Atlantic City | The Quarter at the Tropicana | 2801 Pacific Ave. (S. Iowa Ave.) | 609-348-6700 | www.cubalibrerestaurant.com

"Fabulous" decor meant to evoke 1940s Havana sets the "lively" tone at this casino-city spin-off of the Philly original, a "truly transporting" Cuban in the Quarter serving "good" fare and mojitos that'll make you "forget you're just steps away from losing large sums of cash"; N.B. night owls opt for the weekend late-night menu.

NEW Cuban Pete's ● *Cuban*

17 | 21 | 14 | $29

Montclair | 428 Bloomfield Ave. (S. Fullerton Ave.) | 973-746-1100

Experience "a night in Old Havana" via this "packed" Montclair Cuban BYO serving a "modestly" priced menu in either a "fabulous" indoor setting or in the "beautiful" palm tree-lined patio; still, "inconsistent food" and "spacey service" are letdowns; N.B. bring wine to spike the alcohol in the sangrias.

Cubby's BBQ Restaurant *BBQ*

17 | 7 | 12 | $18

Hackensack | 249 S. River St. (bet. E. Kennedy & Water Sts.) | 201-488-9389

"Bring your favorite carnivore" to this "cafeteria-style" Hackensack BBQ serving up "generous" portions of "finger-lickin' good" 'cue (especially "tender 'n' tasty" ribs) that, for believers, is "right up there with the best."

∅ Cucharamama Ⓜ *S American*

26 | 23 | 20 | $43

Hoboken | 233 Clinton St. (3rd St.) | 201-420-1700

"Unique", "extraordinary" South American fare, a "beautiful" setting to match and "fantastic" drinks all greet those who visit what fans say is "the best of what Hoboken has to offer", celeb-chef Maricel Presilla's venue situated a block away from its counterpart, Zafra; P.S. insiders tout bar dining, which offers a perfect vantage point to "watch food being prepared in the wood-burning oven."

Cucina Rosa *Italian*

23 | 18 | 21 | $33

Cape May | Washington Street Mall | 301 Washington St. (bet. Jackson & Perry Sts.) | 609-898-9800 | www.cucinarosa.com

A "family-friendly" vibe and "bargain" pricing drives fans to this Cape May Italian also recommended for its "very good" cooking and "people-watching", the latter thanks to its "convenient" location in a mall; N.B. though BYO, NJ wines are available.

	FOOD	DECOR	SERVICE	COST

Z NEW CulinAriane ⊠ Ⓜ American | 27 | 18 | 22 | $50

Montclair | 33 Walnut St. (Pine St.) | 973-744-0533

It's "foodie heaven" at this modern New American BYO, a "great addition" to Montclair's dining scene thanks to the "stellar", "adventurous" cooking of husband-and-wife-team Michael and Ariane Duarte (pastry chef and executive chef, respectively), both ably backed by a "pleasant" staff; though it's hard to ignore the "tiny size and no waiting area", sidewalk seating almost doubles the capacity.

Cup Joint Ⓜ American | ▽ 20 | 12 | 25 | $17

Hoboken | 732 Jefferson St. (8th St.) | 201-222-2660 | www.thecupjoint.com

"Comforting, aim-to-please" service and "simple, but delicious" chow (think "amazing" breakfasts) are what keep this "friendly" Hoboken coffee shop/diner joint popular; correspondents concur "cheap" tabs are what's great here, though the "life-altering" pretzel bread may not be far behind.

NEW DabbaWalla Indian | 19 | 19 | 18 | $33

Summit | 427 Springfield Ave. (Summit Ave.) | 908-918-0330 | www.dabbawalla.com

A "funky" design and "interesting concept" define this new Summit Indian, whose name (which means 'lunch box') describes the premise: the fare is served in lunch boxes in a communal seating arrangement; food disputes aside ("flavorful" vs. "bland"), fans applaud it as an "alternative to the usual."

NEW daddy O American | 18 | 20 | 17 | $46

Long Beach Township | daddy O | 4401 Long Beach Blvd. (44th St.) | 609-494-1300 | www.daddyorestaurant.com

"Dress to be seen" at this new "sharp-looking", retro Long Beach New American (in the eponymous boutique hotel) bringing "a little NYC to LBI" while drawing "hip" patrons; the "average" eats seem secondary to the main show here, namely the "fun" bar scene.

da Filippo Autentica Cucina Italiana ⊠ Italian/Seafood | 24 | 17 | 23 | $40

Somerville | 132 E. Main St. (Meadow St.) | 908-218-0110 | www.dafilippos.com

The background "piano" music gets a lot of attention at "wonderful" chef-owner Filippo Russo's "convivial" Somerville BYO, but the real show may be the food, in this case "superb", "authentic" Italian-style seafood; what's more, the staff seems to treat everyone "like a long-lost relative."

Dai-Kichi ⊠ Japanese | 22 | 14 | 20 | $28

Upper Montclair | 608 Valley Rd. (Bellevue Ave.) | 973-744-2954

Surveyors are hooked on this "neighborhood" sushi bar in Upper Montclair; the BYO's "basic" digs take a back seat to the "consistently fresh", "quality" (and "reasonably" priced) fish served by a "wonderful" staff.

Dante's Ristorante *Italian* | 21 | 17 | 21 | $36 |

Mendham | 100 E. Main St. (Cold Hill Rd.) | 973-543-5401

"Attentive" service, "excellent" pizzas and "substantial" portions of "good" food sit well with "families" at this Mendham Italian BYO standby; devotees tout takeout as your best option, especially when the conditions start to look "a little overcrowded."

Z NEW David Burke Fromagerie Ⓜ *American* | 26 | 25 | 24 | $67 |

Rumson | 26 Ridge Rd. (Ave. of Two Rivers) | 732-842-8088 | www.fromagerierestaurant.com

Culinary icon David Burke (of NYC renown) has "ratcheted things up" at this "great reincarnation" of a Rumson landmark that now sports new decor and, more importantly, "exciting", "unique presentations" of New American fare (like cheesecake lollipops) on which the toque's fame rests; "attentive" service rounds out an experience at "one of New Jersey's finest" – and priciest – restaurants.

Z David Drake, Restaurant Ⓩ *American* | 27 | 24 | 26 | $66 |

Rahway | 1449 Irving St. (Cherry St.) | 732-388-6677 | www.daviddrakes.com

A bona fide "destination for gourmets", David Drake's eponymous Rahway New American townhouse eatery is a "brilliant" "symphony of food, decor and service", with "fantastic" prix fixe meals and tasting menus ("order anything and be satisfied") and "attentive" servers who ably maneuver through a series of "intimate", "jewel"-like rooms; yes, it's "very expensive", but that's the price of "perfection."

Dayi'nin Yeri *Turkish* | - | - | - | I |

Cliffside Park | 333 Palisade Ave. (Cliff St.) | 201-840-1770 | www.dayininyeri.com

Turkish pizza might not be the most popular dish in the Garden State, but it is at this Cliffside Park BYO where the toppings (feta, lamb, spinach) certainly give away the cuisine; its modest space is infused with appeal, thanks partly to an owner who's often on the floor to act as a culinary guide.

Z DeLorenzo's Tomato Pies Ⓜ⊄ *Pizza* | 28 | 8 | 17 | $14 |

Trenton | 530 Hudson St. (bet. Mott & Swann Sts.) | 609-695-9534

"No salads, no appetizers, no ambiance", just "amazingly delicious", "brilliant" pizzas are served at this state "classic" in Trenton, the "best of the best" where "lines wrap around the block" and "house rules" are to be obeyed; all agree it's "worth the hype", "waits" and discomfort - there are no bathrooms, so "plan accordingly."

Delta's Ⓜ *Southern* | 22 | 22 | 20 | $36 |

New Brunswick | 19 Dennis St. (bet. Hiram Sq. & Richmond St.) | 732-249-1551 | www.deltasrestaurant.com

"When you want to clog your arteries, Southern-style", this "busy" New Brunswick soul fooder has "all the fat and sass you need"; a "party atmosphere" prevails since there's a "great" bar scene (the "killer" martinis are a catalyst), weekend jazz and "comfy", "loungey" decor; N.B. valet parking is available.

Dim Sum Dynasty *Chinese*   21 | 18 | 19 | $26

Ridgewood | 75 Franklin Ave. (Oak St.) | 201-652-0686 | www.dimsumdynastynj.com

"Excellence in dim sum" should be the award bestowed upon this Ridgewood BYO, which some say is the "best Chinese for miles around" and is "raising the bar" with "consistently good" cooking and "eager-to-please" service; in contrast to the regal, gold-toned setting, prices here are relatively "inexpensive."

⛋ Dining Room, The ⑤Ⓜ *American*   26 | 26 | 26 | $71

Short Hills | Hilton at Short Hills | 41 JFK Pkwy. (Rte. 24, exit 7C).| 973-379-0100 | www.hiltonshorthills.com

Be "pampered" by the "wonderful" New American cuisine and service at this Hilton Short Hills "special-occasion" destination that "sets the standard for luxury, style" and "romance"; yes, jackets are required and you'll have to "load your wallet in advance", but diners concede the reward is an "enchanted evening."

Dish ⑤Ⓜ *American*   22 | 15 | 18 | $39

Red Bank | 13 White St. (Broad St.) | 732-345-7070 | www.dishredbank.com

"Well-prepared" New Americana served in a "small" space with "pleasant" if "minimal" decor is the dish on this "cozy" (read: the "tables are close together") Red Bank BYO; the "hospitable" staff adds to the "no-pretense" ambiance.

Dock's Oyster House *Seafood*   26 | 20 | 23 | $49

Atlantic City | 2405 Atlantic Ave. (Georgia Ave.) | 609-345-0092 | www.docksoysterhouse.com

Since 1897, this "venerable" Atlantic City seafood house has been a picture of "consistency", still turning out "fantastic" fare from its "impeccably fresh" fish that includes the "best" oysters, all in a "wonderful", wood-filled room; P.S. the extensive selection at the raw bar is "everything you could ask for."

Don Pepe *Portuguese/Spanish*   21 | 15 | 19 | $37

Newark | 844 McCarter Hwy. (Raymond Blvd.) | 973-623-4662
Pine Brook | 18 Old Bloomfield Ave. (Changebridge Rd.) | 973-882-6757
www.donpeperestaurant.com

"Overeating is easy" at these "busy" Iberians where "abundant" amounts of garlicky surf 'n' turf specialties and "amazing" sangria are delivered by "friendly", "quick servers; if the "tired" settings need pepping up, "reasonable" prices – especially in light of the quantity – present an offer you "can't refuse."

Don Pepe's Steakhouse *Steak*   22 | 17 | 20 | $42

Pine Brook | 58 Rte. 46 W. (Old Bloomfield Ave.) | 973-808-5533 | www.donpepesteakhouse.com

"Serious meat eaters" (and lobster lovers) don't mind the "absence of decor" at this Pine Brook chophouse (an offshoot of the Newark original) where mammoth steaks, colossal crustaceans and "fantastic" sangria take center stage; "friendly" service and "fair" prices come with the turf.

Doo Rae Myun Ok *Korean* ▽ 21 | 12 | 17 | $23

Fort Lee | 166 Main St. (Palisade Ave.) | 201-346-1331

Check out this Korean BYO, one of Fort Lee's "gems" that vends "spicy", "satisfying" delights backed by "reliable" service; proponents pick it as their "favorite", and it doesn't hurt that it's an "excellent" value.

Doris & Ed's Ⓜ *American* 25 | 19 | 22 | $58

Highlands | 348 Shore Dr. (bet. King & Matthews Sts.) | 732-872-1565 | www.dorisandeds.com

"Every which way but plain" describes the "delightful" seafood and menus (one traditional, the other more modern) that turn up in this "civilized" Highlands venue; if the "simple" decor "could use an update", most find this mainstay's "reputation well deserved", especially when you factor in the "marvelous" wine list.

Drew's Bayshore Bistro Ⓜ *American* ▽ 28 | 16 | 24 | $34

Keyport | 58 Broad St. (W. Front St.) | 732-739-9219 | www.bayshorebistro.com

Cajun-Creole influences inform the "original", "excellent" New American cuisine at this "quaint" BYO a few blocks off Keyport's waterfront; the "loveliest" staff supplements the "friendly" ambiance, while an expansion provides more tables for the "increasing number of clientele."

E & V Ⓜ⇥ *Italian* 24 | 11 | 21 | $32

Paterson | 320 Chamberlain Ave. (bet. Preakness & Redwood Aves.) | 973-942-8080 | www.evrestaurant.com

"Down-home" "red-sauce" Italiana keeps fans flocking to this Paterson establishment, where the decor "doesn't impress" but the "delicious", "on-the-money" cooking does; the seating is "cramped" and the "lines long", but "it's worth the wait" since "huge" portions mean you "eat for days on leftovers."

East *Japanese* 18 | 14 | 15 | $27

Teaneck | 1405 Teaneck Rd. (bet. Rte. 4 & Tryon Ave.) | 201-837-1260

"Pick your pieces" from the "varied" selection traveling via "conveyor belt" at this "busy" Teaneck Japanese sushi house catering to fans of all ages; though "not five star" and perhaps "unremarkable", the fish still "satisfies", especially when you consider the "bang for the buck"; P.S. sampling some sake may help obscure decor that "could use a makeover."

⧫ Ebbitt Room, The *American* 27 | 24 | 26 | $60

Cape May | Virginia Hotel | 25 Jackson St. (bet. Beach Dr. & Carpenter Ln.) | 609-884-5700 | www.virginiahotel.com

"Elegant, refined" atmosphere syncs up nicely with the "wonderful" food at this "romantic" Cape May New American (that resides in the

Virginia Hotel), the epitome of "gourmet dining at its finest" thanks in no small part to the "great" service; "charming" nightly jazz trio caps the "beautiful", "classy" scene.

Eccola Italian Bistro *Italian*

FOOD	DECOR	SERVICE	COST
23	18	19	$39

Parsippany | 1082 Rte. 46 W. (N. Beverwyck Rd.) | 973-334-8211
"The vibe is electric" (as in, the setting is "loud") at this "established" Parsippany strip-mall Italian dealing in "delicious" dishes (including "wonderful" specials for lunch and dinner), many from the wood-burning oven; P.S. the "no-reservations" policy makes for "crowded" conditions.

Echo ⌧ *Eclectic*

FOOD	DECOR	SERVICE	COST
▽ 19	18	18	$35

Red Bank | 79 Monmouth St. (Maple Ave.) | 732-747-8050 | www.echo-redbank.com
"More watering hole than restaurant", this dimly lit Red Bank venue features crowds that congregate over drinks at the bar, where "ogling is sport"; the "ok" Eclectic small plates don't provide much of a match for the "hipster"-central scene.

Edo Sushi *Chinese/Japanese*

FOOD	DECOR	SERVICE	COST
20	11	17	$27

Pennington | Pennington Shopping Ctr. | 25 Rte. 31 S. (bet. Delaware & Franklin Aves.) | 609-737-1190
"Somehow, it works" say supporters of this Pennington Chinese-Japanese strip-mall BYO proffering a combination of "good" sushi and "pretty good Chinese"; it's "friendly" and "familial", though the "refreshed" setting doesn't score when it comes to decor.

Egan & Sons *Irish*

FOOD	DECOR	SERVICE	COST
17	20	18	$28

Montclair | 118 Walnut St. (Forest St.) | 973-744-1413 | www.eganandsons.com
For a "bit of Dublin in New Jersey", try this "congenial" consistently "crowded" Montclair Irish restaurant/brewery specializing in "comforting" gastropub fare that's usually very "solid"; furnishings and artwork from the mother country complete the vibe, as does the "off-the-charts noise levels"; N.B. an expansion is planned for summer 2007.

El Azteca *Mexican*

FOOD	DECOR	SERVICE	COST
21	12	19	$18

Mount Laurel | Ramblewood Shopping Ctr. | 1155 Rte. 73 N. (Church Rd.) | 856-914-9302
"Get in and out fast" at this *muy bueno* strip-mall Mount Laurel BYO Mexican serving "good" eats, and "plenty of them" ("leftovers are a given"); "good" service and "reasonable" prices rank high above the "lacking decor."

El Cid *Spanish*

FOOD	DECOR	SERVICE	COST
21	15	19	$41

Paramus | 205 Paramus Rd. (bet. Century Rd. & Rte. 4 W.) | 201-843-0123
Be prepared to "loosen your belt a notch" at this Paramus Iberian, "home of the dinosaur prime rib" and other "obscenely large portions" of "good" Spanish surf 'n' turf; though some respondents give fewer *olé's* for the "run-down" digs, most don't seem to mind.

Elements Asia *Pan-Asian*

23 | 20 | 19 | $28

Lawrenceville | Village Commons | 4110 Quakerbridge Rd. (Village Rd.) | 609-275-4988

"Inspired" fusion that's "beautifully presented" is what pleased partisans prefer about this strip-mall Lawrenceville BYO Pan-Asian also prized for its "on-point", "accommodating" service; all seem elementally enthralled with a dining room that's "photo-shoot" "lovely."

Elements Café 🚫Ⓜ *American*

21 | 15 | 19 | $35

Haddon Heights | 517 Station Ave. (White Horse Pike) | 856-546-8840 | www.elementscafe.com

"Tantalizing" "tapas" is just the element needed to draw diners to this Haddon Heights New American BYO "proffering" an "assortment" of small plates that quickly add up to "satisfying" meals; overall, regulars recommend this "unique" experience.

Elephant & Castle ● *Pub Food*

11 | 15 | 14 | $23

Cherry Hill | Clarion Hotel | 1450 Rte. 70 E. (I-295) | 856-427-0427 | www.elephantcastle.com

Fish 'n' chips and shepherd's pie give away the British theme at this Cherry Hill chain pub where TVs, darts and pool hold sway; but even the "nice" selection of brews can't rescue "bland", "unimaginative" chow that should only be reserved for when "nothing else is open."

El Familiar *Colombian/Mexican*

- | - | - | M

Toms River Township | Stella Towne Ctr. | 1246 Rte. 166 (Hilltop Rd.) | 732-240-6613

Colombian cooking pairs up with Mexican specialties in this storefront BYO in Toms River Township, an alternative to the area's Italian eateries; the homely decor is handily offset by the interesting – and modestly priced – fare that's there.

Ⓩ El Meson Cafe *Mexican*

24 | 14 | 20 | $23

Freehold | 40 W. Main St. (Court St.) | 732-308-9494

"As close to south of the border" as it gets in central Jersey, this BYO dishes out "huge" portions of the "very best" Mexican that ultimately "generates crowds"; "friendly" service and "attractive" prices are pluses, as is the attached market that's perfect for bodega browsing.

Elysian Cafe *French*

21 | 22 | 20 | $33

Hoboken | 1001 Washington St. (10th St.) | 201-798-5898 | www.elysiancafe.com

All the neighborhood seems to turn up for the "good" food and the "great" bar at this "lovingly restored" and "beautifully detailed" Hoboken French bistro (owned by the proprietors of Amanda's); P.S. as far as "people-watching", insiders know all about the patio, considered the "best in town."

Emerald Fish 🚫 *Seafood*

23 | 16 | 21 | $31

Cherry Hill | Barclay Farms Shopping Ctr. | 65 Rte. 70 E. (Kings Hwy.) | 856-616-9192 | www.emeraldfish.com

Mall-goers turn to this "perfect" Cherry Hill BYO "hideaway for a quiet conversation" whose location belies "top-quality" seafood (dispensed from the open kitchen), a "cozy" ambiance made even better by "beautiful" piscine paintings and a "friendly" staff.

Epernay 🅼 *French*　　　21 | 18 | 18 | $41

Montclair | 6 Park St. (Bloomfield Ave.) | 973-783-0447 |
www.epernaynj.com

Montclair's Gallic-loving gourmands say *oui* to this "traditional" bi-level BYO French bistro proffering "plentiful" portions of "fabulous" steak frites and assorted "standout" "comfort" foods; the jury's still out on service ("brusque" vs. "friendly"), but most avow it's worth your time if just to "feel transported" to the Left Bank.

Eppes Essen *Deli*　　　18 | 9 | 12 | $21

Livingston | 105 E. Mt. Pleasant Ave. (S. Livingston Ave.) | 973-994-1120 |
www.eppesessen.com

"What's not to like?" at this classic (50 years and counting) Livingston kosher-style deli serving "freakishly huge", "top-quality" corned beef and pastrami sandwiches; it's true, the place may "not be pretty", but at least the crew is "much nicer" now that it's under new management.

Espo's ⊘ *Italian*　　　21 | 9 | 18 | $24

Raritan | 10 Second St. (bet. Anderson & Thompson Sts.) |
908-685-9552

"Thriving for decades", this Raritan "diamond-in-the-rough" is known for "huge" portions (expect "doggy bags") of "great", "rib-stickin'" red-sauce Southern Italian brought to table by a "friendly" staff; as for the "basic" bar decor, that's "part of the charm" too.

Esty Street 🆂 *American*　　　23 | 18 | 21 | $51

Park Ridge | 86 Spring Valley Rd. (Fremont Ave.) | 201-307-1515 |
www.estystreet.com

"Dining with family and friends" is a joy at this "pricey" Park Ridge New American that is also known to be "great for business lunches"; a "prompt" staff and a "good" all-American wine list place it a "cut above"; N.B. the Decor score may not reflect a recent renovation.

Eurasian Eatery 🅼 *Eclectic*　　　20 | 11 | 20 | $21

Red Bank | 110 Monmouth St. (bet. Maple Ave. & Pearl St.) |
732-741-7071

The "variety" is as large as the portions served at this BYO opposite Red Bank's Count Basie Theater; while the "not-much-atmosphere" decor may not please everyone, most applaud the "different", "well-prepared" Eclectic eats offered at a "low cost."

NEW Europa at Monroe 🅼 *Mediterranean*　　　– | – | – | E

Monroe Township | 146 Applegarth Rd. (Old Church Rd.) |
609-490-9500 | www.europanj.com

Channeling Italy and Spain through its cuisine, this Monroe newcomer turns out pastas, paellas and other Mediterranean fare, along with a separate slate of tapas, the latter enjoyed at the bar; within the main dining room is a stone fireplace and wine display, both ably underscoring the inviting ambiance.

	FOOD	DECOR	SERVICE	COST

Europa South *Portuguese/Spanish*

| 20 | 15 | 19 | $38 |

Point Pleasant Beach | 521 Arnold Ave. (Rte. 35 S.) | 732-295-1500 | www.europasouth.com

One helping can "feed two" at this Point Pleasant Beach outpost specializing in "authentic" Portuguese and Spanish cooking backed by "energetic" waiters; though it's "been around a long time" – and it shows in the "drab" decor – the deal for devotees is that the goods served here are "reliable."

Fantasea Reef Buffet *Eclectic*

| 17 | 18 | 16 | $27 |

Atlantic City | Harrah's | 777 Harrah's Blvd. (Brigantine Blvd.) | 609-441-5052 | www.harrahs.com

"Help forget gambling losses" by indulging in the array of Eclectic offerings (especially a "good" variety of seafood) at this "undersea-themed" "traditional" buffet docked in Harrah's; the fare's "above average" for some, but critics contend the eats aren't any better than "blah."

☑ Far East Taste Ⓜ *Chinese/Thai*

| 26 | 7 | 22 | $21 |

Eatontown | 19 Main St./Rte. 35 (Broad St.) | 732-389-9866

The kitchen turns out "masterpieces" at this Eatontown Chinese-Thai BYO helmed by Richard Wang, who has a knack for cooking "fantastic" fish dishes; sure, it "defines hole-in-the-wall", but the decor is easy to overlook considering the quality – and low prices – offered here.

Farnsworth House, The *Continental*

| 21 | 16 | 19 | $36 |

Bordentown | 135 Farnsworth Ave. (Railroad Ave.) | 609-291-9232 | www.thefarnsworthhouse.com

Perfectly "suited to romantic evenings" given its "charming", "historic" (circa 1682) house setting, this Bordentown Continental delights diners with "surprisingly good" preparations; casual comers endorse the downstairs bar dining, while others opt for upstairs, which provides more of a "treat" for the eyes.

☑ Fascino Ⓢ *Italian*

| 26 | 21 | 24 | $52 |

Montclair | 331 Bloomfield Ave. (bet. Grove & Willow Sts.) | 973-233-0350 | www.fascinorestaurant.com

"Fascinating" and "fantastic" are some of the superlatives used to describe this BYO "star" in Montclair, the home of the "incredible" DePersio family, and to the "superb" modern Italian cuisine of chef Ryan (and of "mom" Cynthia's "amazing" desserts); to get into the "place that has it all", fans are deterred by neither the "tough reservation" nor "pricey" tabs.

Fat Kat, The Ⓢ Ⓜ *American*

| 24 | 15 | 22 | $38 |

Little Ferry | 201 Main St. (Liberty St.) | 201-814-0234

Chef-owner Antonio Goodman "works wonders in the kitchen" at his New American BYO in a Little Ferry storefront; proponents add that the "hidden treasure" (near Teterboro Airport) is also "worth the trip" for its "excellent" service and "cozy, tavernlike" setting that includes a fireplace.

Federici's ⌒ *Pizza* 21 | 10 | 18 | $22

Freehold | 14 E. Main St. (South St.) | 732-462-1312 | www.federicis.com

"What would we do without the Fed's?" wonder groupies of this 86-year-old Italian stronghold in "Boss-loving" Freehold, a "staple" for "terrific" thin-crust pizza; pros point out it's best to stick with the pies and avoid the rest of the "so-so", "serviceable" menu.

Fedora Cafe Ⓜ *Eclectic* 19 | 19 | 16 | $19

Lawrenceville | 2633 Main St. (bet. Craven Ln. & Phillips Ave.) | 609-895-0844

The setting seems lifted from an "episode of *Friends*" say followers attracted to this "quirky", "funky" Lawrenceville BYO hosting "trendy young" patrons who sit on "comfy couches" to sip coffee or nosh on "comforting" Eclectic vittles; "spacey" service completes the "relaxed" scene.

⚡ Fernandes Steakhouse II *Steak* 26 | 20 | 24 | $34

Newark | 152-158 Fleming Ave. (Chapel St.) | 973-589-4099

Be sure to "take a double dose of your cholesterol" meds before you load up on the "enormous" portions of "terrific", "melt-in-your-mouth" reef 'n' grilled beef delivered by an "attentive" staff at this "excellent" Ironbound Iberian-Brazilian steakhouse; carnivores like that for $23, you can "eat all you can."

Ferrari's Ristorante *Italian* 22 | 17 | 21 | $34

Freehold Township | A & M Plaza | 3475 Rte. 9 N. (Three Brooks Rd.) | 732-294-7400

"Enthusiastic" servers make meals here "feel like you're eating at home" at this Freehold Township shopping-center BYO, where the "good" Italian food pleases; P.S. some suggest the "seafood is the best in town."

⚡ Ferry House, The *American/French* 25 | 20 | 22 | $48

Princeton | 32 Witherspoon St. (Spring St.) | 609-924-2488 | www.theferryhouse.com

"Too many fabulous dishes to choose from" is a common refrain at Bobby Trigg's BYO "winner", one of the only "special-event" venues in Princeton whose French–New American cooking excels even more with backup from a staff that "shows the right amount of attentiveness"; as expected, it's not cheap, but it's near unanimous that the operation is "first-rate."

Filomena *Italian* 20 | 20 | 18 | $36

Berlin | 13 Milford Cross Keys Rd. (White Horse Pike) | 856-753-3540 | www.filomenasberlin.com

Clementon | Commerce Plaza | 1380 Blackwood-Clementon Rd. (Millbridge Rd.) | 856-784-6166 | www.filomenalakeview.com

Deptford | 1738 Cooper St. (Almonesson Rd.) | 856-228-4235 | www.filomenalakeview.com

"Southern Italian as it should be" sums up this "affordable" South Jersey trio that is likely to "never let you down"; Berlin and Deptford are showcases for "great" evening entertainment, and Clementon's "new location is an improvement" over its former spot.

	FOOD	DECOR	SERVICE	COST

Fiorino 🛇 *Italian*
23 | 20 | 21 | $49

Summit | 38 Maple St. (Springfield Ave.) | 908-277-1900 |
www.fiorinoristorante.com

Those out for "special occasions" hardly do wrong when dining at this Summit Northern Italian "mainstay" hitting high notes with "delicious" meals "every time" and offering lots of libations at the "active bar"; the cream on the tiramisu, though, is a seat in the wine cellar for a "true food and drink experience."

NEW 503 Park 🛇 *Eclectic*
▽ 20 | 15 | 16 | $36

Scotch Plains | 503 Park Ave. (Westfield Ave.) | 908-322-5880 |
www.503park.com

This "informal" neighborhood BYO bistro in Scotch Plains has early fans delighted with the "good" Eclectic menu priced at a "bargain"; while some say things here "are getting better", "unseasoned service" doesn't measure up to the "well-prepared" food.

Fleming's Prime Steakhouse *Steak*
22 | 23 | 22 | $57

Edgewater | City Pl. | 90 The Promenade (River Rd.) | 201-313-9463 |
www.flemingssteakhouse.com

"What a lovely way to blow your cholesterol count" quip carnivores at this upscale Edgewater chain chophouse, the "pricey" cousin of the Outback Steakhouse proffering "nicely prepared" steaks and sides; now, if only the "great" view of NYC was visible from your seats ("lower the windows!").

Food for Thought *American*
24 | 24 | 22 | $40

Marlton | Marlton Crossing Shopping Ctr. | 129 Marlton Crossing (Rte. 70) | 856-797-1126 | www.foodforthoughtnj.com

Although slotted away in the corner of Marlton Crossing, this strip-mall BYO "pearl" isn't an afterthought for those who endorse its "well-prepared" New American savories, "good" desserts and "warm" service; the "less than glamorous" setting belies the "romantic" possibilities here in an overall "impressive" operation.

🛇 Fornos of Spain *Spanish*
23 | 17 | 20 | $39

Newark | 47 Ferry St. (Union St.) | 973-589-4767 |
www.fornosrestaurant.com

Considered by many the "king of the Ironbound", this "large" Newark "institution" is synonymous with "abundant" portions, "reasonable" prices and Spanish fare that's bound to "leave you satisfied"; expect a "busy", "crowded" scene, but it's "worth the wait" – the food is "great" and the "parking lot is a plus."

🛇 410 Bank Street *Creole*
27 | 21 | 24 | $51

Cape May | 410 Bank St. (bet. Broad St. & Lafayette Ave.) | 609-884-2127

"Intoxicating", "complex" Creole cooking is the 411 on this Cape May mainstay whose combination of "culinary razzle-dazzle" (the work of chef Henry Sing Cheng) and "cozy" Victorian atmosphere like "Key West" makes a visit here "better than a week in New Orleans"; if the "waits" grate, "engaging" servers help ease the pain; N.B. although BYO, the restaurant offers a short list of New Jersey wines.

	FOOD	DECOR	SERVICE	COST

Frankie & Johnnie's *Steak*   23 | 20 | 21 | $51
Hoboken | 163 14th St. (Garden St.) | 201-659-6202 |
www.frankieandjohnnies.com
Yes, this Uptown Hoboken steakhouse may be somewhat "pricey",
but that's no problem for fans who describe "cooked-to-perfection"
beef and other chophouse favorites, an "excellent" bar and "charming" late-19th-century ambiance; P.S. they offer validated parking, a
"priceless" commodity in this town.

Frankie Fed's Ⓜ *Italian*   20 | 10 | 17 | $22
Freehold Township | 831 Rte. 33 E. (Weaverville Rd.) | 732-294-1333
The thin-crust pizzas may even "equal those of big brother Federici's"
argue backers of this "busy", "friendly" Freehold Township Italian,
who some say has a "nicer atmosphere" than its famous relative;
plus, there's no need to bring cash since "they take plastic."

Frenchtown Inn, The Ⓜ *Eclectic/French*   23 | 22 | 21 | $52
Frenchtown | 7 Bridge St. (Rte. 29) | 908-996-3300
Right alongside the Delaware River in "bucolic" Frenchtown, this
"country" inn "treasure" is "a pleasure" for "wonderful" meals given
the Eclectic-French menu and "classy", "romantic" rooms; N.B. the
adjacent grill room is an alternative for more dress-down dining.

Frescos *Italian/Mediterranean*   24 | 20 | 22 | $42
Cape May | 412 Bank St. (Lafayette Ave.) | 609-884-0366
A "distinctive" menu of Italian-Mediterranean specialties delivered
in "warm" environs makes some ask "why go to Italy?" when there's
this "Tuscan"-inspired, BYO-friendly Cape May trattoria hitched to
its relative, 410 Bank Street; P.S. seafood that's "fresher than fresh"
steals the show.

Fresco Steak & Seafood Grill *Seafood/Steak* 23 | 19 | 19 | $37
Milltown | Heritage Shopping Plaza | 210 Ryders Ln. (Blueberry Dr.) |
732-246-7616 | www.restaurantfresco.com
Most agree the fare really "is that good" at this Milltown reef 'n' beef
BYO that relies on its offerings to override the strip-mall surroundings; it seems always "busy" – maybe it's because here, you get the
"most food for your money."

Ⓩ Frog and the Peach, The *American*   26 | 23 | 24 | $57
New Brunswick | 29 Dennis St. (Hiram Sq.) | 732-846-3216 |
www.frogandpeach.com
"Amazing in every respect", this multilevel New Brunswick New
American "gastronomic paradise" is the home of Bruce Lefebvre's
"flawless" cooking (with new lunch and dinner prix fixe options), "top-
notch" service and wines, and an "extraordinary", "modern" ambiance
reflecting the building's industrial history; you may have to "mort-
gage a friend" for the experience, but then, what are friends for?

Full Moon *Eclectic*   17 | 13 | 16 | $21
Lambertville | 23 Bridge St. (Union St.) | 609-397-1096
The name says it all at this "quirky" BYO Eclectic in Lambertville that's
"only open for dinner during a full moon" but nevertheless draws

raves for a "well-executed menu" served by a "friendly staff"; at other times of the month, you can settle in for "big breakfasts", "really good" lunches and brunches that last "until 4 PM on weekends."

☒ Gables, The *Eclectic* 26 | 25 | 22 | $63

Beach Haven | Green Gables Inn | 212 Centre St. (bet. Bay & Beach Aves.) | 609-492-3553 | www.gableslbi.com

Thanks to a major renovation, a "new look" awaits diners familiar with this Eclectic "oasis of elegance" and "fine dining", an LBI "standard" that retains its high status and still "oozes romance in every corner"; kudos to the "great" B&B setting and "charming" porch, the latter the site of "delightful" afternoon teas; BYO, but they offer NJ wines.

Gaetano's *Italian* 19 | 15 | 16 | $33

Red Bank | 10 Wallace St. (Broad St.) | 732-741-1321 | www.gaetanosredbank.com

More "steady Eddie than special night out", but this "dependable" BYO (with only NJ wines sold) Italian is nonetheless a "good everyday" alternative thanks in part to a "relaxed" atmosphere that's a change from the hip Red Bank scene; "routinely inattentive service", however, is a shortcoming for some.

Gagan Bistro ☒ *Indian* - | - | - | M

Marlton | 150 Rte. 73 N. (Rte. 70) | 856-988-8751 | www.gaganindianbistro.com

Settling into Burlington County is this low-key Marlton Indian BYO that features all the staples sought by locals who crave curries, tandoor-baked breads and an extensive list of vegetarian goods; at $7.95, the lunch buffet is a magnet for budget hounds.

NEW Gallagher's Steak House *Steak* 22 | 23 | 21 | $57

Atlantic City | Resorts Atlantic City Casino & Hotel | 1133 Boardwalk (North Carolina Ave.) | 609-340-6555 | www.resortsac.com

"Cholesterol here I come" say brave-hearted fans more than willing to indulge in "great" beef served at this "sleeper", an Atlantic City offshoot (of the NYC original) tucked away in the Resorts Casino Hotel and looking like "an old steakhouse should" – and costing as much (you'll need a "thick bankroll").

Garlic Rose Bistro *Eclectic* 21 | 15 | 20 | $35

Cranford | 28 North Ave. W. (N. Union Ave.) | 908-276-5749
Madison | 41 Main St. (bet. Green Village Rd. & Waverly Pl.) | 973-822-1178
www.garlicrose.com

These Eclectics in Madison (BYO) and Cranford (serving alcohol) stay true to their name, with garlic-infused offerings that are "satisfying" and "unexpectedly interesting"; the settings are "casual", all the better so you can focus on meals that "help maintain clear blood vessels."

Gaslight *American/Italian* 20 | 16 | 21 | $30

Hoboken | 400 Adams St. (4th St.) | 201-217-1400 | www.gaslightnj.com
"Off the beaten path" in Hoboken, this "comfortable" bar/restaurant has something for everyone, including a "hopping" front bar with

an "extensive martini menu" and a "lovely back room" for dining on "unexpectedly" "decent" American-Italian eats; the "best deal" "for a night with the girls" is on Tuesdays, however, when gals get "a complimentary entree with a $10 purchase" of appetizers, drinks or desserts.

NEW Gaucho Steak Argentinean Grill *Argentinean/Steak*

-	-	-	M

Montclair | 381 Bloomfield Ave. (N. Willow St.) | 973-233-1520

Grass-fed Patagonian beef helps explain the appeal of this Montclair Argentinean BYO whose emphasis is steak but also offers inspired seafood; the tabs are just right for local gauchos who've checked the place out.

Gazelle Café & Grille ⊠ *American*

-	-	-	E

Ridgewood | 11 Godwin Ave. (Franklin Ave.) | 201-689-9689

At this Ridgewood New American BYO near Whole Foods, the open kitchen of chefs Jim Miceli and Ron Norrell invites diners to watch the toques turn out health-conscious dishes; decorwise, the small, low-lit room is graced by figurines of the namesake.

Gianna's Ⓜ *Italian*

▽ 25	19	23	$42

Atlantic Highlands | 42 First Ave. (Bay Ave.) | 732-872-3309 | www.giannasnj.com

A "treasure" in tiny Atlantic Highlands, this BYO "find" of an Italian storefront distinguishes itself with truly "delicious" cooking supported by a "accommodating" staff; despite "tight" quarters, the air of "intimacy" prevails here.

Ginger & Spice *Asian*

-	-	-	M

Ramsey | Kohl's Shopping Ctr. | 1300 Rte. 17 N. (Spring St.) | 201-934-8900 | www.gingerandspice.com

Asian fusion cuisine with a Thai bent kicks this Ramsey BYO into high gear nightly, as adventurers arrive for tom yum soup, squid with chiles and aïoli, and whole fishes; perfectly appropriate is the name, which sums up both the edgy cuisine and scene.

Ginger Thai *Thai*

▽ 15	14	15	$29

Freehold Township | A & M Plaza | 3475 Rte. 9 N. (Three Brooks Rd.) | 732-761-2900

This Freehold Township BYO Thai is applauded for "reasonable" prices and a "comfortable" dining area; but "disappointing" fare up-ends the experience, so some say try ordering items from the "Indian menu" offered at Aangan, which is adjacent.

Girasole *Italian*

25	22	21	$53

Atlantic City | Ocean Club Condos | 3108 Pacific Ave. (bet. Chelsea & Montpelier Aves.) | 609-345-5554 | www.girasoleac.com

"In a word – *magnifico!*" is this "chic" Southern Italian near the Tropicana sporting a "beautiful" blue-black-yellow Versace design and boasting "delicious" dishes, particularly "great" seafood; one look at the celeb- and power-crowd-filled room and you'll know it's the "place to be" in AC; N.B. jacket suggested.

Girasole *Italian*

25 | 19 | 24 | $39

Bound Brook | 502 W. Union Ave. (Thompson Ave.) | 732-469-1080 | www.girasoleboundbrook.com

"Superb" Italian food (from "bruschettas to desserts") isn't the sole reason why this "so-popular" Bound Brook BYO is a "tough reservation", since there's also "excellent", "welcoming" service and prices "low" for the quality of the fare; it's been around for over a decade, so it's no shock that it's a "well-oiled machine."

Giumarello's 🅂 Ⓜ *Italian*

25 | 24 | 24 | $46

Westmont | 329 Haddon Ave. (bet. Cuthbert Blvd. & Kings Hwy.) | 856-858-9400 | www.giumarellos.com

The "best" martinis help keep turnout high for this "all-time area favorite" in Westmont, a "friendly" family-run Northern Italian prized for consistently "wonderful" food, "lively" quarters and "great" bar, where "single diners" feel at home; no, it's "not cheap", but fans who chirp about the early-bird "couldn't be happier."

GoodFellas Ristorante 🅂 *Italian*

- | - | - | E

Garfield | 661 Midland Ave. (Plauderville Ave.) | 973-478-4000 | www.goodfellasnj.com

All the classic Italian bases are covered at this airy Garfield eatery serving a deep savory lineup including veal scaloppine and shrimp scampi; hand-painted walls and cherry wainscoting attract, as does the private party potential, since the restaurant can accommodate up to 100 people.

🔁 Grand Cafe, The 🅂 *French*

25 | 25 | 26 | $62

Morristown | 42 Washington St. (Rte. 24 W.) | 973-540-9444 | www.thegrandcafe.com

Embodying "elegance" to the hilt, this "formal" Morristown French set in a townhouse is surely "pricey", but the "wonderful" cuisine and "top-notch" "veterans" for servers more than compensate; "what can you say?", for it's "one of the last bastions of classic fine dining around."

Grand Colonial, The *Eclectic*

25 | 23 | 20 | $49

Union Township | 86 Hwy. 173 W. (Rte. 78, exit 12) | 908-735-7889 | www.grandcolonialnj.com

"Wow!" gush gastronomes about the "inventive, delicious" Eclectic cuisine – including "fun small plates" and a raw bar – at this "spectacular" yearling situated in a "beautifully" remodeled Colonial building (formerly the Coach & Paddock) in Hunterdon County; although some squawk about "hit-or-miss" service, most consider it "a pleasure" given its "warm, tasteful ambiance", "large wine selection" and "fantastic" cheese cave.

Grand Shanghai *Pan-Asian*

21 | 16 | 15 | $23

Edison | 700 US Hwy. 1 (Old Post Rd.) | 732-819-8830

For "dishes you don't see everywhere" else, try this clubby Pan-Asian in Edison that seats 200 and offers "interesting", "inventive cuisine" like braised sea cucumber as well as more familiar fare (e.g. "don't-miss pork buns" and sushi); a few find the service "gruff", so go here "for a fast meal" or, better yet, opt for takeout.

Grenville, The *American*

FOOD	DECOR	SERVICE	COST
21	22	19	$44

Bay Head | Grenville Hotel | 345 Main Ave. (bet. Harris & Karge Sts.) | 732-892-3100 | www.thegrenville.com

The "lovely" Grenville Hotel complements the "delightful" repasts for patrons who check in to this "special-occasion" New American in Bay Head, the standby for "elegant" Victorian dining; some swear brunch on Sunday "couldn't be more perfect."

Grill 73 Ⓜ *American*

FOOD	DECOR	SERVICE	COST
22	15	20	$39

Bernardsville | 73 Mine Brook Rd. (Woodland Rd.) | 908-630-0700 | www.grill73.com

Adding "upscale" touches to "casual" chow helps keep things "tasty" at this "lively" New American Bernardsville BYO where you get "quality treatment"; some say the "trendy" retro "luncheonette" look is part of the perfect union of food and decor.

Grimaldi's Pizza *Pizza*

FOOD	DECOR	SERVICE	COST
25	13	17	$19

Hoboken | 133 Clinton St. (2nd St.) | 201-792-0800 | www.grimaldis.com
It's the "one you want" counsel pros who've hit this Downtown Hoboken Italian pizza parlor slinging "tantalizing" thin-crust pies topped with "real mozz" and other "fresh" ingredients; it's obviously "a damn fine choice", but remember: no slices here.

Grissini Restaurant *Italian*

FOOD	DECOR	SERVICE	COST
22	20	19	$51

Englewood Cliffs | 484 Sylvan Ave. (Palisade Ave.) | 201-568-3535 | www.grissinirestaurant.com

It may be "showy", but that's the point of this "fashionable" Englewood Cliffs Italian where the "beautiful people" meet to "see and be seen"; the open kitchen's food is "always good", there's a "great" wine list that goes with the "great" vibe at the bar and the service is "attentive", so all in all, it's *"bella."*

GRUB Hut Ⓜ *BBQ*

FOOD	DECOR	SERVICE	COST
-	-	-	I

Manville | 307 N. Main St. (Knopf St.) | 908-203-8003
Although this Manville BYO had to rename itself, nothing about the unique BBQ-Southwestern grub has changed – and pork partisans are already spreading word of the pit-inspired fare on offer.

NEW Gusto Grill *American*

FOOD	DECOR	SERVICE	COST
-	-	-	M

East Brunswick | 1050 Rte. 18 N. (Rues Ln.) | 732-651-2737 | www.gustogrill.com

Open late-night and clubbier with each passing hour, this East Brunswick American boasts a vast martini list and a bounty of brews on tap, all the more to fuel the goings on; the casual vittles – burgers, sandwiches and pizzas – are perfect for a little stomach lining.

NEW Habana Latin *Cuban/Mexican*

FOOD	DECOR	SERVICE	COST
-	-	-	M

Ridgefield Park | 206 Main St. (bet. Grove & Mt. Vernon Sts.) | 201-641-5588

Mexican and Cuban merge at this suddenly popular Ridgefield Park Latin BYO that manages to straddle not only two culinary worlds, but both standard and inventive styles of cooking; candles and tropical plants add some spice to the modest quarters.

Hamilton's Grill Room   *Mediterranean* | 24 | 20 | 21 | $46 |

Lambertville | 8 Coryell St. (N. Union St.) | 609-397-4343 | www.hamiltonsgrillroom.com

"There's a reason why it's hard to nab a reservation" at this Med BYO that "sets the standard" for Lambertville with chef Mark Miller's "amazing" grill work (the result is "excellent" fish and seafood); the courtyard setting near the Delaware Canal only "adds to the wonderful ambiance."

Hard Grove Cafe ◗ *American/Cuban* | 14 | 12 | 13 | $19 |

Jersey City | 319 Grove St. (Christopher Columbus Dr.) | 201-451-1853 | www.hardgrovecafe.com

The verdict is mixed on this diner "institution" in Jersey City: while diehards dig its "kitschy", "fun" decor and "consistent" Cuban-American "favorites", detractors dis it for having a "tacky ambiance" and "slow" service; nevertheless, a "location opposite the PATH station" ensures this joint's "always bustling" with "a diverse clientele."

Harrison, The   *American* | ▽ 24 | 15 | 19 | $41 |

Asbury Park | 808 Fifth Ave. (Main St.) | 732-774-2200

"Outdoor dining is one great way to enjoy this jewel" in Asbury Park serving "interesting" New American items that turn out "well prepared"; the snug space (24 seats) seems appropriate given the "romantic" ambiance.

Harry's Lobster House   *Seafood* | ▽ 22 | 11 | 17 | $57 |

Sea Bright | 1124 Ocean Ave. (New St.) | 732-842-0205

Sea Bright's seafood standby (since 1933) still shows what the "best" stuffed lobsters are all about, even if the "expensive" tabs that accompany them are daunting to some; "accomodating" service helps counterbalance any issues with the "plain", "vanilla" setting.

Harvest Bistro ☒ *French* | 22 | 25 | 20 | $52 |

Closter | 252 Schraalenburgh Rd. (Bergenline Ave.) | 201-750-9966 | www.harvestbistro.com

In the small town of Closter, this French bistro is fertile ground for folks who like the "gorgeous" decor (featuring copper, stone and wood), "loungey" vibe and "busy" bar scene, all abetted by "good" (although "pricey") food; no, "hearing aids aren't necessary", but that's just the sound of fans happy to have something "right out of NYC" in town.

Harvest Moon Inn ☒ *American* | 24 | 22 | 22 | $51 |

Ringoes | 1039 Old York Rd. (Rte. 202) | 908-806-6020 | www.harvestmooninn.com

"They put the 'excel' in 'excellent'" at this "wonderful" New American nestled in a "lovely" stone house in Ringoes; whether you're enjoying "outstanding gourmet fare" in the "romantic" dining room or chowing down on "pub-style dinners" in the tavern, it's "never a bad decision to spend the evening" at this "all-round favorite", especially given its "cozy" fireplaces and "deep wine list."

	FOOD	DECOR	SERVICE	COST

Harvey Cedars Shellfish Co. ☞ *Seafood*   22 | 10 | 18 | $30

Beach Haven | 506 Centre St. (Pennsylvania Ave.) |
609-492-2459
Harvey Cedars | 7904 Long Beach Blvd. (bet. 79th & 80th Sts.) |
609-494-7112
www.harveycedarsshellfishco.com

"Any real LBI'er" considers this cash-only BYO seafood duo a "staple" for its "relaxed" vibe and "simple", "fresh" affordable fish; note that to enjoy the "essence of beachiness" at these "true summer dining experiences", expect "long lines" and "crowds."

☑ Highlawn Pavilion *American*   24 | 27 | 23 | $61

West Orange | Eagle Rock Reservation | Eagle Rock Ave. (Prospect Ave.) |
973-731-3463 | www.highlawn.com

"Astonishing NYC views" aren't the only draw at this "stunning" "occasion" New American housed in a grand, late-19th-century building atop an overlook in West Orange, since the food is "to die for" ("no wonder the place is so close to heaven!"); plus, the staff makes "your every wish their command", so acolytes aver it's all "well worth the $$$"; N.B. the large wine cellar is reserved for private parties.

High Street Grill *American*   ▽ 23 | 18 | 22 | $36

Mount Holly | 64 High St. (bet. Brainerd & Garden Sts.) | 609-265-9199 |
www.highstreetgrill.net

"Good" New Americana is on offer at this spot brightening up downtown Mount Holly; the hosts "meet and greet" diners in a space divided by an "intimate" upstairs and a tavernlike downstairs, where lunch is served every day.

Ho-Ho-Kus Inn, The *Continental/Italian*   21 | 21 | 21 | $50

Ho-Ho-Kus | Ho-Ho-Kus Inn | 1 E. Franklin Tpke. (Sheridan Ave.) |
201-445-4115 | www.hohokusinn.com

You'll "step back in time" when you enter this Ho-Ho-Kus mainstay (housed in an 18th-century Dutch Colonial) offering Continental Italian meals and "excellent" service; food issues aside ("up and down" to "wonderful"), dedicated diners insist the "romantic" setting is a winning feature.

Homestead Inn ☞ *Italian*   ▽ 23 | 9 | 19 | $47

Trenton | 800 Kuser Rd. (bet. Hamilton & Whitehorse Aves.) |
609-890-9851

Known as Chick & Nello's to insiders, this family-run Trenton institution (since 1939) dishes up "old-school", "no-nonsense" Italiana and "no printed menus" (the waiters tell you what's on offer); "minimal" decor and "sketchy service" (unless "you're a regular") is somehow part of the appeal.

House of Blues ◑ *Southern*   16 | 19 | 17 | $31

Atlantic City | Showboat Casino | 801 Boardwalk (Pacific Ave.) |
609-236-2583 | www.hob.com

Thanks to the "to-die-for" Sunday gospel brunch, "great" music and "good" drinks, there's "a better return on your money" than playing at the casino reason backers of this Showboat Southerner in Atlantic

City; still, "dark" digs detract, and some say the "food may give you the blues."

Hunan Chinese Room *Chinese*   23 | 19 | 21 | $25

Morris Plains | 255 Speedwell Ave. (W. Hanover Ave.) | 973-285-1117
The "cool" decor is "eye catching" at this Morris Plains Chinese also setting itself apart with its array of "top-notch" Cantonese, Hunan and Szechaun specialties; the especially "attractive" bar is a dispensary for some seriously "potent" potables.

Hunan Spring *Chinese*   19 | 10 | 16 | $22

Springfield | 288 Morris Ave. (Caldwell Pl.) | 973-379-4994
This "basic", "efficiently" run Springfield Chinese BYO (relative of Morris Plains' Hunan Chinese Room) is considered a "standby" for "solid" "albeit not very imaginative" cooking; the "no-frills" digs "could use an update", but most insist the place "sates" any hot 'n' sour cravings.

Hunan Taste *Chinese*   23 | 24 | 21 | $31

Denville | 67 Bloomfield Ave. (Broadway) | 973-625-2782 | www.hunantaste.com
"Great", "gracious" service plus "delicious" food equals success at this Denville Chinese that's the talk of the town not only for its fare, but for the "elaborate" "over-the-top" decor featuring a number of fish tanks, especially the 20-ft. one near the bar; the quasi "formality" here may help explain tabs on the slightly "expensive side."

Hunt Club Grill *Seafood/Steak*   20 | 20 | 20 | $45

Summit | Grand Summit Hotel | 570 Springfield Ave. (Morris Ave.) | 908-273-7656 | www.grandsummit.com
This "clubby", American Summit surf 'n' turf hotel "standby" (debuted in 1929) keeps its audience partly thanks to servers who "go out of their way to please"; while sometimes "good", sometimes "bland" sums up the food for some, optimists say that though the setting's "not lively at all", at least "you're able to talk with your companions."

☒ Huntley Taverne *American*   22 | 24 | 19 | $47

Summit | 3 Morris Ave. (bet. Broad St. & Springfield Ave.) | 908-273-3166 | www.thehuntleytaverne.com
With its "ski-lodge" decor, this "handsome", "pricey" Summit New American warms its clientele with a "cozy" high-ceilinged setting replete with fireplaces (it feels like "you're in a remote lodge") and with food that "shines"; the "porch is the place to be" in summers, and the "lively" bar is the place to be seen year-round.

Iberia Peninsula ☻ *Portuguese/Spanish*   21 | 16 | 19 | $35

Newark | 63-69 Ferry St. (bet. Prospect & Union Sts.) | 973-344-5611
Iberia Tavern ☻ *Portuguese/Spanish*
Newark | 80-84 Ferry St. (bet. Congress & Prospect Sts.) | 973-344-7603
www.iberiarestaurants.com
They may be "busy", "noisy" and "need updated decor", but these Ironbound Iberians keep the crowds "coming back" with their "mounds of paella", "best-buy lobster specials" and "plentiful" por-

tions of "delicious meat" ("one word: rodizio"); given "fun people-watching" and a "carnival atmosphere", "don't skip the sangria" – it's "homemade and very potent!"

I Cavallini ⓜ Italian
25 22 21 $51

Colts Neck | 29 S. Rte. 34 (Hwy. 537) | 732-431-2934

"Superior" Italian dishes emerges from the kitchen at this destination for upscale dining, a "rustic" yet elegant eatery in Colts Neck; thanks to the combination of food, setting and service, it's no shock this site is among the "very best" Monmouth County has to offer.

Ichiban Japanese
17 12 17 $28

Princeton | 66 Witherspoon St. (bet. Hulfish St. & Paul Robeson Pl.) | 609-683-8323

This "simple storefront Japanese tries to please" Princeton natives with "standard sushi" and "quick lunch boxes" "at an affordable price"; "they have all the basics, but not much more", with picky patrons pointing to its "bare-bones setting" and minimal service – "don't expect to finish your conversation" at dinner, as "they turn the tables quickly"; N.B. it's BYO.

Ikko Japanese
▽ 22 17 21 $26

Brick | Brick Plaza Mall | 107 Brick Plaza (Chambers Bridge Ave.) | 732-477-6077 | www.ikkosteakhouse.com

"One of Brick's better choices" is the word on this Japanese BYO proffering a large menu including sushi, tempura and the like; if you're "looking for excitement", bring the "family" with you – the hibachi chefs put on a "show."

Il Capriccio ⓢ Italian
26 25 25 $63

Whippany | 633 Rte. 10 (Whippany Rd.) | 973-884-9175 | www.ilcapriccio.com

A "high-class", "dressed-up" ambiance infuses this Whippany Italian winner for "food beyond compare" accompanied by "extensive" wines and a staff that knows "when you want to be fawned over, or left alone"; in sum, "everything you're looking for in fine dining is here" – "as long as you can afford it."

Il Forno Trattoria ⓜ Italian
23 14 21 $32

Montclair | 18 S. Fullerton Ave. (bet. Bloomfield Ave. & The Crescent) | 973-233-0800

At this "small" but "intimate" "neighborhood trattoria" in Montclair, a "warm" staff will "make you feel like family" as you dig into brick-oven pizza and "giant portions" of "rustic" Southern Italian fare; the "unpretentious atmosphere" extends to the "reasonable prices" and BYO option (although you can also order a selection "from a Jersey winery"); N.B. dinner only.

Il Michelangelo Italian
21 19 20 $39

Boonton | 91 Elcock Ave. (Powerville Rd.) | 973-316-1111 | www.ilmichelangelo.com

"Tucked away" in Boonton, this "old-world" ristorante residing in a restored 1856 stagecoach inn is welcomed for its "large" portions of "homestyle" Italian fare and "warm, cozy" vibe; if the fare's a touch "inconsistent" at times, most note it's "worth the trip", and "sitting out on the porch" is certainly "a nice touch."

☑ Il Mondo Vecchio 🖼 Italian

25 | 20 | 21 | $48

Madison | 72 Main St. (Central Ave.) | 973-301-0024 | www.scalinifedeli.com

Michael Cetrulo's Madison storefront (the slightly dressed-down alternative to Scalini Fedeli) serves "consistently excellent" Italian fare that some say is on par with the Chatham flagship; the "warm" storefront invites, BYO keeps prices to a relative "bargain", and thanks to the "crowds" and "tin ceiling", expect a healthy amount of "noise."

Il Tulipano 🖼 Italian

23 | 23 | 22 | $56

Cedar Grove | 1131 Pompton Ave. (bet. Lindsley Rd. & Stevens Ave.) | 973-256-9300 | www.iltulipano.com

The staff "attends" to your needs at this "fancy-night-out" NJ Italian in Cedar Grove that offers "good" food and the kind of setting for "your best clothes"; as you guessed, it's more about "dining than eating" here, and steep prices mean many keep it for "special occasions."

Il Villaggio 🖼 Italian

23 | 16 | 24 | $50

Carlstadt | 651 Rte. 17 N. (Passaic Ave.) | 201-935-7733 | www.ilvillaggio.com

"A diamond in the shadow of the Meadowlands", this "incredible" Carlstadt Italian is "the place to go before or after the game" for "old-style cuisine that never disappoints" served by an "attentive" staff; it's all set in "dated but comfortable" digs that have recently been expanded, a change which may outdate the above Decor score.

India on the Hudson Indian

19 | 13 | 16 | $26

Hoboken | 1210 Washington St. (bet. 12th & 13th Sts.) | 201-222-0101 | www.indiaonthehudson.com

For "a taste of India" in Hoboken, try this "reliable" choice for "standard" subcontinental cuisine that includes a "can't-beat" lunch buffet; given "average service" and decor that "could use a redo", "you may want to [opt for] takeout", especially since delivery can be so "slow", you'll wonder if they "had to go to Bombay, grow the vegetables and bring them back."

Indigo Moon 🖼 French

26 | 21 | 22 | $42

Atlantic Highlands | 171 First Ave. (Navesink Ave.) | 732-291-2433 | www.indigochef.com

This "country" French BYO in Atlantic Highlands showcases meals "cooked to perfection", a relatively "elegant" setting where "noise level is low" and consistently "attentive" service; the "respectable" costs confirm the appeal here, but one that most want to keep a "secret."

Indigo Smoke BBQ

22 | 17 | 17 | $29

Montclair | 387 Bloomfield Ave. (Willow St.) | 973-744-3440 | www.indigosmoke.com

"Loosen your belt and leave your diet at the door" before entering this Montclair BYO dishing out "to-die-for" Kansas City BBQ ("great" babybacks) and Southern soul food ("delish" fried chicken, mac 'n' cheese, etc.); the "funky", recently expanded space allows room for all the extra "pounds you may put on."

Inlet Café *Seafood*

19	15	17	$35

Highlands | 3 Cornwall St. (Shrewsbury Ave.) | 732-872-9764 | www.inletcafe.com

"What could be better on a summer day" than a "bite and a beer"? at this "casual" seafooder overlooking Sandy Hook Bay and offering "gorgeous" views; "good, basic" fare is as pleasing as the "friendly" service.

Inn at Millrace Pond *American/Continental*

21	25	20	$46

Hope | 313 Johnsonburg Rd. (Rte. 611) | 908-459-4884 | www.innatmillracepond.com

The building alone – a "charming", converted 18th-century mill in "lovely" Hope – "is reason enough to visit" this "romantic" American-Continental supplying "sophistication in spades"; although the food is "generally very good" and the service is "correct", there are "no bells and whistles", "just straightforward" "grace and style in the woods."

Inn of the Hawke *American*

18	17	18	$28

Lambertville | 74 S. Union St. (Mount Hope St.) | 609-397-9555

An "easygoing" "local spot" with the aura of an old English pub, this "lovely" Lambertville bar/restaurant proffers a "fine selection of beers" and an "eclectic" American menu; it's best enjoyed on the "beautiful flagstone garden patio", although the "cozy indoor dining rooms" are winning in winter too.

Irish Pub & Inn ●⊜ *Irish*

18	15	19	$16

Atlantic City | 164 St. James Pl. (Pacific Ave.) | 609-344-9063 | www.theirishpub.com

The "cheapest" chow and drinks are on tap at this "dark" AC warhorse still packing the house with the "coldest" beers and "standard" Irish vittles; the place seems like "it's been open every hour since it opened", a godsend to its huge fan base.

NEW Isabella's American Bistro Ⓜ *American*

22	19	20	$36

Westfield | 39 Elm St. (bet. Franklin & Hill Sts.) | 908-233-8830 | www.isabellasbistro.com

"Another winner from the owners of Mojave Grille and Theresa's", this adjacent BYO storefront is "a great addition" to Westfield, offering "delectable spins on old favorites" on its "creative" New American menu; a "comfortable" ambiance adds to the mix, but a few still feel the newcomer "needs to come up to par with area restaurants."

Island Palm Grill Ⓜ *American*

▽ 18	15	19	$36

Spring Lake | 1321 Third Ave. (bet. Jersey & Washington Aves.) | 732-449-1909

"Creative" comestibles are cobbled together at this New American Spring Lake BYO bringing a touch of "Key West" to town (think bamboo, along with reds and blues); some say it's a "find" that still seems to be a "secret."

	FOOD	DECOR	SERVICE	COST

Italian Bistro *Italian*
17 | 16 | 17 | $27

Cherry Hill | 1509 Chapel Ave. (Chapel Ave.) | 856-665-6900 | www.italianbistro.com

There's "always something to take home" after a meal at this Cherry Hill chain churning out "hearty" portions of Italian sold at "reasonable" prices; ok, the "overly decorated" digs are "cheesy" and the food for some "run-of-the-mill", but pros propose it's all "good" if you "keep it simple" and just "order pasta."

Z It's Greek To Me *Greek*
18 | 12 | 16 | $22

Cliffside Park | Vitos Plaza | 352 Anderson Ave. (bet. Jersey & Morningside Aves.) | 201-945-5447
Englewood | 36 E. Palisade Ave. (bet. Dean & Engle Sts.) | 201-568-0440
Fort Lee | 1636 Palisade Ave. (Main St.) | 201-947-2050
Hoboken | 538 Washington St. (6th St.) | 201-216-1888
NEW **Jersey City** | 194 Newark Ave. (Jersey Ave.) | 201-222-0844
Ridgewood | 21 E. Ridgewood Ave. (bet. Broad & Chestnut Sts.) | 201-612-2600
Westwood | 487 Broadway (Westwood Ave.) | 201-722-3511
Holmdel | 2128 Hwy. 35 (S. Laurel Ave.) | 732-275-0036
Long Branch | 44 Centennial Dr. (Chelsea Ave.) | 732-571-0222
www.itsgreektome-taverna.com

Whether you find the food "passable" or "perfect" or the settings "comfortable" or ready "to be updated", the consensus is this chain-gang of BYO Greek eateries offers "large" helpings of "yummy" Hellenic vittles that often arrive "quickly"; pricewise, the "cheap" tabs are just ouzo special.

Ixora Ⓜ *French/Japanese*
25 | 20 | 23 | $53

Whitehouse Station | 407 Hwy. 22 E. (Rte. 523) | 908-534-6676 | www.ixoranj.com

For "superb" Japanese-French fusion, track down this "contemporary" Whitehouse Station strip-maller that "tantalizes the senses" and whose "super"-fresh fish are used to assemble the "unique" offerings; no one said it was cheap, but at least BYO "takes some sting out of the bill."

Jack Cooper's Celebrity Deli *Deli*
19 | 9 | 15 | $21

Edison | Tano Mall | 1199 Amboy Ave. (Rte. 1) | 732-549-4580 | www.jackcoopersdeli.com

All the "old faves" are doled out at this "old-fashioned" kosher-style Edison deli selling "high-quality" corned beef and pastrami sandwiches among other items, all served "fast and gruff"; beware of bloat before noshing on all the "wonderful" free pickles.

Jamie's Restaurant *Italian*
- | - | - | E

Clifton | 915 Bloomfield Ave. (Brighton Rd.) | 973-779-8596 | www.jamiesrestaurant.com

Supplying clientele with an upscale ambiance in Clifton, this Italian addition serves classic dishes (notably pastas) along with a selection of prime chops (T-bones, porterhouses and filets); given the food and setting, it's not a stretch to expect suitably expense-account tabs.

	FOOD	DECOR	SERVICE	COST

Java Moon *American*
| 19 | 15 | 16 | $23 |

Edison | 3126 Woodbridge Ave. (Amboy Ave.) | 732-738-5282
Brick | 515 Brick Blvd. (Cedar Bridge Ave.) | 732-477-4555
Jackson | 1022 Anderson Rd. (Rte. 537) | 732-928-3633
Manalapan | 345 Hwy. 9 S. (Rte. 520) | 732-294-1675
Shrewsbury | 431 Broad St. (Rte. 520) | 732-530-0141
NEW **Toms River Township** | 941 Rte. 37 W. (Mule Rd.) | 732-281-1234
Wall | 2420 Hwy. 35 (bet. Church St. & Lakewood Rd.) | 732-292-4592
Lawrenceville | Avalon Commons Mall | 4110 Quakerbridge Rd. (Village Rd. W.) | 609-275-7447
www.javamooncafe.com

"Fresh, healthy, tasty" could be the motto for this chain and its "eclectic" American Traditional fare, namely "fancy", "unusual" sandwiches, "giant", "terrific" salads and other items vended in "offbeat" digs; and as always, the "great" coffee surprises no one; N.B. Jackson has a no alcohol policy, while the other locations are BYO.

Jerry & Harvey's Noshery *Deli*
| 18 | 8 | 14 | $19 |

Marlboro | Marlboro Plaza | 96 Rte. 9 (Rte. 520) | 732-972-1122 | www.jerryandharveys.com

Devotees deli up for "delectable" goods (chopped liver, corned beef) at this kosher-style Marlboro venue that's "like the old neighborhood" for nostalgists; the "dingy" digs could use some "uplift", but at least the "countermen cut lox as thin as it gets."

Je's Ⓜ *Soul Food*
| ▽ 26 | 13 | 17 | $17 |

Newark | 34 William St. (Halsey St.) | 973-623-8848

Even Essex County "politicians" speak with one voice and agree they've "never had better" Southern food than what's dished at this Newark soul fooder, a specialist of "delectable" cornbread and mac 'n' cheese; "good" breakfasts – and long "waits" – are both common here.

Jimmy's *Italian*
| 24 | 14 | 21 | $42 |

Asbury Park | 1405 Asbury Ave. (Prospect Ave.) | 732-774-5051

The "best" veal chops and other "fantastic" cooking straight "from the old-school" Italian repertoire bring down the house at this "always packed" Asbury Park workhouse, where the fare is "served without bells and whistles"; the authentically "old-time" ambiance makes it seem like "Frank and the Rat Pack" could strut in at any moment.

Joel's Malibu Kitchen Ⓜ *Eclectic*
| – | – | – | M |

Ridgewood | 14 Oak St. (bet. E. Ridgewood & Franklin Aves.) | 201-493-9477

Eat under the glow of lava lamps at this Eclectic Ridgewood BYO that proffers a menu that's both original and far-flung; as the name suggests, the vibe is pure paradise for the laid-back.

Joe's Peking Duck House Ⓜ🤍 *Chinese*
| 23 | 8 | 18 | $21 |

Marlton | Marlton Crossing Shopping Ctr. | 145 Rte. 73 S. (Rte. 70) | 856-985-1551

"Awesome" fare, including the signature ("go nowhere else for duck", or for soups), is the calling of this affordable Marlton Chinese

BYO; save for "drab", "take-out decor", all agree this spot is "all it's quacked up to be."

John Henry's Seafood Ⓜ *Seafood*
21 | 17 | 19 | $36

Trenton | 2 Mifflin St. (bet. Franklin & Washington Sts.) | 609-396-3083 | www.johnhenrysseafood.com

This family-owned "standby" in Trenton "has stood the test of time", offering "fresh, well-prepared", "inventive" seafood "with an Italian flair" that's "good enough you can ignore" the drab decor; it's "a favorite" among locals, making "reservations a must on weekends", so consider a stop at the in-house retail market instead and pick something up for home.

Jonathan's on West End *Eclectic*
22 | 14 | 19 | $38

Atlantic City | 672 N. Trenton Ave. (West End Ave.) | 609-441-1800

While the "progressive" roster of "interesting" dishes gives a good reason for diners to head to this Atlantic City Eclectic on the West End, it's the "unbeatable" early-bird (at $11.95) that "rules" – and where you're bound to see all the "locals."

Jose's *Mexican*
▽ 22 | 7 | 16 | $17

Spring Lake Heights | 101 Rte. 71 (Jersey Ave.) | 732-974-8080

"Nothing fancy", just "really good", "homestyle" Mexican is served up in this "little" Spring Lake Heights BYO also applauded for its "cheerful" service; if the "hole-in-the-wall" atmosphere "demands that you take the food home", "great" prices compensate.

Jose's Mexican Cantina *Mexican*
19 | 16 | 18 | $25

New Providence | 24 South St. (Springfield Ave.) | 908-464-4360
Warren | Quail Run Ctr. | 125 Washington Valley Rd. (Morning Glory Rd.) | 732-563-0480
www.josescantina.com

Tuck into *muy* "generous" servings of "home-cooked" Mexican at these "not-just-another-taco-joint" BYOs, colorfully "kitschy", typically "tacky" cantinas that tend to get "crowded"; "decent" pricing is part of the deal here.

Juanito's *Mexican*
23 | 17 | 19 | $25

Howell | 3830 Rte. 9 S. (Aldrich Rd.) | 732-370-1717
Red Bank | 159 Monmouth St. (West St.) | 732-747-9118

"Chain Mexicans can't compare" with these south-of-the-border BYOs proffering "enormous" portions of "tried-and-true" food, all of them "well prepared"; "colorful" decor and "competent", "friendly" service explain why it's consistently "crowded."

Karen & Rei's 🎔 *American*
▽ 27 | 22 | 24 | $45

Clermont | 1882 Rte. 9 N. (1 mi. north of Avalon Blvd.) | 609-624-8205 | www.karenandrei.com

Deserving of all its accolades is this Clermont New American BYO, the "best fine-dining spot in the area" thanks to chef Karen Nelson's "superb" dishes and the hospitality from the staff, including "gracious" co-owner Rei Prabhakar, who ensures the "super-friendly" service; the consensus: all the above make this a truly "great" restaurant.

	FOOD	DECOR	SERVICE	COST

Z Karma Kafe *Indian*
| 25 | 18 | 20 | $24 |

Hoboken | 505 Washington St. (bet. 5th & 6th Sts.) | 201-610-0900 |
www.karmakafe.com

You can "feel the karma" from the "incredibly tasty" Indian cooking
at this "cute" Downtown Hobokenite (relative of Uptown's India on
the Hudson) where the cuisine and "intimate" ambiance translate
into "a spicy evening out" "if you can get a seat"; P.S. veterans vouch
for the lunch buffet that's the "best $8.95 you'll ever spend."

Kaya's Kitchen M *Vegetarian*
| – | – | – | M |

Belmar | Belmar Mall | 817 Belmar Plaza (bet. 8th & 10th Aves.) |
732-280-1141 | www.kayaskitchen.com

"Even serious meat eaters" enthuse about this Belmar vegetarian
BYO for its "yummy", "healthy" offerings on its "varied" menu; the
"great", "earthy" staff supplies the perfect counterpoint to the food
and mood here.

Kibitz Room *Deli*
| 24 | 8 | 13 | $17 |

Cherry Hill | Shoppes at Holly Ravine | 100 Springdale Rd. (Evesham Rd.) |
856-428-7878

The cholesterol crowd kvells over the "great" Jewish "soul food"
found in this Cherry Hill deli issuing "really big" corned beef and
pastrami sandwiches, matzo ball soup and whatnot; slightly "surly
servers" notwithstanding, it's still "the closest thing to the Carnegie
in South Jersey."

Kinchley's Tavern ● ⊟ *Pizza*
| 21 | 8 | 15 | $20 |

Ramsey | 586 N. Franklin Tpke. (Spring St.) | 201-934-7777
Although "badly in need of a makeover", most ignore the decor and
the other "passable" chow in favor of the "best" thin-crust pizzas
purveyed at this "legendary", cash-only 70-year-old Ramsey Italian
tavern; "affordable" tabs even make it worth "the speeding ticket
you may get on the way."

NEW Kitchen 233 *American/French*
| ▽ 22 | 25 | 20 | $48 |

Westmont | 233 Haddon Ave. (Ardmore Terr.) | 856-833-9233 |
www.kitchen233.com

"Delicious" dining attracts at this French-American Westmont
addition distinguished by a wine bar (abetted by a very solid vino selection) and decor featuring dark woods and banquettes; though
"costly", it's nice to "not have to drive all the way to Philadelphia to
get this kind of quality."

Klein's Fish Market & Waterside Cafe *Seafood*
| 20 | 13 | 17 | $32 |

Belmar | 708 River Rd. (bet. 7th & 8th Aves.) | 732-681-1177 |
www.kleinsfish.com

For Jersey Shore "on-the-dock" dining ("watch the boats sail by"),
it's hard to avoid this roomy seafooder marketing "fresh" fish and a
come-as-you-are atmosphere; there's "not much decor" here, but
few care, and even the paper and plastic place settings please;
N.B. there are sushi and raw bars on the premises.

	FOOD	DECOR	SERVICE	COST

K.O.B.E. *Japanese*
▽ 25 | 23 | 18 | $30

Holmdel | The Commons at Holmdel | 2132 Rte. 35 S. (Laurel St.) | 732-275-0025 | www.kobecuisine.com

Despite what the name suggests, this Holmdel Japanese BYO's focus is fish, as in "beautiful" presentations of the "best" sushi served in a "modern" space featuring slate and glass; to experience the "terrific" offerings for even less money, check out the "excellent" bento box lunches.

Komegashi *Japanese*
24 | 18 | 21 | $33

Jersey City | 103 Montgomery St. (Warren St.) | 201-433-4567
Jersey City | 99 Pavonia Ave. (Washington Blvd.) | 201-533-8888
www.komegashi.com

These Jersey City Japanese boast unique features: while some prefer the Montgomery Street locale for its more "traditional" eats including "excellent" sushi, others opt for Pavonia's "interesting" selection of fusion-style food and "wonderful" ambiance featuring a waterside "view of NYC and docked yachts"; either way, "quality and consistency" are guaranteed.

Konbu 🅜 *Japanese*
▽ 25 | 17 | 23 | $29

Manalapan | Design Ctr. | 345 Rte. 9 S. (bet. Gordon's Corner & Taylor Mills Rds.) | 732-462-6886

Though specializing in "fantastic" sushi, chef James Tran also presents "innovative" takes on Japanese at his "friendly" Manalapan shopping-center BYO; the "relaxing" vibe complements a setting featuring private rooms that are "good for families."

Krakus *Polish*
- | - | - | M

Wallington | 208 Main Ave. (Alden St.) | 973-779-1922

From borscht to kielbasa, pierogi to potato pancakes, this Wallington BYO spares no classic from the Polish repertoire; it's all gutsy, filling and robust and served in a humble dining space draped in thick, gold curtains and outfitted with sturdy wood appointments.

Kunkel's Seafood & Steakhouse 🅜 *Seafood/Steak*
▽ 20 | 24 | 22 | $38

Haddon Heights | 920 W. Kings Hwy. (bet. Black Horse & White Horse Pikes) | 856-547-1225

Something you may find "in Manhattan", this Haddon Heights chophouse purveys "good" beef and seafood that's enhanced by the banqueted, mahogany adorned space; if "just another steakhouse" to foes, fans think the place "charms."

Labrador Lounge *Eclectic*
23 | 17 | 20 | $35

Normandy Bch | 3581 Rte. 35 N. (Peterson Ln.) | Normandy Beach | 732-830-5770 | www.kitschens.com

"Offbeat" for the Shore, this "funky" Normandy Beach BYO offers something other than the area's standard eats, with a "tasty" Eclectic slate including sushi (there's "not one dog" on the menu) served by a "good" staff; P.S. it's even more "worthwhile if you sit outside."

	FOOD	DECOR	SERVICE	COST

La Campagna *Italian*
NEW **Millburn** | 194 Essex St. (Main St.) | 973-379-8989
Morristown | 5 Elm St. (South St.) | 973-644-4943
www.lacampagnaristorante.com

| 24 | 18 | 20 | $44 |

"Superlative", "comforting" Italian preparations bring plaudits to this "consistent" Morristown BYO whose floor is guided by "efficient" servers who work a "tight" space; just about everybody "likes it here", plus, the newer Millburn spin-off is "wonderful."

La Campagne *French*
Cherry Hill | 312 Kresson Rd. (bet. Brace & Marlkress Rds.) | 856-429-7647 | www.lacampagne.com

| 24 | 21 | 20 | $51 |

Cherry Hill's "elegant" "country" French "farmhouse" BYO "never disappoints" given the "adorable" setting and "flavorful" fare that brings diners close to France; indeed, the food and decor help counterbalance "uneven service."

Laceno Italian Grill *Italian/Seafood*
Voorhees | Echelon Village Plaza | 1118 White Horse Rd. (Rte. 561) | 856-627-3700

| 25 | 17 | 20 | $40 |

"Hello, Tuscany" say acolytes who tip their hats to this Voorhees mall BYO specializing in the "best", "freshest" seafood on its "great" menu that's "worthy of a nice bottle of wine"; the "very busy" scene attests to the consensus: "Italian doesn't get any better."

La Cipollina Ⓜ *Italian*
Freehold | 16A W. Main St. (South St.) | 732-308-3830

| 23 | 20 | 21 | $41 |

Holding on to its "special-occassion" appeal, this Freehold Italian BYO is a go-to for "leisurely, upscale" dining accompanied by "eager-to-please" service and "excellent" cooking; while "on the pricey side", there's high regard for the "value" prix fixes.

La Esperanza Ⓜ *Mexican*
Lindenwold | 40 E. Gibbsboro Rd. (Arthur Ave.) | 856-782-7114 | www.mexicanhope.com

| ▽ 24 | 13 | 20 | $23 |

"Hummers and work trucks" in the lot give away the diverse crowd that frequents this Lindenwold Mexican where a visit is "like a quick trip over the border" when you factor in the "real-deal" cooking; tequila fans tout the selection, deeming it "impressive for the 'burbs."

La Focaccia *Italian*
Summit | 523 Morris Ave. (Aubrey St.) | 908-277-4006 | www.lafocaccianj.com

| 24 | 18 | 22 | $41 |

Much is *buono* about this "busy" BYO in Summit and its Italian offerings, "tried-and-true" specialties that are "well prepared" and brought to table by a "humorous", "veteran" staff; P.S. the "attractive" expansion may even help ease the "squeeze."

Laguna Grill *American/Eclectic*
Brigantine | 1400 Ocean Ave. (14th St.) | 609-266-8367 | www.lagunagrill.com

| ▽ 22 | 19 | 21 | $39 |

"The best view going" – the "beach and ocean provide the ultimate" decor – gives this Brigantine American-Eclectic near the Borgata a leg up, though the food is "good" too; the "friendly" bar area baits fans, thanks partly to the "great" martinis.

Lahiere's ☒ American
21 | 19 | 20 | $54

Princeton | 11 Witherspoon St. (Nassau St.) | 609-921-2798 | www.lahieres.com

Princeton's "old reliable" (since 1919) has gone New American, with menu changes that "make it better", but still hosts "graduation-day" affairs and "tweedy professor types" who come for the "tradition" and perhaps a bit of that "worn decor"; overall, this "old dowager" "hasn't lost her touch."

☑ La Isla Cuban
26 | 10 | 19 | $21

Hoboken | 104 Washington St. (bet. 1st & 2nd Sts.) | 201-659-8197 | www.laislarestaurant.com

It resembles a "cafeteria", but for "amazing" Cuban comidas, this "tiny" Hoboken all-day BYO delivers what many consider the "best" fare of its kind – and "cheap" at that; it's perpetually "too crowded", so veterans advise you prepare for a "long wait."

Lalezar Turkish
- | - | - | M

Montclair | 720 Bloomfield Ave. (St. Luke's Pl.) | 973-233-1984 | www.lalezarcuisine.com

Sisters Melinda Basaran and Heidi Birson bring a taste of their homeland to Montclair at this chic BYO Turkish (the name means 'tulip garden') featuring char-grilled kebabs supplemented by a variety of vegetarian selections; Friday-night belly dancing should seal the deal.

Lambertville Station American
17 | 20 | 19 | $36

Lambertville | 11 Bridge St. (Delaware River) | 609-397-8300 | www.lambertvillestation.com

"Don't dismiss it as a tourist trap" plead supporters who are "never disappointed" by the "lovely views" of the Delaware River afforded from this brass, glass and oak-filled Lambertville Traditional American set in a former train station; some find "better food in town", but most agree it's a "fine" pit stop.

La Nonna Piancone's Italian
18 | 16 | 17 | $35

Bradley Beach | 800 Main St. (McCabe Ave.) | 732-775-0906 | www.piancone.com

Piancone's South Italian

Brielle | 110 Union Ave. (Agnes Ave.) | 732-528-7833

If "old-fashioned" Italian is the craving, fill up at these relatives dispensing "lotsa food" for "reasonable" prices; "hefty eaters" are pleased, but others note "heavy" eats that are "short on taste"; N.B. there's a bakery attached to the Bradley Beach original.

La Pastaria Italian
19 | 17 | 18 | $30

Summit | 327 Springfield Ave. (Summit Ave.) | 908-522-9088
Red Bank | 30 Linden Pl. (Broad St.) | 732-224-8699
www.lapastaria.com

"Hearty appetites" are welcome at these "crowded" Red Bank and Summit sisters serving up "reliably" satisfying "homestyle"

Italian; feeding "families" is a deal here – prices are as small as the "portions are large."

La Scala ⓂИ *Italian*

22 | 15 | 20 | $39

Somerville | 117 N. Gaston Ave. (bet. Bartine & William Sts.) | 908-218-9300

For a "very ambitious" menu of Northern Italian cuisine that features "exotic meats like ostrich and buffalo", head to chef-owner Omar Aly's BYO in Somerville; "the decor doesn't do the restaurant justice", but surveyors suggest you "get past it and enjoy the food" as well as the "polished", "easygoing service"; P.S. a seat on the patio makes for a "pleasant evening."

La Spiaggia *Italian*

▽ 26 | 20 | 27 | $48

Ship Bottom | 357 W. Eighth St. (Barnegat Ave.) | 609-494-4343 | www.laspiaggialbi.com

The "place to go when you want more than beach food", this "elegant", softly lit Ship Bottom Italian BYO is staffed with "professional" servers who deliver straight-up "fabulous" preparations; few question, then, just why this winning venue is still "raising the bar on LBI dining."

La Strada *Italian*

22 | 19 | 21 | $42

Randolph | 1105 Rte. 10 E. (bet. Canfield & Eyland Aves.) | 973-584-4607 | www.lastradarestaurant.com

With an "extensive" menu of "very good, traditional Italian" fare and "a staff that treats you like family, why go anywhere else?" ask admirers of this "upscale", "old-world restaurant" in Randolph; even better, the "wonderful evening" includes "an elegant atmosphere" highlighted by "a piano player that entertains on weekends."

La Tapatia *Mexican*

– | – | – | I

Asbury Park | 703 Main St. (Sewall Ave.) | 732-776-7826

You won't find cheese slathered over every dish at this Asbury Park Mexican BYO selling truly authentic south-of-the-border cuisine including a range of tacos and tamales washed down by horchatas, creamy beverages made with rice or almonds; the shoebox-size setup doesn't detract from the place's popularity.

Latitude 40N *Seafood*

23 | 13 | 20 | $36

Point Pleasant Beach | 816 Arnold Ave. (bet. Lincoln Ave. & Woodland Rd.) | 732-892-8553 | www.latitude40n.com

"All you have to do is sit back and enjoy" the "delicious" dishes that turn up in this "tucked-away" Point Pleasant Beach BYO, where "moderate" pricing is as welcoming as the "fresh" seafood; while the nautical decor is "nondescript", "attentive" service isn't.

☑ Latour ⓂИ *French*

27 | 21 | 25 | $52

Ridgewood | 6 E. Ridgewood Ave. (Broad St.) | 201-445-5056

"Warm greetings" from chef-owner Michael Latour enhance the "first-rate" repasts at his Ridgewood BYO, a standby and "standard-setter" for Classic French cookery, from savories to sweets; once you walk in, you're "instantly delighted to be here", with admirers affirming it's "adorable" – every inch of it; P.S. to "cut the expense", call ahead to check when they offer prix fixes.

Lawrenceville Inn *American*   22 | 22 | 22 | $51

Lawrence Township | 2691 Main St. (Gordon Ave.) | 609-219-1900 | www.lawrencevilleinn.com

Set in a "restored" Victorian, this "friendly", "French-inspired" New American BYO (with a few NJ wines) in Lawrence Township is a relatively "little-known charmer", where the "lovely" (if "pricey") food utilizes "local ingredients"; P.S. "get the chef's table in the kitchen."

Le Fandy 🗷 Ⓜ *French*   26 | 16 | 20 | $46

Fair Haven | 609 River Rd. (Cedar Ave.) | 732-530-3338

Behind a "humble storefront" lies this "great" BYO hideaway, the home of Luke Peter Ong's "impeccable" French bistro preparations abetted by a "sincere", "helpful" staff; overall, the "small" quarters belie the quality, "high-end" food – and "matching prices."

🇿 Legal Sea Foods *Seafood*   20 | 17 | 18 | $39

Paramus | Garden State Plaza | 1 Garden State Plaza (Rte. 17) | 201-843-8483
Short Hills | Short Hills Mall | 1200 Morris Tpke. (Rte. 24 W.) | 973-467-0089
www.legalseafoods.com

"Good, fresh" fish is the hook at this nautical twosome in Paramus and The Short Hills Mall that "upholds the chain's reputation", offering a "diverse" seafood selection that's appreciated by hordes of fans, including "kids"; hence, it's easy to fathom the appeal, and while "always crowded", "efficient" service keeps things flowing.

Le Petit Chateau Ⓜ *French*   25 | 22 | 25 | $65

Bernardsville | 121 Claremont Rd. (Rte. 202) | 908-766-4544 | www.thelepetitchateau.com

"Haute" "country" French "at its finest" is the signature of "talented" chef-owner Scott Cutaneo's "fabulous" Bernardsville destination also prized for a "wine list to behold"; as "one of Jersey's elite" eateries, you can bet it's "expensive", but for less of an expense, the $65 prix fixe is one "smart" way to go.

🇿 Le Rendez-Vous Ⓜ *French*   26 | 18 | 24 | $51

Kenilworth | 520 Boulevard (21st St.) | 908-931-0888 | www.lerendez-vousnj.com

For a "bit of Provence" in the midst of Kenilworth, this BYO "dead-ringer" of a French bistro offers a "total Gallic experience", with a "personable" staff and "cozy" quarters supporting the "outstanding" dishes; the meals are "expensive", but bargain-hunters meet up for the tasting menus, which are "fabulous values" considering the quality.

Liberty House Restaurant Ⓜ *American*   20 | 25 | 19 | $50

Jersey City | Liberty State Park | 76 Audrey Zapp Dr. (Freedom Way) | 201-395-0300 | www.libertyhouserestaurant.com

The food's "good", but it's the "unbeatable, unobstructed" views of NYC and "beautiful" wraparound porch for alfresco dining that are the selling points of this Jersey City Traditional American camped out in Liberty State Park; it's so perfect for "celebrations", the restaurant has added an 80-ft. yacht nearby for parties.

Light Horse Tavern, The *American*

22 | 24 | 21 | $39

Jersey City | 199 Washington St. (Morris St.) | 201-946-2028 | www.lighthorsetavern.com

"A slice of old Greenwich Village on the other side of the Hudson", this "upscale" Jersey City tavern (housed in a circa-1850 brick building) boasts a "beautiful" bar in its "gorgeous" split-level space, all the better to frame the kitchen's "delicious" New American pub food; a "bounty" of microbrews and a "good" wine list help transform the place into a "neighborhood destination."

Lilly's on the Canal *Eclectic*

21 | 19 | 19 | $35

Lambertville | 2 Canal St. (on Bridge St., ½ block before Penn. bridge) | 609-397-6242

This industrial-chic Lambertville Eclectic proffers "flavorful" fare within its bi-level digs; whereas some favor the "quiet" upper deck to the "frenetic" but "interesting" first floor and its open kitchen, the "beautiful" waterside patio is an all-around crowd-pleaser; N.B. it's BYO, but they sell a few local wines.

Limestone Cafe **M** *American*

22 | 18 | 19 | $43

Peapack | 89 Main St. (Holland Ave.) | 908-234-1475

Fans of Traditional American "comfort" cookery consider this "quaint" eatery in a converted Peapack Victorian "worth a ride out to horse country"; if the decor "needs a little uplift" and the "friendly" service is "spotty", the "good" food helps atone for any shortcomings.

Lincroft Inn *Continental*

18 | 17 | 19 | $39

Middletown | 700 Newman Springs Rd. (Middletown Lincroft Rd.) | 732-747-0890 | www.lincroftinn.com

"Cold winter nights" bring local loyalists to this "warm" 'n' "cozy" Middletown Continental in business since 1697; aside from an "excellent" wine list, it's "great for burgers at the bar" or for just "filling" up, but foes feel that the operation "needs to move into the 21st century."

Little Café, A **S** **M** *Eclectic*

25 | 17 | 23 | $37

Voorhees | Plaza Shoppes | 118 White Horse Rd. E. (Burnt Mill Rd.) | 856-784-3344 | www.alittlecafe.com

"The cutest, quaintest" setting frames the "gorgeous" food, the handiwork of Marianne Cuneo Powell, who's "at the top of her craft" with this Eclectic BYO in a "nondescript" Voorhees strip mall; depending on perspective, you get "cramped" conditions or enough "intimacy" for "romantic" dinners.

Little Tuna, The **M** *Seafood*

20 | 18 | 19 | $36

Haddonfield | 141 Kings Hwy. (S. Haddon Ave.) | 856-795-0888

This Haddonfield BYO is a "reliable" choice for seafood, with generally "well-prepared" fish on a menu that "pleases"; those who land in the "deafening downstairs" can always opt for the calmer upstairs on future visits.

	FOOD	DECOR	SERVICE	COST

LoBianco Coastal Cuisine Ⓜ *American* ▽ 25 | 18 | 20 | $41

Margate | 8409 Ventnor Ave. (Jerome Ave.) | 609-822-0600
"Personable" service and "wonderful" New American offerings
come together in this family-run Margate BYO a block from the
ocean; "crowded" conditions and tables "very close together" make
the seating slightly "uncomfortable", but all is "forgotten" once
the food arrives.

Lobster House *Seafood* 20 | 17 | 18 | $36

Cape May | Fisherman's Wharf | 906 Schellenger Landing Rd.
(Rte. 109 S.) | 609-884-8296 | www.thelobsterhouse.com
"A must" for some of "the freshest" catch in Cape May, this spacious
docksider, a "true summer tradition" and "tourist" destination,
proves you "don't need to be cutting-edge to be great"; for diehards,
the "absurd" waits are "worth it", for others, there's always the takeout window; N.B. open year-round.

Lodos *Mediterranean/Turkish* ▽ 21 | 18 | 18 | $29

New Milford | 690 River Rd. (Henley Ave.) | 201-265-0004
For "delicious", "consistent" Turkish-Mediterranean "treats" in
New Milford, make sure to check out this "terrific" BYO storefront;
all acknowledge that the prices are "reasonable", especially if
you go for the "great deal" of a lunch, when you "get so much food"
for the money.

Lola's *Spanish* 22 | 23 | 20 | $36

Hoboken | 153 14th St. (Bloomfield St.) | 201-420-6062
"Just what Hoboken needed" is what you're bound to hear about this
bi-level Iberian and its "consistently good" tapas, "moderate" pricing and "great" selection of Spanish wines (the cellar holds some
6,000 bottles); the "old-world" ambiance makes some say it feels
like they're "sitting on a veranda in a Spanish town."

Look See *Chinese* 19 | 14 | 17 | $28

Ramsey | 295 N. Franklin Tpke. (Rte. 17) | 201-327-1515
"One of the better" Chinese restaurants in the area is this BYO servicing Ramsey locals with "tasty" dishes; given the undistinguished,
"nothing-fancy" digs and "grumpy" service, is it any surprise that
"takeout is an excellent" alternative?

Ⓩ Lorena's Ⓜ *French* 27 | 21 | 25 | $56

Maplewood | 168 Maplewood Ave. (off Valley St.) | 973-763-4460 |
www.restaurantlorena.com
"Good things come in small packages" marvel fans of this super-
"small" Maplewood French BYO where chef-owner Humberto
Campos Jr. (ex Ryland Inn, Nicholas) uses "wonderful" ingredients
to showcase his "stunning" preparations while his partner, Lorena
Perez, presides over the "attentive" staff; the consensus: it's the
town's "crown jewel."

Los Amigos *Mexican* 23 | 18 | 20 | $27

Atlantic City | 1926 Atlantic Ave. (bet. Michigan & Ohio Aves.) |
609-344-2293

| | FOOD | DECOR | SERVICE | COST |

(continued)

Los Amigos

West Berlin | 461 Rte. 73 N. (Franklin Ave.) | 856-767-5216 Ⓜ
www.losamigosrest.com

The "best" "down 'n' dirty" Mexican fare makes this twosome (in Atlantic City and West Berlin) an obvious choice, though the "ultimate" margaritas are a draw themselves; a "friendly" vibe and the "right" prices set the duo up for several "*olés*"!

Lotus Cafe *Chinese* | 24 | 12 | 18 | $24 |

Hackensack | Home Depot Shopping Ctr. | 450 Hackensack Ave. (Rte. 4) | 201-488-7070

It "doesn't look like much of anything", but even the "uninspired" decor can't keep fans away from this "crowded" BYO Hackensack strip-maller touted for its "outstanding", "reasonably" priced Chinese cooking; "aim-to-please" service and "fast and friendly" delivery also attract advocates.

LouCás *Italian/Seafood* | 24 | 18 | 21 | $38 |

Edison | Colonial Village Shopping Ctr. | 9 Lincoln Hwy. (Parsonage Rd.) | 732-549-8580 | www.loucasrestaurant.com

"You never leave hungry" – or disappointed – with the "overly generous" portions of consistently "delicious" Italian and seafood offerings in store at this bi-level Edison strip-mall BYO overseen by chef and co-owner Loucás Sofocli; a "warm welcome" is a given, as are "crowds" keen on getting a "great" value.

Lua *Pan-Latin* | 22 | 25 | 19 | $48 |

Hoboken | 1300 Sinatra Dr. N. (Independence Ct.) | 201-876-1900 | www.luarestaurant.com

For what's considered the "best scene" in Hoboken – both inside and outside – hit this huge, "gorgeous" Pan-Latin offering "incredible" views of Manhattan visible from the "fantastic" oval neon bar, the site of "eye candy galore"; as to be expected, though the fare's "tasty", it's more "scene than cuisine" at this "South Beach on the Hudson", where a good credit limit is necessary to cover the (unsurprisingly) "pricey" tabs.

Luchento's Ⓜ *Italian* | 20 | 12 | 18 | $36 |

Millstone | 520 Hwy. 33 W. (Dugans Grove Rd.) | 732-446-8500 | www.luchentos.com

"Generous" helpings of "good", if "basic" Italian is the calling card of this "family-friendly" Millstone BYO that also proffers a handful of Cajun-Creole dishes; "nothing to write home about" describes the decor, not the "reasonable" prices.

NEW Lucky Bones ❍ *American* | 18 | 14 | 16 | $32 |

Cape May | 1200 Rte. 109 S. (3rd Ave.) | 609-884-2663

A popular choice for "casual dining" on Cape May, this relatively recent American doubles as both a meet-and-greet "scene" for bar fans and as a "family" eatery serving a range of "tasty" offerings; weekends bring live bands, and good-"value" prices are there every day.

	FOOD	DECOR	SERVICE	COST

Luigi's *Italian*
19 | 15 | 20 | $36

East Hanover | Berkeley Plaza | 434 Ridgedale Ave. (McKinley Ave.) |
973-887-8408 | www.luigisitalianrestaurant.com

A "congenial" mood fills this East Hanover storefront Italian purveying a "solid" menu and "decent" portions, some of which usually end
up in "doggy bags"; no, there's "nothing spectacular" here – just a
"pleasant place for a pleasant meal" that's a "great" value.

Luka's ⓈItalian
22 | 13 | 19 | $32

Ridgefield Park | 238 Main St. (Park St.) | 201-440-2996 |
www.lukasitaliancuisine.com

"Delicious", "high-quality" Italian at "reasonable" prices make this
Ridgefield Park BYO "worth seeking out"; perhaps a little "plain", the
settting is warmed by both the presence of "charming" Luka Sinishtaj
and the "crowds" that visit.

Lulu's Bistro *American*
21 | 17 | 21 | $40

Livingston | 498 S. Livingston Ave. (Northfield Ave.) | 973-994-0150

This "charming" "hideaway" in a Livingston strip mall is "definitely
worth a try" for its "eclectic menu" of "creative" New American fare
and its "romantic, relaxing" ambiance; for most, it "tries hard to
please" and succeeds, offering a "warm", "pleasant" staff and "lots
of attention to the little extras"; P.S. "you can BYO, which is a plus!"

Lu Nello ⓈItalian
25 | 18 | 24 | $56

Totowa | 331 Union Blvd. (Rte. 46) | 973-790-1410 | www.lunello.com

"Never less than wonderful", this Totowa temple of "soul food" the
Italian way is a "gastronome's delight" on account of its "great"
cooking and "exceptional" list of specials; it pays to be an insider,
though, as some say only "regulars get special treatment."

Madame Claude Cafe Ⓜ⑂ *French*
23 | 15 | 20 | $26

Jersey City | 364½ Fourth St. (Brunswick St.) | 201-876-8800 |
www.madameclaudecafe.com

"Simple, honest" French bistro fare keeps this "teeny, tiny", "cute"
and "quirky" cash-only Jersey City BYO a "delight" for fans of sweet
and savory Gallic fare; while the location is unlikely, inside, the
"charming", sunny vibe seems pure Left Bank.

Mad Batter *American*
21 | 19 | 19 | $30

Cape May | Carroll Villa Hotel | 19 Jackson St. (bet. Beach Dr. &
Carpenter Ln.) | 609-884-5970 | www.madbatter.com

"Fantastic" breakfasts and brunches including "outrageously" good
pancakes and "delicious" omelets are the specialty of this "friendly"
venerable American staple set in a Cape May B&B; it's overall an "enjoyable" experience, and "especially if you sit outside" on the porch.

Madeleine's
Petit Paris Ⓜ *Continental/French*
24 | 18 | 23 | $48

Northvale | 416 Tappan Rd. (Paris Ave.) | 201-767-0063 |
www.madeleinespetitparis.com

For "incredible" fare, Gallic-ing gourmets go to this "refined"
Northvale French-Continental renowned as much for its "heavenly"

soufflés and other dishes (courtesy of chef Gaspard Caloz) as for the "gracious" service of wife Madeleine, a "terrific" hostess; no surprise, this "very special" place is "date" central.

Madison Bar & Grill *American*

21 | 20 | 19 | $36

Hoboken | 1316 Washington St. (14th St.) | 201-386-0300 | www.madisonbarandgrill.com

Stop in to this "reliable" north "Hoboken classic", as "beyond the bar" lies a "separate", "nicely appointed dining room that sets the tone" for the "solid" menu of "well-executed" New American "basics" and "adventurous specials"; "when you'd rather just drink", however, the "packed bar" provides a "great singles scene", especially on Tuesday's "crazy" half-price martini night.

Magic Pot Ⓜ *Fondue*

19 | 13 | 19 | $41

Edgewater | 934 River Rd. (bet. Dempsey & Hilliard Aves.) | 201-969-8005 | www.themagicpotfonduebistro.com

This Edgewater BYO "hits the spot" for fondue fans who dig "cheesy goodness" along with "to-die-for" desserts; though some find it somewhat "pricey considering you're doing all of the cooking", most maintain it all adds up to a "fun evening."

Mahogany Grille *American*

23 | 23 | 21 | $50

Manasquan | 142 Main St. (Parker Ave.) | 732-292-1300

"Excellent" fare accompanied by "professional" service, an "attractive" setting and "nice" wines make this Manasquan New American so "loved by many"; it's a "comfortable" "class act" and "dependable" option – usually "when cost doesn't matter."

Mahzu *Japanese*

22 | 16 | 18 | $31

Aberdeen | Aberdeen Plaza | 1077 Rte. 34 (Lloyd Rd.) | 732-583-8985
Freehold Township | 430 Mts. Corner Dr. (Rte. 537) | 732-866-9668
www.mahzujapaneserestaurant.com

It's "hard to choose" between the "wide variety", from "fresh" sushi to "tasty" hibachi and teppanyaki selections at these BYOs, whose names suggest "pine tree" in Japanese; the "friendly" service pleases, even though it tends to be "spotty."

Main Street Bistro *American*

21 | 19 | 19 | $39

Freehold | 30 E. Main St. (Spring St.) | 732-294-1112 | www.bistro1.com

An "upscale crowd" is attracted to this "noisy" split-level New American BYO whose reliably "good" food and scene help "spruce up the dining" situation in Freehold; P.S. some suggest the outdoor dining qualifies as a "people-watching event."

Main Street Euro-American
Bistro & Bar *American*

18 | 15 | 17 | $33

Princeton | Princeton Shopping Ctr. | 301 N. Harrison St. (Valley Rd.) | 609-921-2779 | www.mainstreetprinceton.com

Vintage posters lend to the "quaintness" of this seemingly "always full" yet "comfortable" Princeton shopping-center American whose fare is "good" to partisans and "ordinary" to others; still, all agree the bar is "wonderful" and outdoor seating "pleasant."

	FOOD	DECOR	SERVICE	COST

Maize ☒ *American* — 21 | 22 | 19 | $43

Newark | Robert Treat Hotel | 50 Park Pl. (bet. Center & E. Park Sts.) | 973-639-1200 | www.maizerestaurant.com

This "pretty", Tony Chi-designed Traditional American in a Downtown Newark hotel opposite NJPAC is a sound alternative to the area's Iberian offerings; not surprisingly, concert nights draw crowds that choose the "great", though "limited" pre-theater option that most consider "the way to go."

Makeda *Ethiopian* — 23 | 23 | 20 | $34

New Brunswick | 338 George St. (bet. Bayard St. & Livingston Ave.) | 732-545-5115

"Be a little adventurous" and try this "unique experience" on New Brunswick's Restaurant Row, where you "use your fingers" (plus "spongy" injera bread) "to scoop up authentic Ethiopian" eats that "burst with flavor"; it's all set in a "beautiful" space, and while the "service can vary greatly, the food" – and "hip" weekend music (jazz, funk, reggae) – "makes up for it."

Malabar House *Indian* — - | - | - | I

Piscataway | 1665 Stelton Rd. (Ethel Rd.) | 732-819-0400

This BYO in Piscataway is known for its dosas and rare renditions of affordable, authentic Southern Indian classics such as black lentil balls with yogurt; though the strip-mall surroundings may not engage the senses, the fare might.

Mama Tucci ☒ *Italian* — - | - | - | E

Livingston | Livingston Town Ctr. | 4245 Town Center Way, 2nd fl. (N. Livingston Ave.) | 973-597-3700 | www.mamatucci.com

Northern Italian cuisine is in the spotlight at this Livingston BYO thanks to what emerges from the kitchen, whether savory (the signature pistachio-crusted scallops in lemon–white wine glaze) or sweet (coconut cream pie); warmth is supplied by the decor, noted for its gold tones and brick accents.

Manhattan Steakhouse *Steak* — 22 | 19 | 19 | $55

Oakhurst | 2105 Rte. 35 N. (W. Park Ave.) | 732-493-6328 | www.manhattansteakhouse.com

"Easier than going to the city" reason fans of this manly Oakhurst chophouse dispensing some "good and pricey" "red meat and red wine"; aside from arguments over the manly setting ("terrific" vs. "no atmosphere"), "if you are in the mood for beef, this is the place."

Manon ☒ *French* — 25 | 21 | 23 | $44

Lambertville | 19 N. Union St. (Bridge St.) | 609-397-2596

"Like being transported" to "a bistro in Provence", this "tiny" BYO "charmer" in Lambertville "remains a favorite" for its "stellar" country French cuisine and "delightful" setting (an "eye-catching" mural of 'Starry Night' blankets the ceiling); although tables are "elbow to elbow" and they don't take credit, most maintain this is "a real gem" whose facets include a "caring" staff; N.B. open for dinner only, Wednesday–Sunday.

	FOOD	DECOR	SERVICE	COST

Z Manor, The M *American*   23 | 25 | 24 | $61

West Orange | 111 Prospect Ave. (Woodland Ave.) | 973-731-2360 | www.themanorrestaurant.com

"From the driveway, gardens and fountains" to the "over-the-top" dining room, expect "opulence galore" at this Traditional American in West Orange, a "standby that rarely disappoints" with its "delicious food", "excellent wines" and "accommodating staff"; this "local landmark" may be "overwhelming, but that's nice when celebrating."

Marco & Pepe M *American*   22 | 19 | 19 | $35

Jersey City | 289 Grove St. (Mercer St.) | 201-860-9688 | www.marcoandpepe.com

"A hip place for dinner" or brunch, this "chic" yet "low-key" storefront New American in Jersey City is a destination for small and large plates of deliciously "comforting" New American food; for some, "it doesn't get better", and ex-NYCers ask "who needs Manhattan now?"

Margherita's M *Italian*   22 | 12 | 17 | $25

Hoboken | 740 Washington St. (8th St.) | 201-222-2400

"Always a safe bet" for "simple Italian at its best", this "casual" corner BYO in Hoboken serves up "humongous" helpings of "delicious", "homestyle pastas" and other "traditional" dishes plus "can't-beat brick-oven pizza"; it's "tiny", so "make sure to get there early" to avoid the "insufferable waits", or better yet, opt to sit outside.

**Marie Nicole's ● ** *American*   ∇ 23 | 21 | 23 | $48

Wildwood | 9510 Pacific Ave. (Richmond Ave.) | 609-522-5425

The few who've ventured to this "classy", "off-the-beaten-track" Wildwood "jewel" near Diamond Beach report a "good" New American menu, "attractive" quarters and a "well-stocked" bar; in short, advocates add the "Shore needs this spot."

NEW Market in the Middle *Eclectic*   23 | 20 | 21 | $34

Asbury Park | 516 Cookman Ave. (Bangs Ave.) | 732-776-8886 | www.kitschens.com

An "interesting" Eclectic menu and equally interesting concept draw applause for this "welcome", somewhat recent addition to Asbury Park vending "good" fare along with its setting: a bistro-like restaurant within a wine shop and gourmet market offering "unique" items; the "wonderful" bar and "lively" scene prove the newcomer's "popularity."

Marra's M *Italian*   20 | 15 | 17 | $40

Ridgewood | 16 S. Broad St. (E. Ridgewood Ave.) | 201-444-1332 | www.marrasrestaurant.com

"You get exactly" what you expect at this Ridgewood Italian BYO, namely "good" red-sauce cookery, "warm" service and "long waits even with a reservation"; the convivial scene is confirmed by the "noise" and "elbow-bumping" setup.

Marsilio's Z *Italian*   22 | 17 | 19 | $40

Trenton | 541 Roebling Ave. (Chestnut Ave.) | 609-695-1916

For many, this "blast from the past" (1951) in Trenton's Chambersburg section "still sets the standard" for "abundant" portions of "consistent" Italian red sauce that "wins hearts"; lunchtime "people-watching" is a sport: "don't sit with your back to the door" – you wouldn't want to miss all the "local politicians" in the house.

Martino's ⓂCuban

`21` `11` `18` `$25`

Somerville | 212 W. Main St. (Doughty Ave.) | 908-722-8602 | www.martinoscubanrestaurant.com

If you're thinking Cuban in Central Jersey, try this "nothing-fancy" Somerville BYO dishing out "heaping" helpings of "tasty" "economical" eats; hence, it's no surprise that locals keep coming back to this "homey" venue that's a "true success story."

Mastoris ● Diner

`19` `12` `19` `$22`

Bordentown | 144 Hwy. 130 (Rte. 206) | 609-298-4650 | www.mastoris.com

The menu is "longer than *War and Peace*" and the space is just as "huge" at this "landmark", the "big daddy" of diners in Bordentown catering to patrons who go as much for the "to-die-for" cheese bread as for the "mega" portions; incredible "bargains" keep the "unbelievable" crowds pouring in even at "1 AM, when the parking lot is packed."

Matisse ⓈⓂ American

`22` `20` `20` `$46`

Belmar | 1300 Ocean Ave. (13th Ave.) | 732-681-7680 | www.matissecatering.com

"Wonderful" savories and sweets, and ocean views that are even "better" (you "can't get much closer to the Atlantic") paint a picture of success of this Belmar New American BYO that hosts "dates" and is "worth every dollar"; periodic jazz in winter warms the scene.

Mattar's American/Eclectic

`24` `21` `23` `$52`

Allamuchy | 1115 Rte. 517 (Ridge Rd.) | 908-852-2300 | www.mattars.com

A "diamond" in the rough of Warren County, this "middle-of-nowhere" Eclectic-New American provides a bit of "fine dining" to the area with the "best" food around; it "doesn't disappoint", with diehards claiming "it deserves to be in a big city."

Matt's Red Rooster Grill ⓈⓂ American

`25` `21` `23` `$43`

Flemington | 22 Bloomfield Ave. (Spring St.) | 908-788-7050 | www.mattsredroostergrill.com

For a taste of "Manhattan in the middle of Flemington", fans nestle into this "cheery" New American in a restored Victorian for both chef-proprietors Matthew Green and Matthew McPherson's "well-executed" food and their "Danny Meyer"-like (think NYC's Union Square Cafe) "hospitality"; N.B. though BYO, they offer local wines.

ⓏMcCormick & Schmick's Seafood

`20` `19` `19` `$39`

Hackensack | Riverside Square Mall | 175 Riverside Sq. (Hackensack Ave.) | 201-968-9410

Bridgewater | Bridgewater Commons | 400 Commons Way (Prince Rodgers Ave.) | 908-707-9996 www.mccormickandschmicks.com

The majority just "doesn't care" that these seafood emporiums are part of a chain, adding the items seem "so fresh you have to hold

| | FOOD | DECOR | SERVICE | COST |

them down"; there's also "reliable" steaks and other turf proffered amid decor that makes you "forget you're in a shopping mall."

McLoone's *American*
`17` `23` `18` `$43`

Long Branch | 1 Ocean Ave. (Laird St.) | 732-923-1006
Sea Bright | 816 Ocean Ave. (Beach Way) | 732-842-2894
www.mcloones.com

Two "glorious" views (the ocean in Long Branch and the Navesink River in Sea Bright) are what's behind the appeal of these Americans whose fans have "no complaints" with them; detractors decry "amateurish" dishes and "lacking" service, but they're still a "favorite for locals and credit card companies."

Mediterra *Mediterranean*
`20` `22` `20` `$42`

Princeton | 29 Hulfish St. (bet. Chambers & Witherspoon Sts.) |
609-252-9680 | www.terramomo.com

Proponents of this "smart", "sophisticated" Pan-Mediterranean in the heart of Princeton find "fine" food and say the setting is equally suited to "business lunches" or for when "your parents are visiting you at school"; P.S. it's "heavenly to sit outside on a hot summer night."

Meemah ◩ *Chinese/Malaysian*
`24` `10` `19` `$20`

Edison | Colonial Village Shopping Ctr. | 9 Lincoln Hwy. (Parsonage Rd.) |
732-906-2223

"Forget the strip mall" and "lack of decor" and just "enjoy the food" say fans of this "yummy" Malaysian-Chinese BYO in Edison, the "greatest little secret in NJ"; the clincher: the "wide variety" of "consistently excellent" Pan-Asian dishes are "cheap and plentiful."

Megu Sushi *Japanese*
`▽ 22` `18` `23` `$31`

Cherry Hill | Village Walk Shopping Ctr. | 1990 Rte. 70 E.
(Old Orchard Rd.) | 856-489-6228 | www.megusushi.com

The "colorful" decorations are "intriguing" at this Japanese BYO working in a Cherry Hill strip mall; it's "no Japan" when it comes to sushi, some say, but most agree the offerings are "consistent", and likely "as good as you can expect" in the neighborhood.

NEW Mehndi *Indian*
`-` `-` `-` `E`

Morristown | Headquarters Plaza | 88 Headquarters Plaza (Park Pl.) |
973-871-2323 | www.mehtanirestaurantgroup.com

This luxe Morristown Indian from the Mehtani Restaurant Group (Ming, Moghul and Moksha) presents modern fare and specialty cocktails in a bright, split-level space featuring Murano glass and hand-painted enlargements of traditional Mehndi art (elaborate, temporary henna tattoos known throughout India, the Middle East and North Africa); N.B. other options under the same roof include Ming II, a Pan-Asian, and SM23, a posh lounge serving bar food and drinks.

Meil's ⇗ *American*
`23` `15` `19` `$29`

Stockton | Bridge & Main Sts. (Main St./Rte. 29) | 609-397-8033 |
www.meilsrestaurant.com

For "stick-to-your-ribs" Americana served by a staff that is "a hoot", this "cute" BYO cafe in Stockton is a "delightfully quirky" find for breakfast, brunch, lunch and dinner; most agree "you'll always get a good and filling meal" – just make sure you bring cash to pay for your "down-home" meil's.

☑ Mélange Cafe Ⓜ Creole

26 | 16 | 22 | $35

Cherry Hill | 1601 Chapel Ave. (Rte. 38) | 856-663-7339 | www.melangecafe.com

"Joe Brown is the man!" insist believers about the toque who turns out étouffée that'll "blow you away" and "incredible" jambalaya among the "great" menu items at this Cherry Hill BYO, the "real deal" as far as Creole cookery; the setting's "unassuming", but the place is still nice for "celebrations."

Melting Pot, The Fondue

19 | 20 | 19 | $47

Westwood | 250 Center Ave. (Westwood Ave.) | 201-664-8877
Somerville | 190 W. Main St. (Doughty Ave.) | 908-575-8010
Whippany | Pine Plaza Shopping Ctr. | 831 Rte. 10 (N. Jefferson Rd.) | 973-428-5400
Red Bank | The Galleria | 2 Bridge Ave. (W. Front St.) | 732-219-0090
www.meltingpot.com

It may be a "kitschy chain" but fondue fans and even "jaded foodies" have a "blast" dipping into "delicious" pots of "cheesy, brothy, chocolately goodness" at this Jersey quartet; even though it costs a "small fortune for the privilege of cooking your own food", regulars say there's magic in the 'Big Night Out' ($86 per couple), a four-course prix fixe extravaganza.

Memphis Pig Out ⊉ BBQ

19 | 11 | 18 | $28

Atlantic Highlands | 67 First Ave. (Center Ave.) | 732-291-5533
At this Atlantic Highlands barbecue joint, you get the "best" baby-backs and other "excellent" 'cue on its "sinner's paradise" of a menu; overall, it's an "excellent" buy, and the "kinda-grimy", pig-motif interior "somehow works."

NEW Mercy Grill American

- | - | - | M

Hoboken | 230 Washington St. (bet. 2nd & 3rd Sts.) | 201-239-1400 | www.mercygrill.com

Arched ceilings, brick accents and floor-to-ceiling windows help set apart this warmly minimalist, Hoboken split-level newcomer (the brainchild of two Stevens Tech grads) with an unmistakable industrial modern ambiance; the New American slate draws inspiration from Asia and Europe, and the sleek backlit bar may wind up being people-watching central.

Merion Inn, The American

20 | 22 | 22 | $44

Cape May | 106 Decatur St. (bet. Columbia & Hughes Aves.) | 609-884-8363 | www.merioninn.com

This "traditional" Cape May Traditional American hosts diners "charmed" by the nightly piano, "old-fashioned", "unpretentious" ambiance and generally "reliable" eats and "attentive" staff; aficionados affirm it also boasts a "great", "classy" bar reported to be the oldest in town.

	FOOD	DECOR	SERVICE	COST

Metropolitan Cafe *Asian/Eclectic*

| 22 | 21 | 18 | $40 |

Freehold | 8 E. Main St. (South St.) | 732-780-9400

"Lower Manhattan in the middle of Jersey" neatly sums up this "dark", "trendy" Freeholder populated by "pretty people" baited by the bar scene and "great" cocktails, and perhaps the "good" Asian–Eclectic food; it's a "singles" "meat market", especially on weekends, so couples may want to "plan their romance for weekdays" here.

Metuchen Inn *American*

| 22 | 21 | 20 | $51 |

Metuchen | 424 Middlesex Ave. (Linden Ave.) | 732-494-6444 | www.themetucheninn.com

A "lovely old-world" ambiance graces this Metuchen inn New American, a "relaxing" option whose white-tablecloth setting "charms" and where the wines are "solid"; but detractors don't like "lackluster" service that runs "slow"; N.B. a revised menu's in the works thanks to a new chef, whose arrival may not be reflected in the above Food score.

Mexican Food Factory *Mexican*

| 18 | 16 | 17 | $25 |

Marlton | 601 Rte. 70 W. (Cropwell Rd.) | 856-983-9222

"Consistently consistent", if just a "notch up from typical", is the story of the chow at this 30+-year-old Mexican food hall on busy Route 70 in Marlton; no, the "service isn't the greatest" and self portraits of Frida Kahlo "peer at you from every wall", but cronies confess this spot "does the trick."

Mexico Lindo 🗷 *Mexican*

| ▽ 28 | 15 | 23 | $18 |

Brick | 1135 Burnt Tavern Rd. (Sage St.) | 732-202-1930

Chicken mole and chiles rellenos help authenticate the menu at this Brick Township BYO dishing out "excellent" Mexican food for those "on a budget"; the quality of the cooking more than trumps the "minimal" decor.

NEW Meyersville Inn, The *American*

| - | - | - | E |

Meyersville | 632 Meyersville Rd. (New Vernon Rd.) | 908-647-6302 | www.meyersvilleinn.com

A recent renovation has primed this former 19th-century country store–turned-tavern for greater things and set the stage for its New Orleans–influenced American menu; with three comfortable dining rooms and an inviting bar, perhaps folks will soon be able to find Meyersville on a map.

Mia Ⓜ *Italian*

| 26 | 23 | 23 | $58 |

Atlantic City | Caesars on the Boardwalk | 2100 Pacific Ave. (S. Arkansas Ave.) | 609-441-2345 | www.miaac.com

"Georges Perrier had done it again!" with this Caesars on the Boardwalk Italian, where Philly's most celebrated chef has teamed up with protégé Chris Scarduzio to create "unbelievable" fare supported by "tip-top" servers in an airy, column-filled setting; thanks to who's behind this "great" addition, the "quality is as you'd expect", as perhaps is the "arm-and-a-leg" pricing.

| | FOOD | DECOR | SERVICE | COST |

Michael's Cucina Italia ⓜ *Italian*   19 | 11 | 16 | $25

Manalapan | Alexander Plaza | 333 Rte. 9 S. (Gordon's Corner) | 732-409-4777

With "huge" portions, it's no surprise this Manalapan BYO attracts; the "simple", "family-style" Italian cooking pleases, and many confide they'd "return" in spite of atmosphere that "could be improved."

Midori *Japanese*   24 | 14 | 19 | $32

Denville | Denville Commons Mall | 3130 Rte. 10 W. (bet. Franklin & Hill Rds.) | 973-537-8588 | www.midorirestaurant.com

"If you're a sushi buff, this is the place to be" report raw-fish aficionados of this strip-mall Japanese BYO in Denville, where the "fantastic" selections are so "delicious"; the folks here are "friendly" and the price is right, so "why go anywhere else?"

Mie Thai *Thai*   25 | 16 | 20 | $24

Woodbridge | 34 Main St. (Berry St.) | 732-596-9400 | www.miethai.com

All that "fabulous" Thai cooking "stands out" at this Woodbridge BYO whose numerous backers are inspired by all the "spicy" ("mild is hot"!) vittles that come out of the kitchen; the "bargain" lunch specials ($9.95) are a sweet deal.

Mignon Steakhouse *Steak*   23 | 18 | 20 | $45

Rutherford | 72 Park Ave. (Franklin Pl.) | 201-896-0202 | www.villagerestaurantgroup.com

"Local carnivores get their kicks" out of this Rutherford chophouse preparing "perfectly cooked" steaks that some say add up to a "bang for the buck" given the BYO policy; "great" sides are in the offing, as are "warm" service and a "cozy" wood-and-brick space.

Mikado *Japanese*   22 | 16 | 21 | $27

Cherry Hill | 2320 Rte. 70 W. (S. Union Ave.) | 856-665-4411
Maple Shade | 468 S. Lenola Rd. (Kings Hwy.) | 856-638-1801
NEW **Marlton** | Elmwood Shopping Ctr. | 793 Rte. 70 E. (Troth Rd.) | 856-797-8581

"Bargain" tabs make it easy for raw-fish lovers to indulge in the "fresh" sushi at this South Jersey Japanese BYO trio fronted by the "nicest" staff; they're ideal for "families", especially at the Marlton and Maple Shade branches, where hibachi is offered.

Milford Oyster House *Seafood*   – | – | – | M

Milford | 92 Rte. 519 (York St.) | 908-995-9411 | www.milfordoysterhouse.com

Head for all the oysters offered at this vintage Milford landmark where seafood can be both simply and imaginatively prepared; just a quick skip from the Delaware, it's a day's-end stop for river-rafters and cyclists touring this scenic western area of the state.

Mill at Spring Lake Heights ⓜ *American*   20 | 23 | 21 | $44

Spring Lake Heights | 101 Old Mill Rd. (Ocean Rd.) | 732-449-1800 | www.themillatslh.com

Although the space was known more for "weddings" than for the food, this American steak 'n' seafooder in Spring Lake Heights is

	FOOD	DECOR	SERVICE	COST

now associated with a "good" menu and "romance", the latter thanks to its "beautiful" grounds that include a "lovely" lake where swans glide by; penny-pinchers pick the "reasonably" priced lunch prix fixe and early-bird.

Ming *Asian*

	23	21	18	$35

Edison | Oak Tree Shopping Ctr. | 1655-185 Oak Tree Rd. (bet. Grove & Wood Aves.) | 732-549-5051 | www.mingrestaurants.com Ⓜ

NEW **Morristown** | Headquarters Plaza | 88 Headquarters Plaza (Park Pl.) | 973-871-2323 | www.mehtanirestaurantgroup.com

They "don't fool around" with the spices or the cooking at this Edison BYO Indian-Chinese combo putting out "inspired" food in "upscale" quarters; surely, it's a "refreshing alternative" to the area's other options, but note that it's also a little "pricey"; N.B. the sleek Pan-Asian, Ming II, has recently joined Mehndi in Morristown.

Moghul Ⓜ *Indian*

	24	18	20	$32

Edison | Oak Tree Shopping Ctr. | 1655-195 Oak Tree Rd. (bet. Grove & Wood Aves.) | 732-549-5050 | www.moghul.com

"Scintillating aromas" that emanate from this Edison Indian BYO's kitchen "make you crave" the "first-class" curries and "excellent" naan that fans brand the "best in the state"; the "great" lunch buffets are feasts fit for a moghul at pauper's prices ($10.95).

Ⓩ Mojave Grille *Southwestern*

	24	19	20	$37

Westfield | 35 Elm St. (North Ave.) | 908-233-7772 | www.mojavegrille.com

The curved horns are in keeping with the Southwestern motif, and so is the fare at this Westfield BYO "star", a "spicy change of pace" hailed for "consistently terrific" preparations; no doubt, the restaurant is *magnifico*, but no surprise: no reservations makes the place a "tough table."

NEW Moksha Ⓜ *Indian*

	▽ 22	23	22	$29

Edison | Oak Tree Shopping Ctr. | 1655-200 Oak Tree Rd. (Henry St.) | 732-947-3010

From the group behind Ming and Moghul comes this "new kid on the block", "a breath of fresh air" in Edison that serves up "simply delicious" South Indian edibles in a "pleasant", "quiet" setting; the "finger-licking-good" cuisine includes many vegetarian options and "excellent meat dishes too", making this BYO neophyte "definitely worth a try."

Molly Pitcher Inn *American*

	22	25	23	$47

Red Bank | Molly Pitcher Inn | 88 Riverside Ave. (W. Front St.) | 732-747-2500

The "blazer-and-loafer crowd can't get enough" of this hotel Red Bank Traditional American, the place to "have brandy with dad the night before your wedding" that's still keeping "old-guard" supping alive with "old-world" service and "fine" fare enhanced by "terrific" views of the Navesink River; if it exudes "stodginess" for a few, for most, it's what "delightful dining" should be; N.B. jacket required.

| | | | FOOD | DECOR | SERVICE | COST |

Mompou *Spanish* ▽ 20 | 24 | 20 | $32

Newark | 77 Ferry St. (Congress St.) | 973-578-8114 |
www.mompoutapas.com

A "hopping place for tapas" and wine "in the heart of the
Ironbound", this Ferry Street "find" offers "an upscale take" on
Spanish cuisine in a "sophisticated" "lounge atmosphere" that's
"like something out of SoHo" with its "exposed-brick walls" and
marble-topped bar; the "convivial" vibe extends to live music, salsa
lessons and a "fantastic courtyard."

Monster Sushi *Japanese* 19 | 15 | 18 | $31

Summit | 395 Springfield Ave. (Maple St.) | 908-598-1100 |
www.monstersushi.com

"Peter Luger"-size slabs of sushi explain the name and concept behind this "popular" Jersey Japanese (a Summit spin-off sired by the
NYC mini-chain) where "kids love" the "fresh" comestibles that include a peanut butter and jelly version; one thing: those "big portions can be tough to eat."

Ⓩ Moonstruck Ⓜ *Mediterranean* 24 | 24 | 22 | $48

Asbury Park | 517 Lake Ave. (bet. Main St. & Ocean Ave.) |
732-988-0123 | www.moonstrucknj.com

"Dinner on one of the terraces is heaven on Earth" dote devotees of
this "premier" Asbury Park destination, a supremely "popular", multilevel venue serving "delicious" Mediterranean meals and that's
"long on atmosphere" thanks to the "date-worthy", "romantic"
space; as always, "no reservations" frustrates, but then again, the
"bar is so lovely, so who cares?"

Mo' Pho' *Vietnamese* 24 | 10 | 20 | $25

Fort Lee | 212 Main St. (Lemoine Ave.) | 201-363-8886

Saigon R. Ⓜ *Vietnamese*

Englewood | 58 W. Palisade Ave. (William St.) | 201-871-4777
www.saigonmopho.com

Fans want nothing mo' than to hit this "no-decor" twosome (Fort
Lee's the latest) turning out "terrific" Vietnamese vittles; service
is "reliable" and the seating "limited", so it's not a stretch to
expect "cramped" conditions.

Morton's, The Steakhouse *Steak* 24 | 22 | 22 | $63

Hackensack | Riverside Square Mall | 274 Riverside Sq. (Hackensack Ave.) |
201-487-1303 | www.mortons.com

"What you see is what you get" – your server displays the meat you
choose to eat – at this "sure bet" of a Hackensack meat emporium
that, though part of a chain, still delivers "consistency and quality"
when it comes to its steaks and "excellent" sides; if the "great"
chops don't, the "costly" tabs may just give you heartburn.

Mr. Chu *Chinese* 22 | 14 | 18 | $23

East Hanover | 44 Rte. 10 W. (Ridgedale Ave.) | 973-887-7555
The decor's "dated", so keep your eyes on the "delish" dishes at this
East Hanover Chinese BYO where the value is "great"; watch out for

"crowded" confines, and service is generally "excellent", but when busy, it's so "speedy" (they seem "just as eager getting you in as they are getting you out") that you may not have time to chu.

Mud City Crab House *Seafood*   21 | 11 | 16 | $29
Manahawkin | 1185 E. Bay Ave. (Heron St.) | 609-978-3660
The "quintessential crab house" aptly describes this seasonal Manahawkin BYO marketing "fresh", "great" crustaceans, not its somewhat "shady" digs; for some it's "not worth getting eaten alive" by the mosquitoes, but those willing to abide "long waits" weigh in: the place "can't be beat."

Nag's Head ⊭ *American*   ▽ 26 | 10 | 19 | $21
Ocean City | 801 Asbury Ave. (8th St.) | 609-391-9080
Serving Americana (think Tollhouse pie) in an old bank building, this Ocean Cityite is an "excellent" value in light of "fair" prices and "wonderfully prepared" offerings; one of the Shore's "secrets" is open year-round, but there is no alcohol allowed.

Napa Valley Grille *American*   22 | 21 | 21 | $43
Paramus | Garden State Plaza | 1146 Garden State Plaza (Rtes. 4 & 17) | 201-845-5555 | www.napavalleygrille.com
For a "delightful respite" from a Paramus mall "rush" crush, head to this "sophisticated" "California"-esque spot for "good" New American and an "excellent" 500-label West Coast vino selection that's built for "wine lovers"; after all, it's a good place to "splurge after a day splurging in the stores."

☑ Nauvoo Grill Club *American*   16 | 26 | 17 | $40
Fair Haven | 121 Fair Haven Rd. (River Rd.) | 732-747-8777
"Spectacular" Frank Lloyd Wright–inspired, "ski-lodge" looks at this Fair Haven New American are an easy sell for its "hip fortysomething" patrons who also come for the "great" bar scene; as for its other attributes, "unpredictable" fare and "sketchy" service are low points.

Navesink Fishery ⓜ *Seafood*   24 | 10 | 18 | $34
Middletown | A&P Shopping Ctr. | 1004 Rte. 36 S. (Valley Dr.) | 732-291-8017
"A great steady-Eddie", this "eclectic, quirky" Middletown BYO seafooder "maintains its high standards" with fish that you can't find "any fresher"; if the nautical decor supplies "no atmosphere", there's always takeout – plus a retail market up front.

NEW Nazmi's Turkish Kitchen *Turkish*   - | - | - | M
Cliffside Park | 442 Anderson Ave. (bet. Edgewater Rd. & Fulton Terr.) | 201-941-6650
The Turkish enclave in Cliffside Park grew by one with the arrival of this modest BYO serving classics of the genre; the setting's spare, but key in on the fare and you probably won't mind the plain-Jane decor.

Neelam *Indian*   18 | 13 | 18 | $25
South Orange | 115 South Orange Ave. (Irvington Ave.) | 973-762-1100

(continued)

(continued)

Neelam

Middletown | Village Mall | 1178 Rte. 35 (New Monmouth Rd.) | 732-671-8900

These separately owned suburban BYOs quell "cravings for Indian food", which most find easy at the lunch buffet, an "incredible" bargain; all told, the vittles are "reliable but lackluster", and some suggest takeout when "dark", "depressing" decor is factored in.

NEW Neil's Original Oyster M *American/Seafood*

– | – | – | E

Highlands | 1 Willow St. (Shore Dr.) | 732-872-1450 | www.neilsoriginaloyster.com

Chef Neil West has migrated north to this Highlands New American–seafood perch on the bay and brought his signature hearty fare that attracts big appetites; the nautical tavern-cum–dining room holds appeal for casual diners.

Nero's Grille *Steak*

17 | 16 | 17 | $44

Livingston | 618 S. Livingston Ave. (Hobart Gap Rd.) | 973-994-1410

This stuccoed "grande dame" (since 1969) of Livingston still has mileage thanks to its "clublike" atmosphere and bar scene that attracts a crowd, and not necessarily on account of decor that looks "like a reupholstered diner"; foodwise, the steakhouse specialties range from "dependable" to "serviceable."

New Main Taste Thai *Thai*

23 | 14 | 18 | $36

Chatham | 225 Main St. (bet. Hillside & S. Passaic Aves.) | 973-635-7333

"Marvelously complex", "high-quality" cooking en-Thai-ces fans at this Chatham Siamese BYO, a "real surprise" for the 'burbs; "helpful", "sweet" yet slow-as-"molasses" service comes with the territory, but most maintain it's "certainly worth the wait."

Nha Trang Place *Vietnamese*

∇ 24 | 10 | 17 | $18

Jersey City | 249 Newark Ave. (bet. Cole & 2nd Sts.) | 201-239-1988

Go "not for the decor" but for the "excellent" phos and assorted culinary offerings dished out at this Jersey City Vietnamese BYO; the place tends to "fill up" – no shock given the commendably "quick" service and "budget" tabs.

Z Nicholas M *American*

29 | 26 | 28 | $82

Middletown | 160 Rte. 35 S. (bet. Navesink River Rd. & Pine St.) | 732-345-9977 | www.restaurantnicholas.com

Epitomizing "ultrafine" dining, this "modern" (and Most Popular) Middletown New American "utopia of food and wine" near Red Bank is helmed by chef/co-owner (with wife Melissa) Nicholas Harary, whose "extraordinary" cuisine vaults this "amazing" restaurant to the top Food ranking in the state for the third straight year; add in "superlative" service (also No. 1), and even the "jaw-dropping" tabs don't deter devotees of the "absolute best" New Jersey has to offer; P.S. for more a casual experience, the bar/lounge is a "brilliant" alternative.

	FOOD	DECOR	SERVICE	COST

Niecy's M *Southern* ▽ 20 | 17 | 17 | $30
South Orange | 65B South Orange Ave. (Valley St.) | 973-275-1770
"Down-home" Southern cooking "tastes best when served with a helping of Niecy Hanson's personality" attest admirers of this South Orange BYO whose staff "warms your soul as much as the delicious food"; those who know about this place confess "they'd sell their soul to pay" for the goods.

Nikko *Japanese* 24 | 17 | 21 | $34
Whippany | 881 Rte. 10 E. (Rte. 287) | 973-428-0787 | www.nikkonj.com
"You'd have to go fishing" to get fresher seafood say supporters of this Whippany Japanese featuring a variety of "quality" sushi and an impressive sake selection; the "cheerful" service makes the experience even more "genuinely enjoyable."

Nobi *Japanese* ▽ 25 | 14 | 20 | $30
Toms River Township | T.J. Maxx Plaza | 1338 Hooper Ave. (Bey Lea Rd.) | 732-244-7888
"Fast", "friendly" service and "excellent" sushi add up at this "traditional" shopping-center Japanese BYO in Toms River; it "never disappoints" its admirers who've noted its success over the last 10 years.

No. 9 M *American* 24 | 15 | 21 | $41
Lambertville | 9 Klines Ct. (Bridge St.) | 609-397-6380
The allure of this Lambertville storefront BYO New American lies quite simply in the "excellent" cuisine prepared by chef-owner Matthew Kane; true, the "minimalist" decor may be "plain", but beguiled backers are content to let the food steal the show.

Noodle House, The *Asian* 19 | 19 | 17 | $24
North Brunswick | 2313 Rte. 1 S. (bet. Aaron Rd. & Commerce Blvd.) | 732-951-0141
Credit "imaginative", often "tasty" Asian fare and "ultramodern" decor for the success of this North Brunswick BYO featuring an unorthodox ordering policy (you write your order on a notepad) and, as the name suggests, "lots of noodle dishes"; "slow service" is a con, but pros propose the "excellent" weekend lunch buffet.

Nori *Pan-Asian* 22 | 15 | 19 | $30
Caldwell | 406 Bloomfield Ave. (Academy Rd.) | 973-403-2400
NEW **Montclair** | 561 Bloomfield Ave. (Orange Rd.) | 973-655-8805
These "consistent" BYO Pan-Asians purvey "fresh, flavorful" fish and a few "clever" specialty rolls; "reasonable" prices, "neat" decor (including a tatami room in the Montclair branch) and "good" service keep customers contented.

Norma's Mediterranean Restaurant *Mideastern* 21 | 13 | 19 | $23
Cherry Hill | Barclay Farms Shopping Ctr. | 132-145 Rte. 70 E. (Kings Hwy.) | 856-795-1373
"Even less adventurous family members" go for the Middle Eastern dishes at this Cherry Hill BYO whose occasional belly dancing sup-

plies as much of its "cult following" as the "very good", "feast-fit-for-a-king" offerings; the service "charms", and all agree meals here are "the best deal" going.

Nouveau Sushi Pan-Asian

25 | 20 | 20 | $48

Montclair | 635 Bloomfield Ave. (Valley Rd.) | 973-746-9608 | www.nouveausushi.com

Is it the "son of Nobu"? inquire followers who know this Montclair BYO Japanese-Asian specializing in "truly fresh", "amazingly flavorful" sushi and other "creative" morsels that are "true works of art" accompanied by sometimes "good", other times "aloof", service; some say while the decor is "soothing", "sky-high pricing" isn't.

Nova Terra Pan-Latin

22 | 23 | 20 | $41

New Brunswick | 78 Albany St. (Neilson St.) | 732-296-1600 | www.terramomo.com

If you're looking for some "salsa" in New Brunswick, slink into this "stylish" Pan-Latin that has it all – "delicious", "upscale" cuisine and drinks, "efficient" service and a sultry vibe, thanks to live bands on weekends; "lots of pretty people" come with the terra-tory.

Nunzio Ristorante Rustico Italian

23 | 22 | 20 | $39

Collingswood | 706 Haddon Ave. (Collings Ave.) | 856-858-9840 | www.nunzios.net

With its two-story ceiling and life-sized wall painting surrounding the dining room, you'll find yourself in "another world" at this Collingswood BYO Italian cooking up food that's "loved" along with "loud" acoustics; those put off by the latter try hard not to let it "detract from savoring the cuisine."

Oasis Grill Moroccan

▽ 25 | 16 | 21 | $24

Cherry Hill | 2431 Church Rd. (bet. Cooper Landing Rd. & Oak Ave.) | 856-667-8287

"Affordable" tabs make you want to "try everything" (it's all "addictive") at this unsung Moroccan BYO in Cherry Hill purveying an "authentic" menu; the "nice" staff "appreciates" its customers, whose "hearts belong" to this spot.

NEW Oceanos Greek/Mediterranean

- | - | - | E

Fair Lawn | 2-27 Saddle River Rd. (bet. Brookside Ave. & Northern Dr.) | 201-796-0546 | www.oceanosrestaurant.com

Greek goods are preferred at this Fair Lawn Mediterranean offering an array of mezes, a raw bar and whole fish selections; the list of wines (including a number of varietals from Greece) is shipshape for oenophiles.

NEW Octopus's Garden Seafood

▽ 22 | 21 | 24 | $36

Stafford | 771 S. Main St./Rte. 9 (Mayetta Landing Rd.) | 609-597-8828

"Well-cooked", "flavorful" fare finds its way into Stafford via this BYO seafooder a few miles inland from Long Beach Island; its habitués "highly recommend" it, if not for the food then at least for its "friendly" service.

	FOOD	DECOR	SERVICE	COST

Oddfellows *Cajun/Creole*   19 | 17 | 18 | $27

Hoboken | 80 River St. (bet. Hudson Pl. & Newark St.) | 201-656-9009 |
www.oddfellowsrest.com

"A piece of N'Awlins" near the PATH is the deal on this Hoboken
Cajun-Creole where work-weary former "frat boys" dig the reliably
"spicy" "happy-hour" scene at the bar that's chased down with
some "satisfying" bayou vittles; some say it's just the right cure for
a jambalaya "fix", especially if you've "never been to Louisiana."

Old Bay, The 🗷 *Cajun/Creole*   17 | 16 | 17 | $32

New Brunswick | 61-63 Church St. (Neilson St.) | 732-246-3111 |
www.oldbay.com

It's "busy" and "loud", but "what else do you expect, since it's Mardi
Gras every day?" at this New Brunswick Cajun-Creole microbrewery,
where the food is "spicy" and the drinks go down easy; if the fare is
"not exactly at NOLA" level, at least the live entertainment and outdoor "beer garden" maintain the "festive" feeling.

Olde Corner Deli 🗷 *Deli*   ▽ 26 | 12 | 20 | $25

Island Heights | 22 Central Ave. (Ocean Ave.) | 732-288-9098 |
www.simplygourmetcatering.net

"Everything you order is a winner" is the word on this "quaint" Island
Heights BYO serving deli goods up front (lunch) and more "gourmet" American fare in the main dining room for dinner; that the
menu changes frequently allows repeat customers to experience the
"variety" on offer.

Old Homestead *Steak*   25 | 24 | 23 | $68

Atlantic City | Borgata Hotel, Casino & Spa | 1 Borgata Way
(Atlantic City Expwy., exit 1) | 609-317-1000 |
www.theborgata.com

"Heavy eating" is necessary at this Borgata Hotel, Casino & Spa
chophouse (a satellite of the NYC legend) sending out "some of the
best slabs of beef you've ever seen" into a "beautiful" space adorned
with art deco touches; "hit the jackpot" before arriving, but thanks
to "excellent" service, you'll feel "like a high roller" anyway.

🗷 Old Man Rafferty's *American*   19 | 17 | 18 | $26

Hillsborough | 284 Rte. 206 (Triangle Rd.) | 908-904-9731
New Brunswick | 106 Albany St. (George St.) | 732-846-6153
www.oldmanraffertys.com

"Come hungry" to these "dependable", "comfy" American standbys
for "affordable" fare (including "out-of-this-world" desserts) that
suits any occasion, whether for "family" meals or "first dates";
N.B. the New Brunswick locale has a to-go gourmet deli, and a third
branch is set to debut in Asbury Park in summer 2007.

🗷 Ombra 🗷 Ⓜ *Italian*   25 | 27 | 22 | $52

Atlantic City | Borgata Hotel, Casino & Spa | 1 Borgata Way
(Atlantic City Expwy., exit 1) | 866-692-6742 |
www.theborgata.com

Capturing the ambiance of a wine cellar, albeit one that's as "beautiful" as it is "comfortable", this Borgata Italian features stone, wood

and glass decor, "fantastic" Italian cooking from exec chef Luke Palladino and an "amazing" vino selection sourced from some of Italy's smaller producers; it all goes down well with fans, as long as they're ready for the "pricey" bills.

NEW One 53 *Italian*

- | - | - | E

Rocky Hill | 153 Washington St. (Princeton Ave.) | 609-924-1019 | www.restaurantone53.com

Start with gutsy, seasonal Italian fare, add a roster of boutique vinos, place them in a warm setting with an up-and-coming chef (Justin Braun) and you get this new ristorante in Rocky Hill; not surprisingly, fans hope that all the above supplies a recipe for success.

Onieal's *American*

19 | 17 | 18 | $31

Hoboken | 343 Park Ave. (4th St.) | 201-653-1492 | www.oniealshoboken.com

Although its scene is "typical" for a Hoboken pub (i.e. it's "packed solid"), this "dark" "perennial" turns out New American eats that range from "above average" to "good"; Casanovas confirm it's best to "fight your way past the bar" and settle into the back room, a "perfect date-night" choice.

Opah Grille *Seafood*

24 | 22 | 22 | $52

Gladstone | 12 Lackawanna Ave. (Main St.) | 908-781-1888 | www.opahgrille.com

Somehow, the "Shore" seems so close when you're dining in this suburban seafooder in Gladstone noted for "so-fresh" seafood and the "best martinis on earth" augmented by generally "helpful" service; the "beautiful" saltwater tanks "transport" you closer to the beach.

Ora *American*

20 | 17 | 19 | $43

Morristown | 90 South St. (bet. Miller Rd. & Pine Sts.) | 973-326-9200 | www.orarestaurant.com

For "a little Manhattan sophistication" in Morristown, this "modern" high-ceilinged New American BYO near the town's community theater "delivers as advertised" with an "interesting" menu and "hip" atmosphere; best of all, it all comes "without the wannabes."

Orbis Bistro ⓜ *American*

22 | 15 | 19 | $41

Upper Montclair | 128 Watchung Ave. (N. Fullerton Ave.) | 973-746-7611 | www.orbisbistro.com

The "delectable" New American food is as "special" as the treatment you'll get if you travel to this Upper Montclair BYO fronted by Nancy Caballes, who also presides over the kitchen; the setting is akin to a "comfortable" "dining room in someone's home."

ⓩ Origin ⓜ *French/Thai*

26 | 20 | 20 | $36

Morristown | 10 South St. (Morris St.) | 973-971-9933
Somerville | 25 Division St. (Main St.) | 908-685-1344
www.originthai.com

Whether you dine at the origin-al Somerville locale or the Morristown offshoot, these "bustling" BYO French-Thai fusionists are idolized for "spectacularly" conceived and executed preparations accompanied by "friendly", if "quick", service; at both expect to sit "in close proximity" to your neighbors and "deafening" acoustics, but meals at these "winners" are "worth anything."

Osteria Dante *Mediterranean*

FOOD	DECOR	SERVICE	COST
19	17	17	$39

Red Bank | 91 Broad St. (Linden Pl.) | 732-530-0602 | www.osteriadante.net

The fare "rises above the typical" tout followers of this Red Bank BYO who choose from an "expansive" selection of "down-to-earth" Mediterranean items; acolytes applaud the "pleasant" setting, and "sidewalk seating is still tops"; N.B. now under new ownership.

Osteria Giotto *Italian*

FOOD	DECOR	SERVICE	COST
25	18	21	$40

Montclair | 21-23 Midland Ave. (Bloomfield Ave.) | 973-746-0111 | www.osteria-giotto.com

Everything's "spot on" at this Italian BYO, whether it's the "sublime" dishes (accompanied by "hearty", housemade breads), "warm", "informal" wood setting and "good" service; no doubt, "you'll need a lot of pull" to secure a reservation, but for a bona fide "best-of-Montclair" experience, seek divine intervention if necessary.

Ota-Ya Ⓜ *Japanese*

FOOD	DECOR	SERVICE	COST
23	14	19	$35

Lambertville | 21 Ferry St. (S. Union St.) | 609-397-9228 | www.ota-ya.com

"Fantastic" sushi and "noteworthy" cooked items keep 'em "coming back" to this canalside Lambertville BYO that most agree is a "good value"; ok, you may have to "ignore" the setup, but that's easy if you focus on the food; P.S. parents and other patrons like that the "fish tank entertains the kids."

Oyako Tso's *Japanese*

FOOD	DECOR	SERVICE	COST
21	20	19	$30

Freehold | 6 W. Main St. (bet. South & Throckmorton Sts.) | 732-866-1988 | www.oyakotsos.com

Things are tso "good" at this "fun" Freehold Japanese BYO that's a "big hit with families" on account of the "entertaining" hibachi and "fresh" sushi; though service sometimes seems "lost in translation", the staff is always "respectful of any requests."

Pacific Grille Ⓜ *Pacific Rim*

FOOD	DECOR	SERVICE	COST
20	15	20	$30

Mount Laurel | Village II Shoppes | 1200 S. Church St. (Academy Dr.) | 856-778-0909 | www.pacificgrill.com

"There's nothing fishy" with the seafood that's prepared and served in "imaginative ways" at this Mount Laurel BYO purveying a Pacific Rim slate in a strip-center locale that "you'd miss if you weren't looking hard"; in all, most maintain meals here "hit the spot."

Pad Thai *Thai*

FOOD	DECOR	SERVICE	COST
22	13	17	$20

Highland Park | 217 Raritan Ave. (bet. 2nd & 3rd Aves.) | 732-247-9636 | www.pad-thai.com

"Plentiful", "cheap" and "authentic" are the vittles at this Highland Park Thai; the prices are "right", and the "incredible", "knock-your-socks-off" spicy specialties draw a "packed" house, especially the "best pad Thai" in this neck of the woods.

	FOOD	DECOR	SERVICE	COST

Palm, The *Steak*
24 | 21 | 24 | $61

Atlantic City | The Quarter at the Tropicana | 2801 Pacific Ave.
(S. Iowa Ave.) | 609-344-7256 | www.thepalm.com
Now, "that's dining" marvel backers of this Quarter at the Tropicana chainlet and "carnivore's palace" sending out "X-large", "expertly prepared" steaks and lobsters into its signature dining room complete with caricatures of celebs on the walls; the "big bucks" tabs and "loud" acoustics are soothed by "top" service.

Pamir *Afghan*
21 | 16 | 20 | $27

Morristown | 85 Washington St. (bet. Cobb Pl. & Phoenix Ave.) |
973-605-1095 | www.pamirrestaurant.com
"Low-cost", "traditional" Afghan cuisine comes in "large" portions and with a "bouquet of flavors" at this Morristown BYO, a "welcome change" catering to vegetarians and kebab lovers; the location may be "inauspicious", but all the rugs and pillows here add an "exotic" note.

Panico's *Italian*
24 | 21 | 24 | $52

New Brunswick | 103 Church St. (Neilson St.) | 732-545-6100 |
www.panicosrestaurant.com
Book a table here to "impress your boss" with the "top-notch" Italian food, the specialty of this "classy", "dress-up" New Brunswick mainstay (now in its 20th year) also noted for "sophisticated" service; "expense" tabs notwithstanding, its many admired attributes factor into its "delightful-dining" reputation.

Park, The *Seafood/Steak*
24 | 19 | 21 | $55

Park Ridge | 151 Kinderkamack Rd. (bet. Grand & Park Aves.) |
201-930-1300 | www.theparksteakhouse.com
Some of the "best" steaks in Northern Jersey turn up in this "traditional" Park Ridge chophouse also known for its "particularly well-prepared" seafood; what it lacks in the bang-for-the-buck category (think "New York City prices") is partially recovered by the place's "reliability."

☑ Park & Orchard *Eclectic*
22 | 13 | 20 | $39

East Rutherford | 240 Hackensack St. (Union Ave. W.) | 201-939-9292 |
www.parkandorchard.com
The "unusual", "healthy" assortment (from Italian to stir fries) is as "tasty" as ever for fans of this "extremely popular" East Rutherford Eclectic; with its checkered floors and yellow walls, the space looks somewhat "spartan", but "oh, that wine list" – 2,400 labels at last count – that's "nirvana for oenophiles."

Passage to India Ⓜ *Indian*
23 | 17 | 20 | $27

Lawrenceville | Lawrence Shopping Ctr. | 2495 Brunswick Pike/Rte. 1
(bet. Colonial Lake Dr. & Texas Ave.) | 609-637-0800
It's hard to pass up this Lawrenceville Indian BYO making believers out of clientele with "flavorful" fare paired with "helpful" service and "attractive", "peaceful" quarters; for the best "bargain" for miles, check out the "standout" lunch buffet.

	FOOD	DECOR	SERVICE	COST

NEW Passione ⓜ *French*
▽ 23 | 19 | 21 | $42

Montclair | 77 Walnut St. (Grove St.) | 973-233-1006

A "wonderful" assortment of "classic" Gallic items appears in this "traditional" Montclair French BYO, a "reliable" option and relatively recent entry comforting diners with its fare, setting and "attentive" service; N.B. there's sidewalk seating and weekend tasting menus available.

Pasta Fresca Café and Market *American*
▽ 22 | 15 | 19 | $26

Shrewsbury | The Grove | 637 Broad St. (Shadow Brook Rd.) | 732-747-5616

"Soccer moms in SUVs" "love coming" to this Shrewsbury New American BYO offering a "casual" atmosphere and "tasty" fare that seem just right "after shopping" in the "upscale" Grove mall; "strollers" and "alfresco" eating are both popular here.

Pearl of the Sea *Portuguese*
▽ 18 | 10 | 15 | $32

Long Branch | 46 S. Broadway (Ocean Ave.) | 732-263-1050

The wood oven creates "hearty", "hot and plentiful" Portuguese as "authentic" as it comes confirm folks who've found this Long Branch Iberian a block from the ocean; if "not exactly up to Newark" standards, most seem set to return, saying it's "hard to find this type of place" in these parts.

Penang *Malaysian*
20 | 15 | 16 | $24

East Hanover | 200 Rte. 10 W. (bet. Ridgedale Ave. & River Rd.) | 973-887-6989

Edison | 505 Old Post Rd. (bet. Rte. 1 & Vineyard Rd.) | 732-287-3038

West Windsor | Nassau Park Pavilion | 635 Nassau Park Blvd. (Brunswick Pike/Rte. 1 S.) | 609-897-9088

www.penangnj.com

This "tasty" BYO trio vends the "real deal" when it comes to Malaysian cooking with a slate of "spicy", "comforting" items and a number of noodle dishes brought to table "quickly"; in all, the three are as "good" as they are "busy", and the prices are a "bargain."

Ⓩ Perryville Inn ⓜ *American*
26 | 24 | 22 | $56

Union Township | 167 Perryville Rd. (I-78, exit 12) | 908-730-9500 | www.theperryvilleinn.com

"Superlative experiences" are the norm at this Hunterdon County "class act" set in a historic Colonial tavern, where the "wonderful" Traditional American creations seem ideally suited to the "intimate" setting complete with fireplaces; it all adds up to a "great destination at the end of a drive in the country"; N.B. jacket suggested.

Pete & Elda's ◐ *Pizza*
- | - | - | I

Neptune City | 96 Woodland Ave. (Laurel Ave.) | 732-774-6010 | www.peteandeldas.com

Thin-crust lovers line up for this Shore Italian, a must-stop for its crackerlike pies topped with zesty red gravy and fresh toppings; the old-school fare (in the chicken parm vein) carries its own attraction for this staple's supporters.

	FOOD	DECOR	SERVICE	COST

Z Peter Shields Inn M *American* — 26 | 27 | 25 | $55

Cape May | 1301 Beach Dr. (Trenton Ave.) | 609-884-9090 |
www.petershieldsinn.com

It's all "truly wonderful" at this "very special" Cape May BYO where
"memorable" New American dinners are the norm, as are "excellent" service, "great" views of the ocean from the veranda and a
"beautiful" setting, thanks in part to the Victorian B&B the eatery is
housed in; after all that, it's no wonder this "romantic" restaurant is
such a "favorite."

Z P.F. Chang's China Bistro *Chinese* — 21 | 21 | 19 | $31

West New York | 10 Port Imperial Blvd. (Halfmoon Ct.) |
201-866-7790

Atlantic City | The Quarter at the Tropicana | 2801 N. Pacific Ave.
(S. Iowa Ave.) | 609-348-4600 ☽

Marlton | Promenade at Sagemore | 500 Rte. 73 (Rte. 70) |
856-396-0818

www.pfchangs.com

Hordes "go out of their way" for the "yum" vittles and to put up with
"long, long waits" that are standard at this somewhat "high-end",
extra-"busy" Chinese chain that's about as "loud" as they come; the
drinks are "good" too, and if a few notice a "formula", at least
"the formula works."

Pheasants Landing M *Continental* — 17 | 16 | 17 | $31

Hillsborough | 311 Amwell Rd. (Willow Rd.) | 908-281-1288 |
www.pheasantslanding.com

For Continental food with a German-Swiss accent, locals land at this
"comfortable", "homey" Hillsborough eatery for fondue, game and
other seasonal eats, and for its downstairs pub; while the "good" offerings "aren't particularly exciting", the place is "one of the few
around" that serves this kind of food.

NEW Phillips Seafood *Seafood* — - | - | - | E

Atlantic City | Pier at Caesars | 1 Atlantic Ocean (Arkansas Ave.) |
609-348-2273 | www.phillipsseafood.com

Eastern Shore meets Jersey Shore at the new, old-school Maryland-
based seafooder in the Pier at Caesars; with a rolling oyster cart
offering tableside shucking, it's a classy destination to burn
through gambling winnings.

Pho Thang Long *Vietnamese* — - | - | - | I

Jersey City | 749 Bergen Ave. (Montgomery St.) | 201-209-9140
Vietnamese standards stock the extensive menu at this spartan
Jersey City BYO that's built its reputation upon the namesake warming dishes but also on its rolls and salads; nice prices make this addition long on appeal.

NEW Pic-Nic *Portuguese* — - | - | - | M

East Newark | 224 Grant Ave. (Central Ave.) | 973-481-3646
No picnic fare here, just bountiful portions of robust Portuguese
cooking is what it's all about at this East Newark hideaway that quietly competes with its more famous Ironbound brethren; pictures of

the motherland, handmade tiles and an overall rustic ambiance is the deal when it comes to decor.

Pierre's Ⓜ French

| 23 | 22 | 23 | $50 |

Morristown | 995 Mt. Kemble Ave. (bet. N. Maple Ave. & Tempe Wick Rd.) | 973-425-1212 | www.pierresbistro.com

For "delightful" French "every time", Michael Peter's "country", "congenial" Morristown bistro "never disappoints", whether for a "date" or any other occasion; cronies also consider the "fantastic" lunch buffet, deemed a "bargain for such high-quality food", a "great value" treat.

Pine Tavern American

| 22 | 15 | 20 | $33 |

Old Bridge | 151 Rte. 34 (Cottrell Rd.) | 732-727-5060 | www.pinetavern.net

The "unlikely setting" stands in contrast to the New American menu served at this "rusticated", wood-filled Old Bridge tavern applauded for "spot-on" preparations and a "charming", "put-you-at-ease" vibe; it's a true "solid-neighborhood" eatery, where patrons are known to drop by for the "great" live music.

Pino's La Forchetta Ⓜ Italian

| 18 | 20 | 19 | $40 |

Marlboro | 448 Rte. 9 N. (Union Hill Rd.) | 732-972-6933 | www.pinoslaforchetta.com

"Old-world Brooklyn" comes to Marlboro with this Italian where pizza reigns on one side, and the main dining room is the site for more formal affairs; if the entrees are only "decent" for some, most appreciate that the "'za's are the best thing here" and that the staff "makes you feel special."

🆕 Piquant Bread Bar & Grill Indian

| - | - | - | E |

New Brunswick | 349A George St. (Bayard St.) | 732-246-2468 | www.piquantfoods.com

A hip and trendy destination in Downtown New Brunswick, this upscale new Indian features a menu built upon organic ingredients while taking its inspiration from all over the globe with items such as spicy Scottish salmon accompanied by a tomato-yogurt sauce; every stylish detail in the decor syncs up with the food.

🆕 Pithari Taverna Greek

| - | - | - | M |

Highland Park | 28 Woodbridge Ave. (Raritan Ave.) | 732-572-0616 | www.pitharitaverna.com

Classic Greek – dolmades, souvlaki and the like – is the hallmark of this Highland Park BYO that sits next door to a grocery (where, conveniently, wines from the motherland are offered); moderate pricing gives the goods more appeal.

Pizzicato Italian

| 21 | 20 | 20 | $30 |

Marlton | Promenade at Sagemore | 500 Rte. 73 (Rte. 70) | 856-396-0880

It's "a slam-dunk for casual, non-stuffy Italian" assert backers of this Marlton BYO proffers "an array" of "winning" selections including "tasty" brick-oven pizzas; the "aromas are wonderful", and the alfresco option alleviates any stress from shopping.

	FOOD	DECOR	SERVICE	COST

P.J. Whelihan's ◗ *American* | 17 | 16 | 17 | $21 |

Cherry Hill | 1854 E. Marlton Pike (Greentree Rd.) |
856-424-8844
Haddonfield | 700 Haddon Ave. (bet. Ardmore Ave. & Kings Hwy.) |
856-427-7888
Maple Shade | 396 S. Lenola Rd. (Kings Hwy.) | 856-234-2345
NEW Medford Lakes | 61 Stokes Rd. (Tabernacle Rd.) |
609-714-7900
Sewell | 425 Hurffville-Cross Keys Rd. (Regulus Dr.) |
856-582-7774
www.pjspub.com

The "best" Buffalo wings and brew – and "hot waitresses" – bring
"crowds" to this quintet of South Jersey pubs/restaurants purveying
"good ol'" American "game food" that's "exactly what you'd expect";
they're "always fun", plus there are "enough flat-screens to make
sports fans happy."

Plantation *American* | 19 | 20 | 17 | $42 |

Harvey Cedars | 7908 Long Beach Blvd. (79th St.) | 609-494-8191 |
www.plantationrestaurant.com

Those "mojitos at happy hour are worth leaving the beach for" this
Harvey Cedars New American whose islandy ambiance pairs nicely
with the "different", "reliable" menu; even in off season, this "favorite hang" seems to be "always happening."

☒ Pluckemin Inn, The ☒ *American* | 25 | 26 | 24 | $68 |

Bedminster | 359 Rte. 202/206 S. (Pluckemin Way) | 908-658-9292 |
www.pluckemininn.com

This Bedminster New American "covers all the bases" with a "gorgeous" modern-Colonial setting (evocative of a 19th-century farmhouse) that's centered by an "amazing" three-story wine tower and
list (overseen by a "pro" sommelier), not to mention chef David C.
Felton's "exceptional" dishes and "doting" service; you "won't regret
emptying your wallet", since the "prices reflect the quality"; N.B. the
adjacent Plucky Tavern offers quicker, more casual dining.

Ponzio's ◗ *Diner* | 16 | 11 | 16 | $22 |

Cherry Hill | 7 Rte. 70 W. (Kings Hwy.) | 856-428-4808 |
www.ponzios.com

Cherry Hill's unofficial "town hall" and South Jersey's "ultimate"
diner keeps on dispensing "consistent" coffee-shop chow and
"freshly" made sweets from the on-site bakery in "large" digs, and
whose staff "keeps things moving"; if it is "not the Ponzio's of yore",
many, many more still make it their "landmark."

Pop Shop *American* | 18 | 19 | 18 | $16 |

Collingswood | 729 Haddon Ave. (Collings Ave.) | 856-869-0111 |
www.thepopshopusa.com

"Kids" have so much "fun" wearing "PJs" and noshing on "tasty"
treats from the "enormous" American menu at this "old-timey"
Collingswood soda shop from "yesteryear", where shakes, burgers
and grilled cheese sandwiches rule; the "retro" spot is ultra-"friendly",
and the only thing missing is "The Fonz."

	FOOD	DECOR	SERVICE	COST

Portobello *Italian*
20	16	17	$34

Oakland | 155 Ramapo Valley Rd. (Long Hill Rd.) | 201-337-8990 |
www.portobello-restaurant.com

"Solid" is the cooking dished up in "large" portions at this Oakland
Italian "value" and neighborhood "favorite" that some supporters say is just the ticket for those who need to throw a "big party";
others, however, cite an "erratic" operation, describing "tattered"
decor and "inattentive service."

Portofino **M** *Italian*
25	18	23	$46

Tinton Falls | 720 Tinton Ave. (Sycamore Ave.) | 732-542-6068 |
www.portofino-ristorante.com

"Excellent" Italian cookery reigns at this Tinton Falls eatery opposite
an old grist mill; with its "exceptional" 400-label wine list focused on
Italy and "pleasant", "knowledgeable" service, few have no problem
placing it as one of Monmouth's "finer" restaurants.

Porto Leggero **S** *Italian*
23	24	22	$50

Jersey City | Harborside Financial Plaza 5 (Pearl St.) | 201-434-3200 |
www.portoleggero.net

"Fine dining" comes to Jersey City via this "hidden" restaurant (the
brainchild of the Scalini Fedeli outfit) whose Downtown location
draws a diverse crowd (including financial types) that discovers a
treasure trove of "terrific" Italian cookery served in "spacious",
"beautiful" quarters, which mixes modern and old world; yes, it's a
"touch of class" that comes with a "high" price tag, but most are
"happy to find this culinary surprise."

Portuguese Manor *Portuguese/Spanish*
21	15	20	$33

Perth Amboy | 310 Elm St. (bet. Fayette & Smith Sts.) |
732-826-2233

They "accommodate" you well at this Perth Amboy Iberian that fills
the bill with "dependable", "hearty" Portuguese that stops some
from trekking to Newark; fans add the "rough-around-the-edges"
digs may even look better post-sangrias.

Posh *Asian/French*
∇ 23	25	23	$41

Maple Shade | 584 Rte. 38 E. (bet. Alexander Ave. & Mill Rd.) |
856-222-1128 | www.poshbistro.com

"Strikingly beautiful" is the decor of this Maple Shade site selling
a French-Asian slate an "active" bar scene; service is "impeccable", but "exclusionary costs" and calls for "revamping the menu"
should be considered.

Posillipo **S M** *Italian*
22	16	21	$39

Asbury Park | 715 Second Ave. (Bond St.) | 732-774-5819 |
www.posilliporestaurant.com

Exemplifying "what class without fuss" is all about, this "warm"
Asbury Park Italian (now in its 78th year) prepares "very good"
"Mulberry Street"–style food like "nonna"; opera and 'Broadway'
night on Wednesday is the star, and supporters sing about the "bargain" early-bird, offered every day.

	FOOD	DECOR	SERVICE	COST

Primavera *Italian*
20 | 17 | 19 | $47

West Orange | Wilshire Grand | 350 Pleasant Valley Way
(bet. Marmon Terr. & Sullivan Dr.) | 973-731-4779

"Enormous" portions of "steady" Italian cooking are the prima reason why diners end up at this West Orange hotel standby operating in "not the best" of settings; the waiters still run down the "many" specials (you can "go many times and never repeat a dish"), but pros propose that perhaps it would be nice if the place "printed them."

Pronto Cena ⑤ *Italian*
22 | 19 | 19 | $39

Newark | The Legal Ctr. | 1 Riverfront Plaza (McCarter Hwy.) |
973-824-8999

This "down-to-earth" Northern Italian eatery in Newark "rarely disappoints", focusing on the "basics prepared well"; unlike what the name suggests, service runs "on the slow side", but for a "quietly pleasant" meal, it's a neighborhood staple.

Pub, The *Steak*
18 | 14 | 16 | $29

Pennsauken | Airport Circle | 7600 Kaighn Ave. (S. Crescent Blvd.) |
856-665-6440 | www.thepubnj.com

"If you're looking for something cozy, this is not the place" opine observers of this "huge" "hall" in Pennsauken putting out the "best" salad bar and "same-as-it-ever-was" steaks many find "good", but a few "not mouthwatering", in a medieval, knights-and-armor setting that "has a certain charm"; "they don't try to be something they're not" profess advocates who add "they don't mess with what's worked" for over a half century.

Quiet Man, The *Pub Food*
22 | 16 | 18 | $32

Dover | 64 E. McFarlan St. (Hudson St.) | 973-366-6333 |
www.quietmanpub.com

Decked out in memorabilia from the movie of the same name, this quintessential Irish pub provides "Guinness" and "fast bites" of "tasty" treats of the Old Sod along with American offerings; what's more, all the above comes with an authentically "friendly" vibe.

Raagini *Indian*
22 | 20 | 21 | $36

Mountainside | 1085 Rte. 22 E. (Mill Ln.) | 908-789-9777 |
www.raagini.com

The "excellent" lunch buffet and "super" Sunday brunch are big draws when it comes to this "upscale" Mountainside Indian sporting a "nice-looking" room; if dinners are slightly "expensive", the "consistently delicious", "far-above"-the-norm cooking compensates.

Radicchio *Italian*
23 | 19 | 20 | $46

Ridgewood | 32 Franklin Ave. (Chestnut St.) | 201-670-7311 |
www.radicchiorestnj.com

"Inspired" Northern Italian cuisine of "consistently high-quality" sets apart this "relaxed" Ridgewood BYO, where a bevy of the "best", "unusual" daily specials complements the "small" regular menu; "high prices" don't seem to offend its loyal clientele, who bestow on it "favorite" status.

	FOOD	DECOR	SERVICE	COST

Raimondo's *Italian*

| 23 | 15 | 20 | $44 |

Ship Bottom | 1101 Long Beach Blvd. (11th St.) | 609-494-5391

For "good-for-the-soul" Italian, try this ever-"popular" Ship Bottom BYO, "one of LBI's most consistent", with a staff that "takes pride" in its work; prepare for "loud" acoustics, and some say "off season" is your best bet.

☑ Ram's Head Inn Ⓜ *American*

| 26 | 27 | 25 | $55 |

Galloway | 9 W. White Horse Pike (Taylor Ave.) | 609-652-1700 | www.ramsheadinn.com

It's "nice to see all the men in jackets" and to "actually hear your conversation" at this Galloway "old favorite" turning out Caesars prepared tableside ("where else do they do that these days?") along with other Traditional American fare that would "please those with the highest standards"; overall, it's a "true charmer" for patrons who put it in the "solidly classic" category.

☑ Rat's Ⓜ *French*

| 24 | 28 | 24 | $63 |

Hamilton | Grounds for Sculpture | 16 Fairgrounds Rd. (Sculptors Way) | 609-584-7800 | www.ratsrestaurant.org

"Step into a Wonderland" of a setting when you visit this destination New French ranked No. 1 for Decor, where the "beautiful" Grounds for Sculpture (inspired by Monet's legendary Giverny) afford pre- or post-repast strolls; within the restaurant, "exciting" New French cuisine and "phenomenal" wines reign, both delivered by "excellent" servers; N.B. there's also a less formal cafe that accepts walk ins.

Rattlesnake Ranch Café *Southwestern*

| 16 | 14 | 16 | $25 |

Denville | Foodtown Shopping Ctr. | 559 E. Main St. (bet. Fox Hill Rd. & Front St.) | 973-586-3800 | www.rattlesnakeranchcafe.com

"The only place around to fulfill a craving for alligator" is this Denville strip-mall Southwesterner whose "interesting" lineup also includes elk, ostrich and buffalo; happily, "great" margaritas and "moderate" pricing take some of the sting out of "so-so decor" and "unremarkable" eats.

Raven and the Peach *American*

| 24 | 25 | 24 | $56 |

Fair Haven | 740 River Rd. (Fair Haven Rd.) | 732-747-4666

"Romance", "celebrations" and "entertaining clients" all come easy over "delightful" New American food at this Fair Haven "special-occasion" spot sporting a "*Casablanca*-esque" ambiance; thanks to "professional", "attentive" service, you may even be less inclined to notice it's "one of the most expensive meals" you may ever have.

Raymond's Ⓢ *American*

| 21 | 18 | 19 | $27 |

Montclair | 28 Church St. (bet. Fullerton Ave. & Park St.) | 973-744-9263 | www.raymondsnj.com

"Everyone should love" Raymond Badach's "insanely popular" Montclair "institution" that's "always a pleasure" for its "perfectly satisfying" New American "comfort food" all day long; the BYO's "cozy", "retro" look and "friendly" floor crew are "just what you want out of a local restaurant."

	FOOD	DECOR	SERVICE	COST

Ray's Little Silver Seafood ⓜ⊄ *Seafood* — 23 | 10 | 18 | $33

Little Silver | Markham Place Plaza | 125 Markham Pl. (Prospect Ave.) |
732-758-8166

Everything arrives "piping hot" and tastes "delicious" at this storefront BYO in Little Silver vending the "freshest" fish at "reasonable"
prices; "helpful", "efficient" service supplies a ray of sunshine in
these "plain"-Jane digs.

Rebecca's ⓜ *Cuban* — 24 | 19 | 22 | $44

Edgewater | 236 Old River Rd. (River Rd.) | 201-943-8808 |
www.rebeccasedgewater.com

Layout and size help supply the "romance" that fuels this Edgewater
Cuban BYO where the "intimate" ambiance is matched by "wonderful", "vibrant" food; for an even "quieter tête-à-tête", fans endorse
the "charming" back patio.

Red *American* — 20 | 22 | 19 | $45

Red Bank | 3 Broad St. (Front St.) | 732-741-3232 |
www.rednj.com

More about the "chic" ambiance and "social scene" than its "solid"
New American cuisine, this "dark", "late-night" Red Bank site hosts
"beautiful" people "cocktailing" along with sometimes "friendly",
sometimes "pretentious" service; all agree, though, that as lounges
go, the upstairs one is "great."

Red's Lobster Pot *Seafood* — 24 | 13 | 19 | $35

Point Pleasant Beach | 57 Inlet Dr. (Ocean Ave.) | 732-295-6622 |
www.redslobsterpot.com

This Point Pleasant Beach waterside BYO, "shack" and "mainstay"
features an "excellent" outside area (inside's the "size of a phone
booth") to "watch the boats go by" while chowing down on "amazingly fresh" lobsters and other sea fare; P.S. the dockside raw bar
is "excellent" too.

Red Square *Eclectic/Russian* — – | – | – | VE

Atlantic City | The Quarter at the Tropicana | 2801 Pacific Ave.
(S. Iowa Ave.) | 609-344-9100 | www.chinagrillmgt.com

The spirits of Lenin and co. are alive and well at Jeffrey Chodorow's
Soviet-kitschy lounge/restaurant in the Quarter at the Tropicana,
where caviar, Eclectic fare and martinis (try the 'Chernobyl') are
served in a setting filled with agitprop, red velvet, banquettes and a
60-ft. bar made of ice; comrades richer than Croesus can lease one of
several vodka lockers, all icily chilled in the 0-degree Fahrenheit vault.

Renault Winery ⓜ *American* — 22 | 24 | 22 | $47

Egg Harbor City | 72 N. Bremen Ave. (Moss Mill Rd.) | Egg Harbor |
609-965-2111 | www.renaultwinery.com

One of the oldest wineries in America provides an "enchanting" backdrop for this Egg Harbor New American serving up "a treat" of a menu
and "romance at dinner"; the "unique" setting also includes a hotel and
golf course, turning any trip here into a "fine adventure"; P.S. open
Friday and Saturday, and Sunday, which offers an "excellent" brunch.

	FOOD	DECOR	SERVICE	COST

Reservoir Tavern 🗷 Ⓜ *Pizza*   22 | 8 | 16 | $24
Boonton | 90 Parsippany Blvd. (Intervale Rd.) | 973-334-5708
"Exquisite" thin-crust pizza is the story of this Boonton red-saucer, a family-run feedery (since 1936) dispensing 'zas and "no-nonsense" Italiana in "divey", "no-decor" digs; the "consistently delicious" goods keep inspiring all the "committed clientele" to line up.

Restaurant, The Ⓜ *American*   21 | 23 | 22 | $54
Hackensack | 160 Prospect Ave. (bet. American Legion Dr. & Beech St.) | 201-678-1100 | www.therestaurant.net
"High style" comes with "high prices" at this "classy", "dark" and "intimate" New American bar/restaurant improbably located in a Hackensack condo complex; all told though, the "pretty-good" food "takes a backseat" to the "pickup" central scene, a "wolf's den of middle-aged men" and divorcées.

NEW Restaurant L 🗷 *Continental*   - | - | - | E
Allendale | 9 Franklin Tpke. (bet. Mackay Ave. & Waibel Dr.) | 201-785-1112 | www.go2l.com
Comfortable leather seats and a convivial bar set an inviting tone and frame the warming Continental food (from short ribs to veal piccata) at this Allendale entry, a moderately expensive newcomer that's caught on with the neighborhood; N.B. they can seat up to 40 guests for private parties.

Restaurant Latour Ⓜ *American*   - | - | - | VE
Hamburg | Crystal Spring Resort | 1 Wild Turkey Way (Crystal Springs Rd.) | 973-827-0548 | www.crystalgolfresort.com
Part of northwest New Jersey's 4,000-acre golf and spa destination, the Crystal Springs Resort, this 40-seat New American boasts cuisine from chef John Benjamin (an alum of the French Laundry and Aureole), formal service and a glass window in the dining room that affords views of the surrounding mountains; for oenophiles, the uncommonly deep wine list is one of the world's best, featuring 3,600 labels and 50,000 bottles; N.B. there's a tasting room in the cellar, where parties of up to 20 are accommodated.

NEW restaurant.mc *Eclectic*   - | - | - | E
Millburn | 57 Main St. (Millburn Ave.) | 973-921-0888 | www.restaurantmc.com
This pricey Millburn Eclectic is already attracting attention for its globe-spanning ingredients and chic bar scene; at the helm of this hot newcomer is chef Steve Permaul, who regularly reinvents the menu to keep up with the town's sophisticated clientele.

Richard's ⇴ *Deli*   20 | 12 | 19 | $18
Long Branch | 155 Brighton Ave. (Sairs Ave.) | 732-870-9133
"Anything and everything you can imagine or want" from a deli is in this Long Brancher whose artery-"clogging" comestibles (e.g. corned beef and pastrami sandwiches) "satisfy"; the only complaint: "they close too early to be able to eat dinner."

	FOOD	DECOR	SERVICE	COST

Richie Cecere's Restaurant & SupperClub 🗷 *Italian*

21 | **23** | **21** | **$68**

Montclair | 2 Erie St. (Label St.) | 973-746-7811 | www.richiececere.com
"For a big night out", this "cosmopolitan" tri-level supper club-cum-Italian restaurant in Montclair shines with its "good" food, "high-end" space and happening weekend cabaret that includes an 18-piece orchestra, crooner and showgirls ("you expect Ricky Ricardo to waltz in"); this adult "playground" may be "flamboyant" and "pricey", but it's a "favorite" nonetheless.

Rick's Ⓜ *Italian*

- | **-** | **-** | **M**

Lambertville | 19 S. Main St. (Ferry St.) | 609-397-0051 | www.ricksitalian.com
This popular Lambertville BYO offers modestly priced preparations and a warm ambiance, the latter partly due to co-owner Dana Cormier, who presides over the dining room; though the menu is focused on Italian home cooking, chef Alex Cormier's blackboard specials (foie gras, sweetbreads) provide a contrast to the restaurant's looks, with its knotty pine paneling and red-and-white checkered tablecloths.

Ristorante da Benito *Italian*

25 | **21** | **24** | **$53**

Union | 222 Galloping Hill Rd. (Walton Ave.) | 908-964-5850 | www.dabenito.com
For "great" Italian with an "excellent" wine list, local politicians and pedestrians alike head to this "swanky" Union spot whose "top-notch" staff "rolls out the red carpet" for the "see-and-be-seen" clientele; "costly" tabs notwithstanding, fans find it "as good as it gets."

Ritz Seafood Ⓜ *Seafood*

24 | **15** | **20** | **$38**

Voorhees | Ritz Shopping Ctr. | 910 Haddonfield-Berlin Rd. (Voorhees Dr.) | 856-566-6650 | www.ritzseafood.com
"Creative" fare, all so "fabulous" and "tasty", is the real appeal of this slightly "cramped" Voorhees Asian BYO seafooder near the Ritz movie complex; a "gracious", "efficient" front of the house is a bonus, as is the "exotic" tea selection (at nearly 40 varieties).

🛿 River Palm Terrace *Steak*

25 | **19** | **20** | **$58**

Edgewater | 1416 River Rd. (Palisade Terr.) | 201-224-2013
Fair Lawn | 41-11 Rte. 4 W. (Plaza Rd.) | 201-703-3500
Mahwah | 209 Ramapo Valley Rd. (bet. W. Ramapo Ave. & Rte. 17) | 201-529-1111
www.riverpalmterrace.com
"If you love steak you can't miss" this triad of "classy", "very popular" North Jersey meat emporiums that also deliver "consistently good" Continental cuisine and seafood; expect to blow "lots of money", and note that many beef "reservations are meaningless", since you'll likely wind up waiting "too long a time" even if you have one.

Roberto's Dolce Vita *Italian*

22 | **18** | **21** | **$38**

Beach Haven | 12907 Long Beach Blvd. (Indiana Ave.) | 609-492-1001
The staff's "extra-warm touch" lights up this "crowded" Beach Haven BYO "favorite" of LBIers, serving Northern Italian dishes that

"never disappoint" in "comfy" quarters; pros profess "sitting fire-side" in the winter couldn't be sweeter.

Roberto's II ⓂItalian

19 | 13 | 20 | $45

Edgewater | 936 River Rd. (bet. Dempsey & Hilliard Aves.) | 201-224-2524 | www.robertos2.com

Think "Sinatra and the '50s" and you have this family-run Edgewater Italian "landmark" that's been dishing out ample portions of "solid" red-sauce numbers since 1972; things seemingly "haven't changed" here, as evidenced by decor that could "use an update."

Robin's Nest American

22 | 20 | 22 | $32

Mount Holly | 2-4 Washington St. (White St.) | 609-261-6149 | www.robinsnestmountholly.com

A "quaint", "unpretentious" setting frames the "delicious" goings on within this Mount Holly American BYO, a showcase for "superb" sweets and "impressive" dishes backed by "attentive" servers; P.S. "even the iced tea is special here."

Robongi Japanese

25 | 16 | 21 | $31

Hoboken | 520 Washington St. (bet. 5th & 6th Sts.) | 201-222-8388 | www.robongi.net

"Super-friendly" staffers serve the "freshest" fish at this Hoboken Japanese BYO, the town's "popular" mainstay for "excellent" sushi; yes, the "kitschy" decor is very *Gilligan's Island*, but given the food – and "reasonable" prices – no one seems to mind.

Rocca ⓂItalian

22 | 18 | 20 | $38

Glen Rock | 203 Rock Rd. (bet. Glen Ave. & Main St.) | 201-670-4945 | www.roccaitalianrestaurant.com

Chef-owner Craig Levy's (ex NYC's Gotham Bar & Grill) "consistently enjoyable" fare (including the "best" pastas) rules at this "inviting" Glen Rock Italian that overall "does everything well"; N.B. takeout fans can pick up savories and pastries at the market around the corner.

Rod's Olde Irish Tavern Pub Food

19 | 16 | 19 | $29

Sea Girt | 507 Washington Blvd. (5th Ave.) | 732-449-2020 | www.rodstavern.com

"The *Cheers* of Sea Girt" is filled with folks who settle in for the "hospitality" and reliably "good" pub provisions, not to mention to check out games on the myriad TVs; this American "stalwart of suds" has the "right" prices, so it's no surprise that "my husband would eat all his meals there if he could."

Rod's Steak & Seafood Grille Steak

21 | 23 | 21 | $49

Convent Station | Madison Hotel | 1 Convent Rd. (Madison Ave.) | 973-539-6666 | www.rodssteak.com

"All aboard" for the "delicious" steaks and seafood that drive the success of this "classy" Convent Station American where patrons dine in one of the restored antique Pullman Parlour cars, while others opt for the "charming" main dining room decked out in Victoriana; regardless of venue, meals here are "consistently good."

	FOOD	DECOR	SERVICE	COST

Roman Cafe, The *Italian* — 19 | 16 | 19 | $43
Harrington Park | 12 Tappan Rd. (Schraalenburgh Rd.) | 201-767-4245 |
www.romancafe.com

"Meet up with friends and have a leisurely dinner" at this "go-to neighborhood place" in Harrington Park that's "always a solid performer", proferring a "typical but well-done" classic Italian menu; though some say the "decor needs improvement", this establishment compensates with a "quiet" ambiance and "friendly" staff.

Rooney's Oceanfront *Seafood* — 18 | 21 | 17 | $43
Long Branch | 100 Ocean Ave. (Melrose Terr.) | 732-870-1200 |
www.rooneysocean.com

A "breathtaking" scenery (namely, the Atlantic) explains why you have to "fight the crowds" to get a seat at this waterside Long Branch seafooder whose accommodating staff only "rushes you out if there's a hurricane coming"; for some, however, the "passable fare" is certainly "not as good as the view."

NEW Roots Steakhouse *Steak* — - | - | - | VE
Summit | 401 Springfield Ave. (Maple St.) | 908-273-0027 |
www.rootssteakhouse.com

The new classics in steak (think Kobe beef sliders) can be found at this new, marble-and-wood Summit chophouse proffering a diverse menu backed by a mostly American wine list; naturally, the expense-account tabs come with the turf.

Rosemary and Sage ⑤Ⓜ *American* — 26 | 18 | 23 | $51
Riverdale | 26 Hamburg Tpke. (bet. Haycock & Morris Aves.) |
973-616-0606 | www.rosemaryandsage.com

For an "outstanding", "lovingly prepared" meal and "friendly" service in "out-of-the-way" Riverdale, look no further than chef and co-owner Brooks Nicklas' perennially popular, "simply" spruced-up New American recognized for its popular tasting menu; one gripe: "too bad it's only open" Wednesdays–Sundays for dinner.

Ruga Ⓜ *American* — 20 | 18 | 18 | $48
Oakland | 4 Barbara Ln. (W. Oakland Ave.) | 201-337-0813 |
www.rugarestaurant.com

The results on this Oakland New American are mixed: while backers applaud the "beautiful" decor and quality of the preparations (they're "good" and "varied"), some say it's "not what it used to be", countering that the fare is "unimaginative" and the "service slow."

Ⓩ Ruth's Chris Steak House *Steak* — 24 | 20 | 23 | $60
Weehawken | Lincoln Harbor | 1000 Harbor Blvd. (19th St.) |
201-863-5100
Parsippany | Hilton Hotel | 1 Hilton Ct. (Campus Dr.) | 973-889-1400
www.ruthschris.com

Meat eaters have "no beef" with this duo of "classic" chain chophouses known for their "juicy, "sizzling" "butter-covered" chops that are as "rich" as the tabs; carnivores confirm "these are places to go if on a cholesterol holiday"; P.S. equally mouthwatering is the "nice" view of NYC from the Weehawken location.

	FOOD	DECOR	SERVICE	COST

Sabor *Nuevo Latino*
22 | **20** | **19** | **$43**

NEW **Hawthorne** | 1060 Goffle Rd. (Rte. 208) | 973-238-0800
North Bergen | 8809 River Rd. (Churchill Rd.) | 201-943-6366
www.saborlatinbistro.com

These "snazzy" Nuevo Latinos spotlight "upscale", "vivid" cooking backed by "trendy" decor, thus attracting a "hip" crowd intent on "people-watching"; as the night wears on, expect more of a nightclub ambiance, with live entertainment and "skillful" bartenders concocting "fab" cocktails, mojitos naturally among them.

☑ Saddle River Inn 🅢 Ⓜ *American/French*
27 | **25** | **26** | **$62**

Saddle River | 2 Barnstable Ct. (W. Saddle River Rd.) | 201-825-4016 |
www.saddleriverinn.com

"Top flight" is another name for this "rustic" yet "civilized" French–New American near the Saddle River that's been dealing in delightful dining for more than 25 years, serving "haute", "sublime" fare that lends the "quaint" converted farmhouse setting an "elegant" touch; blessedly, BYO helps suppress the cost of this "superlative" restaurant that easily rivals the best.

Saffron Indian Cuisine *Indian*
23 | **19** | **19** | **$29**

East Hanover | 249 Rte. 10 E. (New Murray Rd.) | 973-599-0700 |
www.saffronnj.com

"High-class" Indian is the name of the game at this East Hanover BYO where "fantastic" food (and a "not-to-be-missed" lunch buffet) arrives via "helpful" staffers within quarters "more elegant" than the genre usually offers – along with tabs perhaps a tad "pricier"; but overall, when the check comes, it's "worth it."

☑ Sagami Ⓜ *Japanese*
26 | **14** | **21** | **$36**

Collingswood | 37 W. Crescent Blvd. (bet. Haddon & Park Aves.) |
856-854-9773

The fish is "all it's cut up to be" at this Collingswood BYO, the birthplace of South Jersey's Japanese scene where the "best sushi around" is still served in a "dark", "low-ceilinged" space; but since you can expect "heaven in the raw", "who cares how the place looks?"

Sails *Eclectic*
18 | **24** | **18** | **$43**

Somers Point | 998 Bay Ave. (Goll Ave.) | 609-926-9611 |
www.njsails.com

"Scenic" bay views and a "sexy" atmosphere come together at this "modern", "hip" Somers Point Eclectic where patrons "love the look" of the place along with its "fantastic" martinis and other cocktails at the bar; if critics call the food "a little too weird", others say at least it's "creative."

Sakura-Bana Ⓜ *Japanese*
25 | **13** | **21** | **$34**

Ridgewood | 43 Franklin Ave. (bet. Chestnut & Oak Sts.) |
201-447-6525

Ardent believers in this longtime Japanese Ridgewood BYO (two decades and counting) still hold it up as the best example "this side of the Hudson" for its "deliciously super-fresh" sushi; "tight", "lacking" quarters are a small concession to pay for the "gold standard" in raw fare.

Sakura Spring *Chinese/Japanese*   ▽ 23 | 19 | 22 | $27

Cherry Hill | 1871 Rte. 70 E. (Greentree Rd.) | 856-489-8018

A "wide", unusual mix of "tasty" Chinese and Japanese specialties greets diners at this Cherry Hill BYO that's good "when you want more than just a take-out" experience; if dinner's out of the picture, lunch is a perfect time to drop by, thanks to "great" prices.

Sallee Tee's Grille *American/Eclectic*   21 | 18 | 18 | $34

Monmouth Beach | 33 West St. (Channel Dr.) | 732-870-8999 | www.salleeteesgrille.com

"Where else can you eat a great corned beef sandwich while your partner enjoys sushi?" before "great" water views than at this Monmouth Beach Eclectic catering to "every taste" imaginable with an "interesting", expansive menu; "mobbed in the summer" and "busy the rest of the year" sums up the scene at this "slam for the buck."

Sally Ling *Chinese*   19 | 15 | 17 | $28

Fort Lee | 1636 Palisade Ave. (Main St.) | 201-346-1282

For its many admirers, the food at this popular Fort Lee Chinese is consistently "yummy", with "quick", "efficient" service and a "friendly" vibe as part of the appeal; a few foes, however, find fare that's "nothing special" and a floor staff that's "indifferent."

Salt Creek Grille *American*   20 | 24 | 20 | $43

Rumson | 4 Bingham Ave. (River Rd.) | 732-933-9272 | www.saltcreekgrille.com

The "amazing" architecture is Craftsman-inspired while the location is "perfectly situated" to take in the "wonderful sunsets" across the Navesink at this Rumson Traditional American; the food is "nicely cooked" if "unremarkable", but the wines are "excellent", as is "sitting by the fire pit and savoring cocktails."

Samdan *Turkish*   22 | 14 | 19 | $31

Cresskill | 178 Piermont Rd. (Union Ave.) | 201-816-7343 | www.samdanrestaurant.com

Those with a taste for Turkish head straight for this "cheerful", "simply decorated" ("who cares about decor?") and "always busy" Cresskill Middle Eastern "delight" dispensing "delicious" mezes and meat kebabs; they've got the "right" prices, plus the "nicest" folks work there.

Sammy's Ye Old Cider Mill *Steak*   21 | 9 | 16 | $59

Mendham | 353 Mendham Rd. W. (Oak Knoll Rd.) | 973-543-7675 | www.sammyscidermill.com

"There's no sign", "other than the convoy of Lexuses" outside, "but that doesn't keep away the throngs" who "love" this Mendham "icon", a "speakeasy-turned-restaurant" serving "amazing" if "pricey" steaks and lobsters; P.S. pros note expect to be "ushered downstairs" for an "interminable wait" and then eat at a picnic table amid "arcade"-hall quarters.

	FOOD	DECOR	SERVICE	COST

San Remo *Italian*   22 | 15 | 19 | $39

Shrewsbury | 37 E. Newman Springs Rd. (Rte. 35) | 732-345-8200 | www.sanremoitaliana.com

"Appearances can be deceiving" say followers of this "unassuming" Shrewsbury Italian BYO cooking up "good", "solid" specialties served by "so-friendly" staffers; a "busy" room and "loud" acoustics go to show that everyone seems to be having an "excellent night" here.

Sapori *Italian*   24 | 22 | 22 | $34

Collingswood | 601 Haddon Ave. (Harvard Ave.) | 856-858-2288 | www.sapori.info

"You can taste" the work that goes into the "great" Italian preparations at this rustic Collingswood BYO fronted by a "delightful" owner who often stops by tables to greet guests; it all seems so "authentic" here, some say they "thought they were dining in a trattoria in Italy."

NEW Sapo Verde 🅼 *Mexican*   – | – | – | M

Atlantic Highlands | 99 First Ave. (W. Mt. Ave.) | 732-291-8003

A former ice cream parlor on Atlantic Highlands' main drag has morphed into this affordable Mexican BYO eatery with all the expected favorites plus more upscale specialties; the red, orange and yellow hues of the setting are as enticing as the town's newly aquired hipness.

Savanna *Spanish*   20 | 20 | 19 | $37

Red Bank | The Galleria | 10 Bridge Ave. (W. Front St.) | 732-741-6333 | www.savannaredbank.com

"Worthy" tapas is dished up in "modern", "warmly comforting" quarters (featuring low-hanging lanterns and rich woods) at this Spanish BYO set in an "old-factory" space in Red Bank's historic Galleria complex; one thing: all those small plates can "run up the bill."

NEW Savannah's 🅼 *Eclectic*   – | – | – | M

Stockholm | 2700 Rte. 23 N. (Rte. 515) | 973-697-6000

Sitting on the outskirts of Sussex County ski country is this scenic, snazzy and spacious Eclectic in Stockholm that's part jazz club and part lounge; while only open Thursdays through Sundays, it's already home for a crowd of night owls.

Sawa Steakhouse & Sushi Bar *Japanese*   22 | 20 | 21 | $32

Eatontown | 42 Rte. 36 (Rte. 35) | 732-544-8885
NEW Long Branch | Pier Vill. | 68 Ocean Ave. (Chelsea Ave.) | 732-229-0600
www.sawasteakhouse.com

Fans "go back" after sampling the offerings at these Japanese providing "entertaining" hibachi tables and sushi that may be "West Coast" quality; the huge fish tanks are a "nice" touch, but perhaps better is that "you can't go wrong considering the price."

ⓩ Scalini Fedeli 🅢 *Italian*   27 | 25 | 26 | $69

Chatham | 63 Main St. (bet. Parrott Mill Rd. & Tallmadge Ave.) | 973-701-9200 | www.scalinifedeli.com

"Prepare to be wowed" at top toque Michael Cetrulo's "magical" Northern Italian "in the woods" of Chatham, where the "truly amazing" dining experience "from start to finish" consists of a "sublime" prix fixe meal enhanced by "wonderful" wines, "superb" service and a "lovely, intimate" setting; true, it's "expensive", but all agree it's "worth every penny" you'll have to give up.

Scarborough Fair Ⓜ American — 20 | 23 | 19 | $44

Wall | 1414 Meetinghouse Rd. (Rte. 35) | 732-223-6658 | www.scarboroughfairnj.com

At this "warm", "low-key" Wall New American, the food is "pretty good" and various alcoves along the winding stairway and small rooms guarantee "intimacy"; it's "a little expensive" for some, but "oh, what a lovely place."

Z NEW SeaBlue Seafood — 27 | 25 | 25 | $73

Atlantic City | Borgata Hotel, Casino & Spa | 1 Borgata Way (Atlantic City Expwy., exit 1) | 800-692-6742 | www.theborgata.com

Michael Mina, the celebrated chef of the eponymous San Fran restaurant, has landed in AC's Borgata with this year's No. 1 rated newcomer, a "clear winner" thanks to its "extremely fresh" and "incredibly" prepared, wood-grilled seafood (with fish sourced from around the world), "well-developed" wine list and Adam Tihany's "beautiful" room filled with reds and oranges; in all, this expense-account addition is an undeniable "home run."

Sea Shack Seafood — 20 | 16 | 20 | $44

Hackensack | 293 Polifly Rd. (Rte. 17) | 201-489-7232 | www.seashack.com

Aficionados get shack attacks for this "oldie-but-goodie" Hackensack seafooder where "top-of-the-line" fish is "prepared any way you like it" (and the martinis are "superb"); some argue that the place needs a "face-lift", and you should look out for "high prices", but at least the service ("you feel like family") helps to soothe wounded wallets.

Segovia Portuguese/Spanish — 22 | 13 | 20 | $37

Moonachie | 150 Moonachie Rd. (Garden St.) | 201-641-4266 | www.segoviarestaurant.com

"Paella paradise", this "noisy" Moonachie Iberian in the shadows of the Meadowlands serves "excellent" Portuguese and Spanish in "abundance"; a "friendly" staff has "been there for years – and so, unfortunately, has the decor", but just about everyone ignores the "dark" digs and focuses on their "leftovers."

Senorita's Mexican Grill Mexican — 20 | 19 | 19 | $24

Bloomfield | 285 Glenwood Ave. (Washington St.) | 973-743-0099 | www.senoritasmexicangrill.com

A "great addition" to gentrifying Bloomfield, this colorful, "lively" Mexican offers a "reasonably priced" menu that's a "fiesta for the palate" with its combination of "tasty", "straight-up classics" and "inventive new tastes"; there's also a long list of tequilas and some "very strong margaritas", all brought to table by an "accommodating", "friendly" staff.

	FOOD	DECOR	SERVICE	COST

Sens Asian *Asian*
▽ 22 | 20 | 20 | $23

South Brunswick | South Brunswick Square Mall | 4095 Rte. 1 S. (bet. New & Wynwood Rds.) | 732-355-1919

The "nondescript" strip-mall environs can't hide the "surprisingly good" Asian dishes or the "hip" decor (with a waterfall in back) at this South Brunswick BYO; the consensus is that it "makes a nice impression", as does its "friendly" staff.

☑ Serenade *French*
27 | 26 | 26 | $70

Chatham | 6 Roosevelt Ave. (Main St.) | 973-701-0303 | www.restaurantserenade.com

"Perfect in every way" is the refrain sung by fans of this "charming" New French in Chatham, which hums with "delighted" diners who "never tire" of the "impeccable" "fine dining", courtesy of husband-wife team James Laird and Nancy Sheridan Laird (chef and manager, respectively); the "superb" cuisine and wines, an "elegant" dining room and an "excellent" staff all add up to make it like a "top NYC restaurant transplanted to the suburbs."

Sergeantsville Inn, The ☒ *American*
23 | 24 | 21 | $48

Sergeantsville | 601 Rosemont-Ringoes Rd. (Rtes. 523 & 604) | 609-397-3700 | www.sergeantsvilleinn.com

Emitting a "romantic" ambiance in Sergeantsville, this roadside New American set in a 1734 Colonial building provides "well-prepared" selections (in the main room and more casual tavern) and "great" martinis, both adding to "joyful" repasts; P.S. some say it's best "in winter when the fireplaces are crackling."

Settebello Cafe ☒ *Italian*
22 | 19 | 21 | $37

Morristown | 2 Cattano Ave. (Speedwell Ave.) | 973-267-3355

The "welcoming" atmosphere and "all sorts of delicious" food add up to the "perfect combination" for advocates of this Morristown Northern Italian BYO; high marks go to the outdoor courtyard, a "lovely" choice that somehow feels "like being in Tuscany."

Seven Hills of Istanbul ☒ *Mediterranean/Turkish*
21 | 19 | 19 | $29

Highland Park | 441 Raritan Ave. (bet. 4th & 5th Aves.) | 732-777-9711 | www.7hillsofistanbul.com

"Superb" grilled meats and "good" salads are on offer at this BYO "breath of fresh air" for Highland Park serving Turkish specialties at "hard-to-beat" prices; reinforcing the "authentic" aura is the "attractive" decor, with its various rugs and "enormous" samovar.

Shaker Cafe ☒⊄ *American/Eclectic*
- | - | - | M

Flemington | 31 Main St. (bet. Bloomfield Ave. & Capner St.) | 908-782-6610 | www.shakercafe.com

Not named for a religious order but rather referring to the salt and pepper shakers, this quirky American-Eclectic BYO in outlet-clogged Flemington is where shoppers stop for omelets, salads and sandwiches; another big plus: your pocketbook leaves in generally good shape.

	FOOD	DECOR	SERVICE	COST

Shanghai Jazz ☒ Chinese
21 | 19 | 21 | $39

Madison | 24 Main St. (Green Village Rd.) | 973-822-2899 |
www.shanghaijazz.com

Chinese and jazz hit the right note at this Madison restaurant-cum-
nightclub featuring a "widely diverse" menu of "high-quality" cooking accompanied by a "backdrop of hot and cool jazz", "some of the
best" you can find; factor in the "lively" mood and "efficient" service,
and it's no stretch to say things are "in harmony" here.

Ship Inn, The Pub Food
▽ 19 | 19 | 17 | $28

Milford | 61 Bridge St. (Rte. 519) | 908-995-0188 |
www.shipinn.com

If you're "in the mood for a pint of ale and shepherd's pie", head to
this "very comfortable" Milford mainstay that's nautically themed
and, appropriately, located just a stone's throw from the Delaware;
it's a "real pub" for "sampling microbrewed ales and beers" plus
"classic" British bar food that's "good without pretension" and
served by a "friendly staff."

Shipwreck Grill American
25 | 17 | 20 | $46

Brielle | 720 Ashley Ave. (Evergreen Ave.) | 732-292-9380 |
www.shipwreckgrill.com

"Why would anyone think of going to NYC when we have this in our
backyard?" is the question many would ask after time spent at this
Brielle New American seafooder whose "wonderful" food, "great"
bar and servers who make sure to "satisfy their customers" all bring
accolades; despite "high-level" acoustics, things in this "tip-top"
restaurant seem shipshape.

Shogun Japanese/Steak
18 | 15 | 18 | $30

East Brunswick | Center 18 Mall | 1020 Rte. 18 N. (bet. Gunia St. &
Hillsdale Rd.) | 732-390-1922 | www.shogun18.net
Green Brook | 166 Rte. 22 (Washington Ave.) | 732-968-3330 |
www.shogun22.net
Toms River Township | Bey Lea Golf Course | 1536 N. Bay Ave.
(Oak Ave.) | 732-286-9888 | www.shogunbeylea.com

The hibachi chefs "put on a spectacular show" at these Japanese
cousins that are "fun for kids" and "a favorite for celebrations", proffering "plentiful" portions of "above-average" sushi and grill items;
nevertheless, some feel the food is "nothing special" and note the
"chainlike decor" "needs a makeover"; N.B. the Kendall Park branch
will reopen in March 2007 after renovations.

Shumi ☒ Japanese
25 | 12 | 22 | $35

Somerville | 30 S. Doughty Ave. (bet. Veterans Memorial Dr. W. &
W. Main St.) | 908-526-8596 | www.shumirestaurant.com

"Hidden" in the recesses of a strip mall, this Somerville BYO is "ab-
solutely worth" seeking out for "incredible" raw fin fare that "sets
the standard"; sure, the decor "leaves a lot to be desired, but you
can get over that", perhaps by "sitting at the sushi bar", where the
"wonderfully talented chef-owner" "will guide you to interesting"
specials that are "expensive but worth it."

	FOOD	DECOR	SERVICE	COST

Siam Ⓜ🚭 *Thai* | 21 | 7 | 14 | $25

Lambertville | 61 N. Main St. (bet. Coryell & York Sts.) | 609-397-8128
"If you're looking for authentic, delicious, reasonably priced Thai food", this "casual" storefront BYO in Lambertville will "leave you tongue-Thai-ed"; despite "extremely slow" service and "bland", "unappealing" decor, it's "very popular and deservedly so", making reservations "a must"; P.S. "it's cash-only."

Siam Garden *Thai* | 23 | 20 | 20 | $31

Red Bank | The Galleria | 2 Bridge Ave. (W. Front St.) | 732-224-1233 | www.siamgardenrestaurant.com
This "tasty" Red Bank Thai BYO's menu is "large" enough to "cater to everyone, including children and vegetarians" who'll find some "delicious" dishes; the staff seems "eager to please", and acolytes add up the ways why this place is a "delightful change of pace."

Silver Oak Bistro *American/Southern* | 23 | 12 | 19 | $41

Ridgewood | 26 Wilsey Sq. (W. Ridgewood Ave.) | 201-444-4744 | www.silveroakbistro.com
At this "charming" BYO addition in Ridgewood, chef/co-owner Gary Needham makes a "serious effort at being different", doling out "generous portions" of "innovative", Southern-style New American cuisine that's "great on the taste buds" if "less so on the waistline"; while the "incredible food" "trumps the noisy, shoebox surroundings", the "tiny" interior nevertheless has surveyors suggesting you "arrive early" or reserve in advance.

Silver Spring Farm Ⓜ *French* | ▽ 23 | 20 | 20 | $53

Flanders | 60 Flanders Drakestown Rd./Rte. 206 S. (Theresa Dr.) | 973-584-0202 | www.silverspringfarm.com
"Run by a French family that's been at it for [nearly] 50 years", this "fantastic" Flanders favorite "only gets better with age", offering "country-style" Gallic cuisine in a "quaint", refurbished 1870s inn accessed via "a winding, tree-lined road"; all in all, the "wonderful" experience provides "old-world comfort and elegance" "at a decent price"; N.B. dinner only.

Simply Radishing Ⓢ *American* | 18 | 9 | 15 | $20

Lawrenceville | Lawrence Shopping Ctr. | 2495 Brunswick Pike/Rte. 1 (bet. Colonial Lake Dr. & Texas Ave.) | 609-882-3760
"For a quick lunch or snack between errands", this strip-mall New American in Lawrenceville offers salads "so big a family could share just one" plus a "carb-loading extravaganza" of a bread bar boasting "a tasty assortment of butters"; while it also serves dinner, patrons protest its "dreary-looking" decor, declaring "it desperately needs a makeover"; N.B. it's BYO.

Ⓩ NEW Sirena *Italian* | 23 | 26 | 19 | $53

Long Branch | 27 Ocean Ave. (Laird St.) | 732-222-1119
A "fantastic" setting overlooking the ocean partnered with "high-quality" cuisine is the deal at this relatively new Long Branch entry, an Italian newcomer situated waterside; although the early word is

that the "uneven service" could come with less "attitude", the "excellent" eats help compensate.

Sirin *Thai*

22 | 19 | 20 | $33

Morristown | 3 Pine St. (South St.) | 973-993-9122 |
www.sirinthairestaurant.com

For "quick and easy dining" before or after a show at the Community Theater, head to this "above-average" BYO Thai in Morristown that's "a great find" for an "interesting variety" of "well-prepared food"; it's situated in a "cozy, houselike setting" that seems "understated" and "pleasant" to some and "dark" to others; N.B. closed Tuesdays.

Siri's Thai French Cuisine *French/Thai*

25 | 20 | 23 | $37

Cherry Hill | 2117 Rte. 70 W. (Haddonfield Rd.) | 856-663-6781 |
www.siris-nj.com

The strip-mall locale "deceives" but the cooking doesn't at this Cherry Hill BYO that knits Thai and French in its "amazingly good" fare; though outside is all shopping center, the inside, with its white tablecloths, pleases, as does the "friendly" service.

Sister Sue's *Caribbean*

▽ 21 | 14 | 20 | $27

Asbury Park | 311 Bond St. (Cookman Ave.) | 732-502-8383

"Trek no further than Asbury Park" to experience "true Trini tastes" turning up in this Caribbean BYO whose "pleasant" staff serves "authentic" Trinidadian cookery such as curried goat and oxtail stew; aside from it's "good" value it's a "great change" from the usual.

NEW Skylark Diner ● *American*

19 | 22 | 19 | $23

Edison | 17 Wooding Ave. (bet. Old Post Rd. & Rte. 1) | 732-777-7878 |
www.skylarkdiner.com

"More silver spoon than greasy spoon", this "lively" "upscale diner" in Edison is flying high in the eyes of fans who praise its almost "offensively large portions" of "spiffed-up comfort food", its "ultramodern", "meet-George-Jetson" decor and its "friendly" service; it also boasts an attached bar/lounge with an "impressive drink menu", regular DJs and trivia nights.

Slowly 🅢Ⓜ *American*

23 | 19 | 20 | $41

Toms River | 73 Main St. (bet. Washington & Water Sts.) | 732-914-0102

"Am I really in Toms River?" wonder first-timers who've checked out this New American BYO distinguishing itself with "distinctly well-flavored" preparations within a "contemporary" setting (slate floors, track lighting, etc.); overall, it's a "favorite", since "this kind of quality can't be found everywhere."

Smithville Inn *American*

18 | 21 | 19 | $36

Smithville | 1 N. New York Rd. (Moss Mill Rd.) | 609-652-7777 |
www.smithvillenj.com

Exposed wooden beams and various fireplaces lend "charm" to this Smithville site whipping up Traditional American "throwback" goods to complement the "early American" ambiance; the fare may be "uneven", but there's nothing like "sitting by the fire" to soak up some "coziness."

	FOOD	DECOR	SERVICE	COST

Smoke Chophouse & Cigar Emporium *Seafood/Steak*

22 | 19 | 20 | $56

Englewood | 36 Engle St. (Palisade Ave.) | 201-541-8530 | www.smokechophouse.com

"The place to go for a great meal and a cigar afterwards", this Englewood steak-and-stogie site offers "fantastic" beef and seafood in an "old-world, gentlemen's club" ambiance; if you can't take the "smoky haze", there's a nonsmoking room downstairs, where you'll find the same "top-shelf wine list" and "attentive service"; N.B. you can BYO for a $20 corkage fee.

NEW Smokey's American BBQ ⓂⓅ *BBQ/Southern*

- | - | - | I

Montclair | 312 Orange Rd. (bet. Cedar & Washington Aves.) | 973-233-0087

At this Montclair all-American barbecue specialist, the ribs and wings come fried, BBQ'd or fiery hot, and acolytes appreciate a chopped pork sandwich that's reminiscent of Carolina 'cue; takeout's the thing here, as are the bargain-basement prices.

Sogno *Italian*

23 | 18 | 20 | $44

Red Bank | 69 Broad St. (bet. Monmouth & Wallace Sts.) | 732-747-6969 | www.sognoredbank.com

"Excellent" Italian food fills the room, as does lots of "noise" ("what's that?") and "crowds" at this "narrow", "tightly" packed Red Bank BYO, for some the town's "restaurant of choice" that "bustles" just about every night; no shock – it's best to "call for a reservation."

SoHo on George *American*

23 | 22 | 21 | $48

New Brunswick | 335 George St. (bet. Bayard & Liberty Sts.) | 732-296-0533 | www.sohoongeorge.com

This New American New Brunswick "winner" succeeds with "tasty" savories (and "sinful" desserts), an "elegant" yet "trendy" vibe (complemented by an "airy" space) and "efficient" service; thanks to its "always-hot" bar, expect "loud" acoustics, but for the area, "this is one of the best for a night out."

Soho 33 *American*

19 | 15 | 17 | $33

Madison | 33 Main St. (bet. Green Village Rd. & Waverly Pl.) | 973-822-2600 | www.soho33.com

"Salads and sandwiches" sum up the "light" lunches that "ladies" show up for at this "casual" Madison BYO selling "standard" American food on a menu that seems "to the point"; "when dining locally", it's a "reliably" sound choice.

Solaia Restaurant *Italian*

20 | 21 | 18 | $52

Englewood | 22 N. Van Brunt St. (Palisade Ave.) | 201-871-7155 | www.solaiarestaurant.com

Situated "next to the bustling Bergen Performing Arts Center", this "chic", "upscale" Italian in Englewood is just the ticket "for dinner or drinks before a show" with its "imaginative" seafood-centric menu and equally "lively" bar scene; whether you opt to sit in the "pretty interior" or "outside on warm days", expect to have a "pleasant" if "pricey" experience.

Solari's ☒ *Italian* 21 | 16 | 19 | $41

Hackensack | 61 River St. (Bridge St.) | 201-487-1969 | www.solarisrestaurant.com

Just shy of its 70th anniversary, this "traditional" Italian has been a "Hackensack haven" for lunching "lawyers, judges and politicos" "from the nearby Bergen County courthouse" "for three generations"; it's also a "warm and inviting" destination for dinner courtesy of "gracious" chef, owner and host Marco Solari; P.S. live music keeps it "swinging" on weekends.

Solo Bella *Italian* ▽ 21 | 19 | 19 | $31

Jackson | 426 Chandler Rd. (Genova Ave.) | 732-961-0951

"Dependable" Italian dinners are nice to have around say gratified eaters at this Italian BYO seemingly operating solo in "restaurant-less" Jackson; for "family-style" dining, it scores points, and for the folks in town, it's "worth the wait."

So Moon Nan Jip ● *Korean* ▽ 23 | 11 | 17 | $26

Palisades Park | 238 Broad Ave. (Brinkerhoff Ave.) | 201-944-3998

There's nothing so-so about the "delicious" Korean barbecue and other "homestyle" "standards" served up at this "comfortable" "value" in Palisades Park; there are "many side dishes" to tempt the taste buds plus "great sushi and sashimi", but you'll likely leave "smelling like the food you just grilled", so "don't go in a suit."

Somsak *Thai* 23 | 14 | 20 | $24

Voorhees | Echo Shops | 200 White Horse Rd. (bet. 4th & 5th Sts.) | 856-782-1771

The chef-owners take "great care" in what they prepare at this "popular", longtime Voorhees Thai BYO known for its "consistently excellent" cuisine that uses "fresh" ingredients, "attentive" service and "real-bargain" pricing; P.S. the "homemade ice creams are must haves."

Sono Sushi *Japanese* 26 | 16 | 22 | $32

Middletown | Village Mall | 1098 Rte. 35 (New Monmouth Rd.) | 732-706-3588 | www.sonosushi.com

Watch the "happiest patrons" walk out of this "friendly" Middletown Japanese BYO, the "best sushi house in the area", with "super-fresh", "high-quality" raw fish employed in the "beautiful" morsels; tips: check out the "nicely prepared" hot dishes, and "take advantage of the amazing lunch specials."

NEW Sonsie *Eclectic* - | - | - | E

Atlantic City | Pier at Caesars | 1 Atlantic Ocean (Arkansas Ave.) | 609-345-6300 | www.sonsieac.com

Boston's upscale, casual Eclectic brings its European brasserie setting with this newcomer in the Pier at Caesars; in addition to the hearty brasserie-style selection at lunch and dinner, there's a breakfast menu of eggs and croissants to fuel a busy day at the slot machines.

	FOOD	DECOR	SERVICE	COST

Sophie's Bistro Ⓜ *French* | 22 | 20 | 21 | $36 |

Somerset | 700 Hamilton St. (bet. Baier & Dewald Aves.) | 732-545-7778 | www.sophiesbistro.net

In the "unlikeliest of places" dwells this Somerset French "charmer" lauded for its "affordable" bistro fare accompanied by Gallic wines, "quaint" banqueted quarters (with a copper bar), "congenial" hosts and staff; overall, it easily transports to "gay Paree."

Soufflé Ⓜ *French* | 23 | 18 | 21 | $48 |

Summit | 7 Union Pl. (Summit Ave.) | 908-598-0717 | www.soufflerestaurant.com

"Quiet, understated and worth a visit", this Summit storefront draws praise for its "fine" French cuisine, especially the "spectacular soufflés" "that are certain to please"; factor in "charming decor" and a "wonderful staff", and this Gallic "sleeper" seems "a rare pleasure" "in an area dominated by Italian restaurants"; P.S. the "BYO takes the sting out of the prices."

🄴 South City Grill *American* | 23 | 23 | 20 | $47 |

Jersey City | 70 Pavonia Ave. (Washington Blvd.) | 201-610-9225
Rochelle Park | 55 Rte. 17 S. (Passaic St.) | 201-845-3737
Mountain Lakes | 60 Rte. 46 E. (Crane Rd.) | 973-335-8585
www.southcitygrill.com

Whether you're looking for a "fabulous" meal in a "modern setting" or a "happening bar" with a "hip, young singles scene", you'll have "an amazing experience" at this trio of "trendy", seafood-centric Americans offering a "diverse" menu of "delectable" delights; while the "speed and friendliness of service varies", however, the decibel levels do not: "the food's fine if you can stand the noise, but oh that noise!"

Spain *Portuguese/Spanish* | 21 | 15 | 20 | $35 |

Newark | 419 Market St. (Raymond Blvd.) | 973-344-0994 | www.spainrestaurant.com

"Mammoth amounts" of "tasty" Spanish-Portuguese fare – including "giant lobsters", "brontosaurus-sized steaks" and "hefty desserts" – ensures "everyone carries out a doggy bag" at this Ironbound institution that "caters to families and NJPAC visitors"; while the decor "appears a bit worn", the service here remains "as good as ever."

Spanish Tavern *Spanish* | 22 | 17 | 21 | $39 |

Mountainside | 1239 Rte. 22 E. (Locust Ave.) | 908-232-2171
Newark | 103 McWhorter St. (Green St.) | 973-589-4959
www.spanishtavern.com

"Does paella get any better?" ask aficionados of this "reliable" Iberian duo that delivers "huge" helpings of "Spanish food at its best" – "just come with a loose outfit and enjoy"; "friendly", "attentive service" is also a plus, but while the "more elegant Mountainside branch" boasts a "warm" ambiance, the Ironbound original may be "a little dated."

	FOOD	DECOR	SERVICE	COST

Spargo's Grille Ⓜ *American* | 25 | 18 | 20 | $40 |

Manalapan | Andee Plaza | 130 Rte. 33 W. (Millhurst Rd.) | 732-294-9921 | www.spargosgrille.com

"Don't judge" this place by its strip-mall locale argue fans of this Manalapan BYO presenting "attractive", "well-prepared" New American food that's a "bargain" considering the quality of the preparations; while service gets "spotty when the house is full", it still comes across as "friendly."

Specchio Ⓢ Ⓜ *Italian* | 25 | 25 | 24 | $63 |

Atlantic City | Borgata Hotel, Casino & Spa | 1 Borgata Way (Atlantic City Expwy., exit 1) | 609-317-1000 | www.theborgata.com

An "ethereal" experience awaits at this "high-end" Italian in AC's Borgata where chef Luke Palladino's modern cuisine is "nothing short of outstanding" (and features "fresh" vegetarian options, thanks in part to local sourcing) and where tables are spaced "far enough apart" to lend a "romantic" ambiance to the "beautiful" space; the consensus: "double down your bet – this one's worth the chips."

NEW **Spice Cuisine** *Eclectic* | - | - | - | M |

Bloomfield | 26 Belleville Ave. (Willet St.) | 973-748-0056

Thailand and Italy meet up at this Eclectic low-frills Bloomfield BYO newcomer, where the dishes go either way, sporting Asian or Italian accoutrements; as for the cost, modest pricing easily appeals to fans of East and West.

Spike's *Seafood* | 22 | 7 | 17 | $26 |

Point Pleasant Beach | 415 Broadway (bet. Rte. 35 & St. Louis Ave.) | 732-295-9400

"Fabulously" fresh catch in digs that look "like a shack should" is the appeal of this Point Pleasant Beach BYO seafooder/market that "knows how to cook" and where they serve the stuff "without any hoopla"; if the "waits" are the equivalent to "getting hazed when rushing a fraternity", few mind when they keep in mind the "ultimate goal" – chowing down on the eats.

Squan Tavern Ⓜ *Italian* | 19 | 13 | 19 | $27 |

Manasquan | 15 Broad St. (Main St.) | 732-223-3324 | www.squantavern.com

The "absolute friendliest" folks serve the "best" pizzas that steal the show at this family-run feedery that's been dispensing solidly "good", "heavy" Italian "home cooking" for generations in Manasquan; P.S. the kitchen's been known to "prepare special requests when they're not on the menu."

Sri Thai *Thai* | 24 | 9 | 17 | $19 |

Hoboken | 234 Bloomfield St. (3rd St.) | 201-798-4822

Although "low on decor", this tiny Thai BYO in Hoboken beckons fans with its "sensational" Siamese chow; prices are "cheap, the food "filling" and the staff "friendly", so no wonder lots of folks think it "worth a try."

Stage House
Restaurant & Wine Bar *French*

23 | 22 | 21 | $56

Scotch Plains | 366 Park Ave. (Front St.) | 908-322-4224 |
www.stagehouserestaurant.com

"Prepare to be spoiled" at this "expensive-but-worth-it" *nouvelle*
French in Scotch Plains that's tucked away in a "charming", "rustic"
1737 stagecoach inn highlighted by a "fireplace [for] cold evenings"
and "patio dining in the summer"; they've recently added a "more
casual tavern" side, which some say "has taken away from the restaurant" but most consider a "wonderful", "lower-cost alternative"
for "lighter fare."

☑ Stage Left *American*

26 | 23 | 25 | $64

New Brunswick | 5 Livingston Ave. (George St.) | 732-828-4444 |
www.stageleft.com

"A perfect place for an after-theater meal" or "a celebration night",
this "consistent winner" in New Brunswick "keeps getting better
with age", proffering "excellent" New American cuisine from chef
Anthony Bucco that's complemented by an "incredible cheese table" and "to-die-for wine list"; factor in "superb service" and an "elegant atmosphere" and this is "the definition of fine dining", which
to some means you'd better "bring two credit cards."

Steve & Cookie's By the Bay *American*

25 | 20 | 22 | $47

Margate | 9700 Amherst Ave. (N. Monroe Ave.) | 609-823-1163 |
www.steveandcookies.com

"Consistently good" deliciousness keeps the house "packed" at this
"favorite" of a New American with a "gorgeous" Margate location
and "wonderful" service (including the "best bartenders" at the
"great" bar); off peak is ideal when things are a "little quieter" and
when you can enjoy the fare before one of the "blazing" fireplaces.

Stony Hill Inn *Continental/Italian*

23 | 25 | 22 | $54

Hackensack | 231 Polifly Rd. (Rte. 80) | 201-342-4085 |
www.stonyhillinn.com

"Romance abounds" at this "charming" Italian-Continental in
Hackensack that's set in the "elegant, old-world" ambiance of a converted 1818 farmhouse; a 2006 management and chef change
hasn't diminished its "high reputation", so "whether you're having
an intimate dinner", a "gathering with friends" or a "special event",
this is "the place to go for posh."

Strip House *Steak*

23 | 23 | 21 | $63

Livingston | Westminster Hotel | 550 W. Mt. Pleasant Ave.
(bet. Daven Ave. & Microlab Rd.) | 973-548-0050 |
www.theglaziergroup.com

You "don't have to go through any tunnels" to reach this "swanky"
Livingston spin-off of the Gotham original vending "lusciously"
good steaks proffered in, as the name implies, "sexy", "reddish"
boudoirlike quarters; some say if only they could strip away some of
the "NYC pricing", but for surf 'n' turf supping, it's "major league
all the way."

	FOOD	DECOR	SERVICE	COST

Suez Canal 🖹 *Seafood*
| | - | - | - | I |

Jersey City | 117 Tonnele Ave. (bet. Broadway & Newark Ave.) | 201-333-5305

Serving all things aquatic in nautical, neon-accented quarters, this Egyptian seafooder in Jersey City is noted for its fresh catch, from fried items to charcoal-grilled options; affordable tabs transform it into a must-try for fish fans.

NEW Sultan's Turkish Cuisine 🅼 *Turkish*
| | - | - | - | M |

Hackettstown | 133 Main St. (Liberty St.) | 908-979-9222 | www.sultansturkishcuisine.com

In an area not known for ethnic eats comes this Turkish BYO (run by four women) in Hackettstown; expect a roster of authentic fare (sh-ish kebabs and gyros rule) served in quarters featuring a burgundy-and-brown color scheme.

NEW Sumo *Japanese*
| | - | - | - | M |

Wall | 1933 Rte. 35 (Allaire Rd.) | 732-282-1388

Barely christened but already crowded, this roomy Wall Japanese BYO is emerging as the new fave among Shore dwellers, with a sizable sushi selection in addition to cooked foods created hibachi style.

Sunny Garden *Chinese*
| | 22 | 20 | 20 | $28 |

West Windsor | 15 Farber Rd. (Rte. 1) | 609-520-1881 | www.sunnygarden.net

"Tucked away just off Route 1" in West Windsor, this hard-to-find "upscale Chinese" has "a loyal crowd of regulars" that raves about its "flavorful soups", "elegant entrees" and sushi selection, all "prepared with care and attractively presented"; factor in "attentive service" and "the atmosphere of a four-star hotel", and this BYO is "truly a fine-dining experience."

Surf Taco *Mexican*
| | 20 | 14 | 16 | $13 |

Manasquan | 121 Parker Ave. (Stockton Lake Blvd.) | 732-223-7757
Point Pleasant Beach | 1300 Richmond Ave. (Marcia Ave.) | 732-701-9000
Seaside Park | 212 SE Central Ave. (bet. Franklin & Lincoln Aves.) | 732-830-2111
www.surftaco.com

Bringing "West Coast" Cal-Mex to NJ, these BYO counter-service spots offer up "quick and easy" items – tacos, burritos, wraps and smoothies – that are "fresh" and "cheap"; overall, this "fun" and "casual" trio has quickly become a "necessity on the Shore."

Sushi by Kazu *Japanese*
| | ▽ 28 | 14 | 20 | $35 |

Howell | 2724 Rte. 9 S. (bet. 2nd & 3rd Sts.) | 732-370-2528

Devotees give "thanks" for this Japanese BYO in Howell, chef Kazu Mukai's showcase for "extremely fresh" fish used for his undeniably "great" sushi and other near "perfect" fare; to experience "top quality", get there early – the "very small" space "fills up fast."

Sushi Lounge *Japanese*
| | 24 | 22 | 20 | $37 |

Hoboken | 200 Hudson St. (2nd St.) | 201-386-1117

(continued)

Sushi Lounge

Morristown | 12 Schuyler Pl. (Washington St.) | 973-539-1135 |
www.sushilounge.com

For "high-quality" sushi and a "hip", "clublike" scene, check out these "extra-loud" Hoboken and Morristown Japanese dens and make like sardines ("you have to weigh about 80 pounds to squeeze in when it's full"); with the "best" DJs around, they please lounge lizards who say "the beats are even better than the eats."

NEW Table Ⓜ *American*   – | – | – | VE

Little Silver | Markham Place Plaza | 151 Markham Pl. (Prospect Ave.) |
732-747-2008 | www.tablenj.com

Brand new in Little Silver and set in a shopping mall that already sports several restaurants, chef Martin Bradley's BYO distinguishes itself with its haute New American fare; the tabs are high, but so are hopes that this addition becomes a fixture in town.

Table 8 Ⓜ *American*   23 | 21 | 21 | $45

Montclair | 615 Bloomfield Ave. (bet. Midland Ave. & Valley Rd.) |
973-746-2233 | www.table8nj.com

"In a town full of surprises", this Montclair BYO is an undeniable "delight" that's easy on the eyes (thanks to a "chic" red-and-black design scheme) and on the palate, with a "delicious" roster of New American preparations delivered by "terrific" servers; it's all overseen by a "charming" owner, so it's no surprise this "lively" addition is "worth the price."

Tacconelli's Pizzeria Ⓜ🚭 *Pizza*   20 | 10 | 15 | $17

Maple Shade | 450 S. Lenola Rd. (Rte. 38) | 856-638-0338 |
www.tacconellispizza.com

While there "aren't too many choices" at this Maple Shade spin-off of the Philly original, the "thin-crust" pizzas with "lots of garlic" are "hits" that'll still make "you grin"; "no credit cards" frustrates, and those who think the 'zas "overrated" are overruled.

Ⓩ Taka Ⓜ *Japanese*   26 | 26 | 24 | $37

Asbury Park | 632 Mattison Ave. (Main St.) | 732-775-1020 |
www.takaapnj.com

"Beautiful", "sophisticated" and "sleek" in setting, this Asbury Park BYO is the "current fave", serving "super-fresh", "cleverly" assembled sushi and other "excellent" Japanese "delights" supported by a "pro" staff; in all, admirers are entranced with this "winning" spot that seems "straight out of Manhattan."

NEW Takara *Japanese*   ▽ 25 | 26 | 19 | $28

Ocean Township | Orchard Plaza | 1610 Rte. 35 S. (Willow Dr.) |
Oakhurst | 732-663-1899 | www.takarasteakhouse.com

Hibachi tables, tatami rooms and a koi pond lend allure to this "lovely" Ocean Township BYO that "deserves much praise" since the cooked Japanese fare is "really good", the decor "really nice" and the sushi "super"; though in its infant years, this entry is "excellent" so far.

	FOOD	DECOR	SERVICE	COST

Tapas de Espana *Spanish*
20 | 17 | 18 | $36

Englewood | 47 N. Dean St. (bet. Palisade Ave. & Park Pl.) | 201-569-9999
North Bergen | 7909 Bergenline Ave. (79th St.) | 201-453-1690

"*Viva Espana!*" is what unprompted acolytes exclaim after hitting these "lively" tapas experts serving a "long" menu of Spanish "tasty" bites in old-world Spain environs; though larger portions are available, "bring a group", "explore the menu" then "stick with the small plates."

Taqueria 🅜 *Mexican*
▽ 20 | 12 | 17 | $15

Jersey City | 236 Grove St. (Grand St.) | 201-333-3220

"Roll up your sleeves and enjoy some of the best" – and "cheapest" – Mexican eats around rave admirers of this "friendly" family-run Jersey City BYO whose "honest", "authentic" cooking counterbalances the modest looks; P.S. plus, "where else can you get a cactus taco?"

Taro *Pan-Asian*
21 | 22 | 19 | $36

Montclair | 32 Church St. (bet. S. Fullerton Ave. & S. Park St.) | 973-509-2266 | www.tarorestaurant.com

The food is as "tasty as it looks", and thus fans are "hooked" on this Pan-Asian Montclair BYO with "austere", "minimalist" decor that "soothes" and seems suited to the menu; N.B. though they've been serving it for some time, dim sum rolls around on weekends.

NEW Tashmoo *Pub Food*
– | – | – | M

Morristown | 8 Dehart St. (South St.) | 973-998-6133

Settling in swimmingly off the green in Morristown, this Traditional American pays homage to an inlet of the same name on Martha's Vineyard and seeks to emulate the summery vibe there; for the food, the burgers and other comfort eats are complemented by boutique brews in an upscale-pub setting.

Taste of Asia, A 🅜 *Malaysian*
21 | 13 | 19 | $30

Chatham | 245 Main St. (N. Passaic Ave.) | 973-701-8821 | www.atasteofasianj.com

"Chase away the malaise" at this storefront Malaysian in Chatham that "excites the taste buds" with its "diverse menu" of "well-prepared food"; though some find the space "cavernous" and "bare", this BYO proves a "real bargain" and "a nice alternative to Chinese."

Teak *Pan-Asian*
23 | 22 | 19 | $42

Red Bank | 64 Monmouth St. (Drummond Pl.) | 732-747-5775 | www.teakrestaurant.com

"The food's very good, the drinks are better and the people-watching is the best" ("am I pretty enough?") at "one of Red Bank's hippest" parlors, a Pan-Asian where "low lighting" and "cool" decor suit the young "singles" scene; P.S. for some "quiet" with dinner, sit in one of the "more intimate back rooms."

Teresa's Cafe *Italian*
21 | 16 | 18 | $29

Princeton | Palmer Sq. | 23 Palmer Sq. E. (Nassau St.) | 609-921-1974 | www.terramomo.com

For most, there are no reservations about this no-reservations strip-mall Italian, "one of the best things about" Princeton since the "solid", "high-quality" *ciao* is "affordable and delicious", the atmosphere "bubbly" and the service "friendly" (if "uneven") – oh, and "getting a table on weekends can take as long as getting a PhD."

Terra Ⓜ *Eclectic* | 20 | 15 | 19 | $40 |

Maplewood | 175 Maplewood Ave. (bet. Baker St. & Highland Pl.) | 973-763-4005 | www.restaurantterra.com

An "ambitious" Eclectic menu supplies interest in this "welcoming" BYO Maplewood whose globe-trotting preparations complement the "small" "SoHo-esque" quarters; while a few note "mixed experiences", most cite "well-prepared" eats and a "helpful", "friendly" staff.

Terrace Restaurant *Mediterranean* | 22 | 22 | 23 | $48 |

Short Hills | Hilton at Short Hills | 41 JFK Pkwy. (Rte. 24, exit 7C) | 973-912-4757 | www.hiltonshorthills.com

"A cut above most hotel's second-tier restaurants", this "elegant" alternative to the Hilton at Short Hills' Dining Room delivers "fine" Mediterranean food and "unrushed service" in a "sumptuous" setting; while the "spectacular" "Sunday brunch is their forte" (there's "truly something for everyone"), they also offer tapas, pizza and other light fare at the bar.

Tewksbury Inn Ⓜ *American* | 22 | 20 | 19 | $45 |

Oldwick | 55 Main St./Rte. 517 (King St.) | 908-439-2641

"Mingle with the horsey set" and "rub elbows with the upper crust" at this "rural gem" in "gentrified" Oldwick that proffers "unusual" New American offerings and fine wines in a "charming" former inn; whether you opt for the "warm, comfortable" dining room, the "clubby", "social" tavern or the "lovely outside seating in summer", expect a "relaxing" meal.

Thai Chef *Thai* | 21 | 17 | 19 | $32 |

Hackensack | Riverside Square Mall | 169 Hackensack Ave. (off Rte. 4) | 201-342-7257
Montclair | 664 Bloomfield Ave. (bet. Orange & Valley Rds.) | 973-783-4994
Somerville | 24 E. Main St. (bet. Bridge & Warren Sts.) | 908-253-8300
www.thaichefusa.com

Although distinct in their own ways (Hackensack incorporates French fare and serves alcohol), the Thais that bind these three "treasures" are their "large" menus, "tasty" cooking and "Zen-like" settings even with often "busy" dining rooms; overall, backers applaud that this trio is an "impressively consistent" performer.

Thai Kitchen *Thai* | 23 | 14 | 20 | $22 |

Bridgewater | 1351 Prince Rodgers Ave. (I-287, exit 14B) | 908-231-8822
Bridgewater | Somerset Shopping Ctr. | 327 Hwy. 202/206 (off Rte. 22) | 908-722-8983
Hillsborough | Hillsborough Shopping Ctr. | 649 Hwy. 206 (Amwell Rd.) | 908-904-8038
www.thaikitchennj.com

So what if "the decor is lacking"? ask fans, for these "friendly" Somerset County BYOs offer an "incredible bargain" (lunch is "a steal") on some of the "best" Thai in the Garden State; "fast" "pros" for servers keep the "busy" rooms in order.

Thai Thai *Thai*
`25` `16` `21` `$27`

Stirling | 1168 Valley Rd. (bet. Poplar Dr. & Warren Ave.) | 908-903-0790

"Always crowded" with "a loyal following", this strip-mall "favorite" in Stirling serves up "Thai-riffic food" with such "presentation, taste and quality" that "you'll swear you're in a popular NYC restaurant"; the "fresh, creative" curries come at an "excellent value" that's made even better by the BYO policy and the presence of a "friendly staff."

Theater Square Grill *American/Continental*
`20` `23` `18` `$50`

Newark | New Jersey Performing Arts Ctr. | 1 Center St. (McCarter Hwy.) | 973-642-1226 | www.theatersquaregrill.com

"Your best bet" for "good" pre-performance repasts, this Newark Continental-American in NJPAC proffers a "high-end" menu amid a "beautiful" retro "modern" space; though "hardly cheap", you gain ground by making "curtain call" on time.

Theresa's *Italian*
`23` `17` `21` `$37`

Westfield | 47 Elm St. (bet. E. Broad St. & North Ave.) | 908-233-9133 | www.theresasrestaurant.com

"Good", "solid" "old-time" Italian food and "hard-to-beat" prices add up to a "packed" room at this Westfield BYO "festive" "favorite" that "always satisfies"; expect "loud", "overwhelming" acoustics and, thanks to no reservations, "waits worse than what you get at Great Adventure."

3 Forty Grill *American*
`21` `23` `20` `$40`

Hoboken | 340 Sinatra Dr. (Washington St.) | 201-217-3406 | www.3fortygrill.com

Devotees of this "upscale" Hoboken New American stream in for "fresh" seafood and "interesting" martinis at the "active" bar; "great" views of the NYC skyline and a "trendy" setting augment the "love" factor for many; N.B. the restaurant offers validated parking to those who spend over $50.

⚡ 3 west *American*
`23` `24` `21` `$49`

Basking Ridge | 665 Martinsville Rd. (Independence Blvd.) | 908-647-3000 | www.3westrest.com

"Imaginative" "haute comfort food" keeps admirers attracted to this "frenetic" Basking Ridge American, a "winner" equally prized for its fare and "hot" bar, where "hanging out becomes a career" for some; the "chic", "rustic" space is suited to both "intimate" dinners or "business" meetings, the latter appropriate given the tabs ("the bill can really sneak up on you").

NEW Thyme Square ⓜ *Mediterranean*
`21` `18` `19` `$41`

Red Bank | 45 Broad St. (White St.) | 732-450-1001

This "winning" Red Bank BYO newcomer is already "highly recommended" for its "warm", sophisticated ambiance, not to mention the "interesting" Med menu; first-timers affirm they'll "be back."

	FOOD	DECOR	SERVICE	COST

Tick Tock Diner ◗ *Diner*
17 | 12 | 17 | $18

Clifton | 281 Allwood Rd./Rte. 3 W. (Garden State Pkwy., exit 153) | 973-777-0511 | www.ticktockdiner.com

Time marches on at this 24/7 "roadside" Clifton "classic" diner (since 1948), "ticking along" with its "something-for-everybody" menu and "huge" quantities of "cheaply" priced chow; it "won't let you down", and admirers add it more than transcends the "truck-stop" category.

Tim Schafer's Cuisine Ⓜ *American*
25 | 17 | 22 | $46

Morristown | 82 Speedwell Ave. (bet. Cattano Ave. & Clinton Pl.) | 973-538-3330 | www.timschafersrestaurant.com

This "newly decorated" New American Morristown BYO storefront stays "at the top of the pack" courtesy of its "exotic", "well-prepared" lineup (elk, buffalo and ostrich, many enlivened by beer) coupled with an "effective" front of the house; P.S. it "hasn't skipped a beat" even though Tim Schafer is no longer affiliated with the restaurant.

Tina Louise Ⓜ *Asian*
24 | 15 | 20 | $28

Carlstadt | 403 Hackensack St. (bet. Broad St. & Division Ave.) | 201-933-7133 | www.villagerestaurantgroup.com

A "charming" sister-team of Tina (chef) and Louise (manager) Wong run this "friendly", "little" Carlstadt BYO that spotlights "clean", "light" flavors in its "excellent" fare; best of all, this "fresh approach" to Asian cooking comes at a "bargain."

Tisha's Fine Dining *American*
25 | 21 | 21 | $44

Cape May | 714 Beach Dr. (Stockton Ave.) | 609-884-9119 | www.tishasfinedining.com

"Fabulous" views sync up with the "fantastic" food at this Cape May New American BYO that's "about as close to the water" as possible; acolytes advise alfresco dining is key at this Victorian destination that offers the "best oceanside dining in the area."

Tomatoes *Californian/Eclectic*
24 | 23 | 20 | $47

Margate | 9300 Amherst Ave. (Washington Ave.) | 609-822-7535

The "trendy", "upscale" decor attracts "glitzy", "jet-set" clientele at this "sleek" Margate Cal-Eclectic where "every dish is delicious" and the service "good"; in the "ultimate-scene" restaurant at the Shore, dessert is really "all the eye candy at the bar."

Tomo's Cuisine Ⓜ *Japanese*
- | - | - | E

Little Falls | 113 Rte. 23 (bet. 1st & 2nd Sts.) | 973-837-1117

Purists may be pleased with the arrival of this relatively expensive Japanese BYO in Little Falls offering sushi and a slate of authentic, artistically presented cooked dishes; it's small and frills-free, but raw-fish experts may see a sea dream come true.

Tony Da Caneca *Portuguese/Spanish*
24 | 15 | 22 | $38

Newark | 72 Elm Rd. (Houston St.) | 973-589-6882 | www.tonydacaneca.com

"So much incredible" Portuguese and seafood – "huge" servings of it – are why backers "come back" to this "slightly off-the-beaten-path" Iberian that's branded "one of the best" in Newark; via scene and cuisine, this "unpretentious" place successfully "transports you" to Portugal.

	FOOD	DECOR	SERVICE	COST

NEW Tony Luke's Sandwiches
	-	-	-	I

Atlantic City | Borgata Hotel, Casino & Spa | 1 Borgata Way (Atlantic City Expwy., exit 1) | 609-317-1000 | www.theborgata.com

A Philly favorite has settled into Casino City in the form of this Borgata sandwich specialist drawing slot players with the signature broccoli rabe–topped pork- and steak-stuffed rolls; early lines indicate that the spin-off of the original is going down well with the crowds.

Tortilla Press Mexican
23	19	21	$26

Collingswood | 703 Haddon Ave. (Collings Ave.) | 856-869-3345 | www.thetortillapress.com

Fans "can't say enough" about the "excellent" fare that's "strong on creativity" at this Collingswood Mexican BYO also recognized for its "colorfully decorated" digs; sage respondents say "bring your own tequila" – the place is set up for whipping up margaritas.

Tortuga's Cocina 🕏 Mexican
21	10	17	$22

Lambertville | 11½ Church St. (Union St.) | 609-397-7272

Tortuga's Mexican Village 🕏 Mexican

Princeton | 44 Leigh Ave. (bet. John & Witherspoon Sts.) | 609-924-5143 | www.tortugasmv.com

They're "the bomb" when it comes to food swear fans of these "not-your-ordinary" south-of-the-borderites dispensing "down 'n' dirty" Mexican amid "no decor"; the "best" prices spur "rowdy" crowds to keep coming; N.B. Lambertville serves alcohol, and Princeton is BYO.

Tosca Ristorante Italian
20	23	21	$49

Kenilworth | 572 Boulevard (bet. N. 23rd & 24th Sts.) | 908-709-1200 | www.toscaristorante.net

There's "fine dining" afoot in Kenilworth with this Northern Italian, a "palatial" venue with elegant dining rooms and a "cool" lounge; putting aside disagreements about the food (it ranges from "quite good" to "ok"), supporters say the place shows "promise"; N.B. the cellar wine room holds 20 for private parties.

Trap Rock American
21	21	19	$44

Berkeley Heights | 279 Springfield Ave. (bet. Snyder & Union Aves.) | 908-665-1755 | www.traprockrestaurant.net

"This place rocks" may be the first thing folks say of this "upmarket" Berkeley Heights pub and microbrewery serving "excellent" beers and distinguished by "first-rate" New American fare; the "attractive ski-lodge" decor lends a touch of "romance" to this otherwise "lively gathering place."

Tre Figlio 🖾 Italian
24	21	23	$42

Egg Harbor City | 500 W. White Horse Pike (Mannheim Ave.) | Egg Harbor | 609-965-3303 | www.trefiglio.com

"Not to be missed", this Egg Harbor City Italian is a purveyor of "truly fine" cooking with a "courteous" staff to back it up; plus, the wines are "wonderful", the surroundings "lovely" and bargain-hunters adore the "great" early-bird.

Tre Piani ⑤ *Italian/Mediterranean* | 21 | 20 | 20 | $42

Plainsboro | Forrestal Village Shopping Ctr. | 120 Rockingham Row (College Rd. W.) | 609-452-1515 | www.trepiani.com

"Local ingredients" are given their due at this spacious, "open" Plainsboro Italian-Mediterranean whose fare takes its inspiration from Slow Food U.S.A. (an organization dedicated to upholding the culinary traditions of the country, and to sustainable agriculture); the dishes, however, are sometimes "good", and sometimes "decent."

Triumph Brewing Company *Eclectic* | 18 | 20 | 16 | $28

Princeton | 138 Nassau St. (Washington Rd.) | 609-924-7855 | www.triumphbrewing.com

"Gotta love the beers" – all of them "excellent" – marketed to the "bustling" crowds that populate this "energetic" Princeton micro-brewery that also feeds fans with "unexpectedly" good Eclectic pub vittles; the "spacious", "neo-modern" industrial space (with high vaulted ceilings and an exposed, glass-enclosed brewery) seats 260, "so don't expect a quiet meal."

Tsuki ⑤ *Japanese* | 22 | 14 | 17 | $30

Bernardsville | 23 Mine Brook Rd. (Mt. Airy Rd.) | 908-953-0450

The "strong suit" is the "consistently fresh" sushi sold at this Japanese Bernardsville BYO also purveying "tasty" cooked morsels; while the "lacking atmosphere" and "not-so-hot service" are less appealing, thanks to the fare, few seem to care.

Tuckers Eating & Drinking Establishment *American* | 18 | 18 | 17 | $31

Beach Haven | 101 West Ave. (Engleside Ave.) | 609-492-2300

"Full of cheer", this "nautical" Beach Haven "staple" remains "popular" and the "only game in town" on account of "reliable" American bar food, TVs and, as the name suggests, a "great" bar dispensing assorted drinks; when sports aren't on, at least the bay views are.

Tucker's Steak & Seafood House *Seafood/Steak* | ▽ 19 | 19 | 18 | $44

Somers Point | 800 Bay Ave. (E. New Jersey Ave.) | 609-927-3100

The water view's "spectacular" at this Somers Point house of "above average" reef 'n' beef set in a Victorian inn by the bay; true, you "can't beat the porch seats", but tabs are too "lofty" for some who decry the "overpricing" doesn't add up.

Tun Tavern ◐ *American* | 18 | 17 | 17 | $24

Atlantic City | Sheraton Hotel | 2 Miss America Way (Baltic Ave.) | 609-347-7800 | www.tuntavern.com

"They should call it fun tavern" aver acolytes of this Atlantic City American featuring Marine Corps. memorabilia, burgers and "great" microbrews; thanks to "reasonable" prices, most maintain it's "good for a hearty meal after shopping the outlets."

	FOOD	DECOR	SERVICE	COST

Tuptim *Thai*
22 | 16 | 21 | $29

Montclair | 600 Bloomfield Ave. (bet. Park St. & Valley Rd.) |
973-783-3800 | www.tuptimthaicuisine.com

"Always worth a visit", this Montclair Thai BYO servicing vegetarians
and meat eaters offers "delicious" dishes in a "calming", "down-to-
earth" setting; "attention to detail" from a "caring" staff helps it
"hold its own" against newer competitors.

Tuzzio's *Italian*
21 | 11 | 21 | $28

Long Branch | 224 Westwood Ave. (Morris Ave.) | 732-222-9614 |
www.tuzzioscatering.com

The "veal parms" are the best at this "no-frills" Long Branch long-
timer (over 40 years) still delivering the "best in classic red-sauce"
Italian cooking accompanied by an "old-fashioned", "friendly" atmosphere; when factoring everything in, it's not surprising this
place remains "rock solid."

Two If By Sea Ⓜ *American*
22 | 14 | 19 | $46

Red Bank | 141 Shrewsbury Ave. (Herbert St.) | 732-747-1586 |
www.twoifbysea.com

Backers insist the fare's "underappreciated" at this Red Bank New
American seafooder with an "excellent" wine list and a staff made
up of "nice people"; it's near unanimous, though, that the food "out-
shines" the "characterless decor."

2Senza Ristorante Ⓜ *Mediterranean*
20 | 18 | 20 | $42

Red Bank | The Galleria | 2 Bridge Ave. (W. Front St.) | 732-758-0999 |
www.2senza.com

This "bustling" Red Bank Mediterranean stays "a cut above" its
competitors with "good" food and an ambiance "full of vitality", the
latter thanks to its brick-walled setting and open kitchen; if some get
a senza "pricey" tabs, most find it a "dependable" choice.

Ugly Mug *American*
16 | 14 | 18 | $21

Cape May | 426 Washington St. (Decatur St.) | 609-884-3459 |
www.uglymugenterprises.com

Downing burgers and brews, it's hard not to "feel like a local" at this
"classic" Cape May watering hole selling "standard" American pub
chow and eponymous cups, T-shirts and other items; those who "keep
returning" do it out of "tradition" as much as for the "convivial" vibe.

NEW Underground Café Ⓜ *E Euro.*
13 | 17 | 18 | $28

Princeton | 4 Hulfish St. (Witherspoon St.) | 609-924-0666

"Filling in for Eastern European", this "different" Princeton BYO vends
"large" servings of Bulgarian items (along with French and Italian
dishes) in a suitably "funky", "Euro" ambiance; despite "shaky" vittles, adherents insist this addition is bound for "landmark" status.

Ⓩ Union Park Dining Room *American*
26 | 25 | 25 | $52

Cape May | 727 Beach Ave. (Howard St.) | 609-884-8811 |
www.unionparkdiningroom.com

"Carefully prepared" New American food served on "good china"
makes for "lovely" dining at this "surprise" of a Victorian BYO (with NJ

	FOOD	DECOR	SERVICE	COST

wines) whose "romantic", "special-occasion" appeal is supported by white tablecloths and "informative" service; although the wraparound porch features views of the Atlantic, many marvel "you can't believe" you're in Cape May given the wonderfully "formal" airs here.

Varka Fish House *Greek/Seafood*

25	24	23	$54

Ramsey | 30 N. Spruce St. (E. Main St.) | 201-995-9333 | www.varkarestaurant.com

"Terrific" treats from the sea are the lure at this "chic" Greek, a fish lover's "delight" in Ramsey that impresses with other "amazingly" good Mediterranean fare, all arriving via "efficient" servers; in keeping with the genre, per-the-pound pricing "creeps up on you."

Ventura's Greenhouse *Italian*

17	15	17	$31

Margate | 106 S. Benson Ave. (Atlantic Ave.) | 609-822-0140

"For a taste of the Shore", voters visit this "casual" Margate Italian that's "insanely crowded" when summer rolls around, when most hit the outdoor deck; "so-so" food simply doesn't measure up to checking out the "so-good-looking" people and indulging in "bikini watching."

NEW Verdigre 🗷 Ⓜ *American*

▽ 22	25	21	$49

New Brunswick | 25 Liberty St. (bet. George & Nellson Sts.) | 732-247-2250

A "new discovery" in New Brunswick, this New American–Med proffers a deliciously "hip mix" of club scene and "interesting" (and "expensive") fare within a "dark", "eye-catching" interior; the lounge offers its own menu that's nice for late-night nibbling.

Verjus Ⓜ *French*

25	19	22	$48

Maplewood | 1790 Springfield Ave. (Rutgers St.) | 973-378-8990 | www.verjusrestaurant.com

"Fine dining" in a "comfortable" setting is key to the success of this "superb" Maplewood French (helmed by a wife and husband) where "fantastic" dishes meet up with "pampering" service in decor filled with the works of local artists; whether or not you go for the "bargain" Sunday brunch, this "lovely" restaurant is "well-worth" visiting.

Verve *American/French*

23	19	22	$45

Somerville | 18 E. Main St. (bet. Grove & N. Bridge Sts.) | 908-707-8655 | www.vervestyle.com

Voters vouch for the vibe at this "classy" triple-decker, a "treasure" for Somerville offering "well-done" New American–French bistro meals (and "great" steaks), "quality" service and "good" live jazz; P.S. the "way-cool" lounge is much "appreciated."

Vic's Ⓜ *Pizza*

20	10	19	$22

Bradley Beach | 60 Main St. (Evergreen Ave.) | 732-774-8225 | www.vicspizza.com

"Fill up on the cheap" with "excellent" "thin-crust" pizzas at this "venerable" Bradley Beacher that's been owned by one family for four generations; sure, the main attraction may not be the "old-school" digs, but for the "perfect balance of crust, sauce and cheese", it's hard to go wrong here.

| | FOOD | DECOR | SERVICE | COST |

Village Gourmet *Eclectic*
`21` `17` `17` `$29`

Rutherford | 73-75 Park Ave. (Ridge Rd.) | 201-438-9404 |
www.villagerestaurantgroup.com

This BYO in Rutherford is favored for its "reasonably" priced food,
an Eclectic array of New American, Asian and Southwestern, served
in "quaint, casual" quarters; "solidly satisfying" sums up the dining,
and there's no question – the "liquor store right inside" the dining
room is a nice touch.

Village Green ☒ *American*
`25` `18` `23` `$53`

Ridgewood | 36 Prospect St. (Hudson St.) | 201-445-2914 |
www.villagegreenrestaurant.com

The "small" plates pack "fabulous" flavors at this "sophisticated"
New American BYO featuring "courteous", "knowledgeable" service
and multicourse prix fixes with "selections to satisfy any palate"; the
"high-quality" cooking comes with equally high prices, but tabs are
little concern to fans who like "the best Ridgewood has to offer."

Villa Vittoria *Italian*
`22` `17` `20` `$36`

Brick | 2700 Hooper Ave. (Cedar Bridge Ave.) | 732-920-1550 |
www.villavittoria.com

Italian food "fixes" are fulfilled at this Brick standby serving "very
good" specialties amid the sound of "nice" live piano music; "attentive" service helps keep the operation "consistent", and fans tip
their hats to the "fair" tabs that come with the drinks.

Vine ☒ *American/Mediterranean*
`22` `21` `21` `$54`
(fka Tre Vigne)

Basking Ridge | 95 Morristown Rd. (bet. Maple & N. Finley Aves.) |
908-221-0017 | www.vinerestaurant.net

The "vastly improved" decor's now "more modern" and the re-
worked fare often "delicious" at this retooled Basking Ridge Med-
New American that boasts some "energy"; factor in "attentive" service, and the consensus is the new version is a "success."

Walpack Inn ☒ *American*
`19` `22` `18` `$35`

Wallpack Center | Rte. 615 (Rte. 206 N.) | 973-948-3890 |
www.walpackinn.com

Wall-mounted deer and elk heads "fit in with the surrounding woods"
and line up nicely with a menu of "good", "old-style" Americana at
this Walpack staple whose "rustic" ambiance charms; sure, the all-
you-can-eat salads and breads are "great", but everyone agrees the
"view out back" is worth the trip alone; N.B. open Fridays–Sundays.

Wasabi Asian Plates *Japanese*
`24` `19` `21` `$31`

Somerville | 12 W. Main St. (N. Bridge St.) | 908-203-8881
Wasabi House *Japanese*

East Brunswick | Colchester Plaza | 77 Tices Ln. (Rte. 18) |
732-254-9988

"Inspired" if not "dazzling" food is common to these Asians in East
Brunswick and Somerville, with both prized for their "efficient" and
"friendly" servers; the "chic" Somerville satellite serves "great"

| | FOOD | DECOR | SERVICE | COST |

drinks and is roomier than BYO East Brunswick, which offers more traditional Japanese cuisine, notably "terrific" sushi.

☑ Washington Inn *American*

26 | 26 | 26 | $58

Cape May | 801 Washington St. (Jefferson St.) | 609-884-5697 | www.washingtoninn.com

"High elegance" is achieved at this "pinnacle of Cape May dining" offering "pleasurable" meals considering the "exceptional" Traditional American food, "gracious" service and "excellent" wine list, all within a "lovely" "old" space that was once a plantation home; high prices do nothing to dissuade diners from describing the "across-the-board" excellence here.

Water Lily *Asian/French*

24 | 21 | 23 | $35

Collingswood | 655 Haddon Ave. (Collings Ave.) | 856-833-0998 | www.waterlilybistro.com

"Fabulous" fusion fare backed by "stunning" green-and-burgundy decor justify the accolades given to this Collingswood BYO, where the "interesting" menu combines Asian and French; supporters simply "can't rave enough" – and that's before they talk about the "outstanding" servers.

West Lake Seafood Restaurant *Chinese*

▽ 25 | 15 | 18 | $25

Matawan | Pine Crest Plaza | 1016 Rte. 34 (Garden State Pkwy., exit 120) | 732-290-2988 | www.westlakeseafood.com

That "many customers order from the Chinese language menu" is a sign that this Matawan BYO is serving "exquisitely pure" Cantonese selections, especially "fresh" seafood you "select from one of the fish tanks"; some say it offers one of the more "authentic" experiences in the area.

What's Your Beef? *Steak*

20 | 13 | 18 | $39

Rumson | 21 W. River Rd. (Lafayette St.) | 732-842-6205

It's "been around since 1969, and looks it", but this Rumson red-meat staple has been "solidly" standing by the neighborhood with "slabs" o' beef that you "walk up to a window" and choose pre-gnawing; if the steaks don't sate, the "extensive" salad bar will.

☑ Whispers *American*

27 | 23 | 25 | $56

Spring Lake | Hewitt Wellington Hotel | 200 Monmouth Ave. (2nd Ave.) | 732-974-9755 | www.whispersrestaurant.com

In a "fabulous" Victorian hotel near "beautiful" Spring Lake "lies a mecca of gourmet treats" in the form of this "serene" New American BYO, which specializes in "memorable" meals enhanced by "polished" servers and "consistently excellent" preparations; devoted fans concur the positives easily outweigh any concerns about the "expense" associated with this "oasis of elegance."

☑ White House ⊄ *Sandwiches*

27 | 7 | 15 | $13

Atlantic City | 2301 Arctic Ave. (Mississippi Ave.) | 609-345-1564

"Sub lovers" surrender to the "world's best" hoagies doled out at this South Jersey "legend" (since 1946) where the service is "gruff, the meat ain't tough" and "unreal" bread makes the sandwiches "great";

once you've tasted the goods, you'll understand the "crazed" scene and "lines down the street."

Wild Ginger 🔲 🅼 *Japanese* — 25 | 15 | 19 | $46

Englewood | 6 E. Palisade Ave. (bet. Dean & S. Van Brunt Sts.) | 201-567-2660 | www.wild-ginger.biz

At this Englewood Japanese BYO, let the "chef choose" and then receive "memorable" sushi served by "lovely" staffers within "cramped" quarters; those "shocked" by "sky-high" tabs reason they'll have to "pay dearly" for "Bergen County's answer to Nobu" but add "ask the price of the specials before ordering."

Windansea *Seafood* — 20 | 21 | 18 | $38

Highlands | 56 Shrewsbury Ave. (Bay Ave.) | 732-872-2266 | www.windanseanj.com

"Gorgeous" water views mean many show up to this Highlands seafooder; the food's "fresh", and "families" applaud the scene for lunch or during early-dinner hours, all before "loud", "lively" crowds "invade the place" on the lookout for drinks and a "meat market."

NEW Wolfgang Puck American Grille *American* — 23 | 23 | 21 | $50

Atlantic City | Borgata Hotel, Casino & Spa | 1 Borgata Way (Atlantic City Expwy., exit 1) | 609-317-1000 | www.theborgata.com

"Don't ever leave!" is what enthusiasts ask of Wolfgang Puck, whose arrival at AC's Borgata with this New American brings plaudits for "oh-so-good" fare and Tony Chi's "cool" design in two distinct dining areas: one a "wonderful" tavern, the other for more formal meals; "regardless of where you sit", this "welcome" newcomer is a "real winner."

Wondee's Thai Café *Thai* — - | - | - | I

Hackensack | 296 Main St. (Camden St.) | 201-883-1700 | www.wondeenj.com

The Thai comestibles satisfy at this BYO in Hackensack that operates in obscurity; there's not much in the way of scenery, but bargain tabs mean you leave with cash in your pocket.

Wonder Seafood *Chinese* — ▽ 24 | 12 | 16 | $25

Edison | 1984 Rte. 27 (Langstaff Ave.) | 732-287-6328

"You'll have a memorable meal" at this BYO establishment in Edison that gets "crowded on weekends" for its "variety" of "authentic Chinese" ("not Chinese-American") cuisine, including "must-try dim sum" and lots of seafood; some naysayers note a "lack of service and decor" – it's set in a "noisy, auditoriumlike hall" – but the "Chinatown-quality" eats are "worth it."

Word of Mouth 🅼 *American* — 24 | 24 | 21 | $40

Collingswood | 729 Haddon Ave. (bet. Collings & Washington Aves.) | 856-858-2228

For "tasteful" dining, try this BYO, an "excellent" alternative to other Collingswood eateries for its "comforting" New American food, stained-window ambiance that's "great for special dinners, including dates", and "personable" service.

	FOOD	DECOR	SERVICE	COST

Yankee Doodle Tap Room *American*

| 14 | 20 | 15 | $32 |

Princeton | Nassau Inn | 10 Palmer Sq. (Nassau St.) | 609-921-7500 | www.nassauinn.com

"Tradition is everything in Princeton" and this "classic Ivy League taproom" beneath the "historic" Nassau Inn (circa 1756) "has it all": "simple" American fare, a "warm fireplace", "pictures of famous alumni on the walls" and "a one-of-a-kind Norman Rockwell mural"; some dis the eats as "uninspired", but "for a burger and a beer, it can't be beat."

Ya Ya Noodles *Chinese*

| – | – | – | M |

Skillman | Montgomery Shopping Ctr. | 1325 Rte. 206 N. (Rte. 518) | 609-921-8551 | www.yayanoodles.com

This relatively unknown Chinese BYO in a Skillman shopping center hits the spot with its authentic dishes from a long menu including a host of dim sum offerings; N.B. look out for the bubble tea bar that's adjacent to the dining room.

Yellow Fin *American*

| 25 | 18 | 21 | $50 |

Surf City | 104 24th St. (Long Beach Blvd.) | 609-494-7001

It "would be great anywhere" aver regulars of this "packed" Surf City New American BYO that keeps a following in light of "eclectic", "delicious" (albeit "expensive") dinners and a "chic" vibe; though "good" service can run "snobby", cronies call the place "worth it" just for the "quality of the food."

Yumi *Pan-Asian*

| 26 | 17 | 22 | $39 |

Sea Bright | 1120 Ocean Ave. (Church St.) | 732-212-0881 | www.yumirestaurant.com

Patrons walk away feeling "wonderful" after making their way through the "diverse" offerings at this Sea Bright BYO, proffering flavors of the Pacific Rim while especially noted for "delicious" Japanese items; "super-sweet" service brings a bit of light to the "dark" digs.

Zafra *Pan-Latin*

| 24 | 16 | 19 | $31 |

Hoboken | 301 Willow Ave. (3rd St.) | 201-610-9801

"If you can get a table" at this colorful, compact Hoboken BYO "hideaway" (the casual precursor to nearby Cucharamama), the payoff is "great", since celeb chef and co-owner Maricel Presilla's Pan-Latin fare is "outstanding", the menu "wide-ranging" and the drinks "amazing"; P.S. the "fantastic" brunch is somewhat of a "secret" in this "land of bars and grills."

⊡ Zoe's by the Lake 🅜 *French*

| 26 | 24 | 24 | $54 |

Sparta | 112 Tomahawk Trail (2 mi. east of Rte. 15) | 973-726-7226 | www.zoesbythelake.com

"NYC and Paris" meet in Sussex County at this "out-of-the-way" Sparta French, where the "exceptional" (and "expensive") fare is matched by a "lovely, spacious" bi-level dining room and a "fantastic" lake setting (not surprisingly, "sitting outside is best"); with a staff that "goes above and beyond" to cater to the clientele, few hold no qualms about calling this "jewel" "superb on all fronts."

INDEXES

Cuisines

Includes restaurant names, neighborhoods and Food ratings. ☒ icon indicates places with the highest ratings, popularity and importance.

AFGHAN

Pamir | **Morristown**	21

AMERICAN (NEW)

Acacia | **Lawrenceville**	25
NEW Alphabet Soup | **Audubon**	-
☒ Amanda's | **Hoboken**	26
☒ André's | **Newton**	27
Anton's/Swan | **Lambertville**	22
Arthur's Landing | **Weehawken**	20
Atlantic B&G | **S Seaside Pk**	24
Bacari Grill | **Washington Twp**	21
Bazzini | **Ridgewood**	21
Bell's Mansion | **Stanhope**	18
☒ Bernards Inn | **Bernardsville**	26
Black Trumpet | **Spring Lake**	23
Blu | **Montclair**	25
Blue | **Surf City**	23
NEW ☒ Blue Bottle | **Hopewell**	27
Blueside Grill | **Englewood**	18
Boulevard Grille | **Mahwah**	18
Brandl. | **Belmar**	24
Brannon's Hurricane | **Barnegat**	21
Brass Rail | **Hoboken**	19
Buttonwood Manor | **Matawan**	18
Cafe at Rosemont | **Rosemont**	22
Cafe Loren | **Avalon**	25
☒ Chakra | **Paramus**	21
City Bistro | **Hoboken**	19
Clydz | **New Bruns.**	23
NEW ☒ CoccoLa | **Hillsborough**	22
NEW Continental | **A.C.**	-
Copeland | **Morristown**	25
Copper Fish | **Cape May**	20
Cork | **Westmont**	21
NEW ☒ CulinAriane | **Montclair**	27
NEW daddy O | **Long Beach**	18
NEW ☒ David Burke | **Rumson**	26
☒ David Drake | **Rahway**	27
☒ Dining Room | **Short Hills**	26
Dish | **Red Bank**	22
Doris & Ed's | **Highlands**	25
Drew's Bayshore | **Keyport**	28

☒ Ebbitt Room | **Cape May**	27
Elements Café | **Haddon Hts**	21
Esty Street | **Park Ridge**	23
Fat Kat | **Little Ferry**	24
☒ Ferry House | **Princeton**	25
Food for Thought | **Marlton**	24
☒ Frog & Peach | **New Bruns.**	26
Gazelle Café | **Ridgewood**	-
Grenville | **Bay Hd.**	21
Grill 73 | **Bernardsville**	22
Harrison | **Asbury Pk**	24
Harvest Moon | **Ringoes**	24
☒ Highlawn Pavil. | **W Orange**	24
High Street Grill | **Mt Holly**	23
☒ Huntley Taverne | **Summit**	22
NEW Isabella's | **Westfield**	22
Island Palm Grill | **Spring Lake**	18
Karen & Rei's | **Clermont**	27
NEW Kitchen 233 | **Westmont**	22
Lahiere's | **Princeton**	21
Lawrenceville Inn | **Lawrence Twp**	22
Light Horse | **Jersey City**	22
LoBianco | **Margate**	25
Lulu's Bistro | **Livingston**	21
Madison B&G | **Hoboken**	21
Mahogany Grille | **Manasquan**	23
Main St. Bistro | **Freehold**	21
Main St. Euro-Amer. | **Princeton**	18
Marco & Pepe | **Jersey City**	22
Marie Nicole's | **Wildwood**	23
Matisse | **Belmar**	22
Mattar's | **Allamuchy**	24
Matt's Red Roost. | **Flemington**	25
NEW Mercy Grill | **Hoboken**	-
Metuchen Inn | **Metuchen**	22
Mill | **Spring Lake Hts**	20
Napa Valley | **Paramus**	22
☒ Nauvoo Grill | **Fair Haven**	16
NEW Neil's Original Oyster | **Highlands**	-
☒ Nicholas | **Middletown**	29
No. 9 | **Lambertville**	24

Olde Corner Deli | **Island Hts**	26
Onieal's | **Hoboken**	19
Ora | **Morristown**	20
Orbis Bistro | **Upper Montclair**	22
Pasta Fresca Café | **Shrewsbury**	22
☑ Peter Shields | **Cape May**	26
Pine Tavern | **Old Bridge**	22
Plantation | **Harvey Cedars**	19
☑ Pluckemin Inn | **Bedminster**	25
Raven & Peach | **Fair Haven**	24
Raymond's | **Montclair**	21
Red | **Red Bank**	20
Renault Winery | **Egg Harbor**	22
Restaurant | **Hackensack**	21
Restaurant Latour | **Hamburg**	-
Rosemary & Sage | **Riverdale**	26
Ruga | **Oakland**	20
☑ Saddle River Inn | **Saddle R.**	27
Scarborough Fair | **Wall**	20
Sergeantsville Inn | **Sergeantsville**	23
Shipwreck Grill | **Brielle**	25
Silver Oak Bistro | **Ridgewood**	23
Simply Radish. | **Lawrenceville**	18
NEW Skylark Diner | **Edison**	19
Slowly | **Toms River**	23
SoHo on George | **New Bruns.**	23
Spargo's Grille | **Manalapan**	25
☑ Stage Left | **New Bruns.**	26
Steve & Cookie's | **Margate**	25
NEW Table | **Little Silver**	-
Table 8 | **Montclair**	23
Tewksbury Inn | **Oldwick**	22
3 Forty Grill | **Hoboken**	21
Tim Schafer's | **Morristown**	25
Tisha's | **Cape May**	25
Trap Rock | **Berkeley Hts**	21
Two If By Sea | **Red Bank**	22
☑ Union Park | **Cape May**	26
NEW Verdigre | **New Bruns.**	22
Verve | **Somerville**	23
Village Green | **Ridgewood**	25
Vine | **Basking Ridge**	22
☑ Whispers | **Spring Lake**	27
NEW Wolfgang Puck | **A.C.**	23
Word of Mouth | **Collingswood**	24
Yellow Fin | **Surf City**	25

AMERICAN (TRADITIONAL)

Alchemist/Barrister | **Princeton**	16
Allendale B&G | **Allendale**	16
An American Grill | **Randolph**	21
Avon Pavilion | **Avon-by-Sea**	18
Barnacle Bill's | **Rumson**	21
Basil T's | **Red Bank**	20
☑ Baumgart's Café | **multi. loc.**	19
☑ Bay Ave. Trattoria | **Highlands**	28
NEW Bay Head Bistro | **Bay Hd.**	21
Bell's | **Lambertville**	19
Bell's Mansion | **Stanhope**	18
Bistro 44 | **Toms River**	25
Black Horse | **Mendham**	19
Blue Pig Tavern | **Cape May**	20
Braddock's | **Medford**	22
NEW Brickwall Tav. | **Asbury Pk**	19
Cabin | **Howell**	18
Charley's | **Long Branch**	19
☑ Chart House | **Weehawken**	20
☑ Cheesecake Fact. | **multi. loc.**	19
Christopher's | **Colts Neck**	21
Clark's Landing | **Pt. Pleas.**	17
Country Pancake | **Ridgewood**	19
Cranbury Inn | **Cranbury**	17
Cup Joint | **Hoboken**	20
Doris & Ed's | **Highlands**	25
Gaslight | **Hoboken**	20
NEW Gusto Grill | **E Brunswick**	-
Hard Grove | **Jersey City**	14
Harry's Lobster | **Sea Bright**	22
Inn at Millrace | **Hope**	21
Inn/Hawke | **Lambertville**	18
Java Moon | **multi. loc.**	19
Laguna Grill | **Brigantine**	22
Lambertville Stat. | **Lambertville**	17
☑ Latour | **Ridgewood**	27
Liberty House | **Jersey City**	20
Limestone Cafe | **Peapack**	22
NEW Lucky Bones | **Cape May**	18
Mad Batter | **Cape May**	21
Maize | **Newark**	21
☑ Manor | **W Orange**	23
Mastoris | **Bordentown**	19

McLoone's | **multi. loc.**	17
Meil's | **Stockton**	23
Merion Inn | **Cape May**	20
NEW Meyersville Inn | **Meyersville**	–
Molly Pitcher | **Red Bank**	22
Nag's Head | **Ocean City**	26
☑ Old Man Rafferty | **multi. loc.**	19
☑ Perryville Inn | **Union Twp**	26
P.J. Whelihan's | **multi. loc.**	17
Ponzio's | **Cherry Hill**	16
Pop Shop | **Collingswood**	18
Quiet Man | **Dover**	22
☑ Ram's Head Inn | **Galloway**	26
Robin's Nest | **Mt Holly**	22
Rod's Olde Irish | **Sea Girt**	19
Sallee Tee's | **Monmouth Bch**	21
Salt Creek | **Rumson**	20
Shaker Cafe | **Flemington**	–
Smithville Inn | **Smithville**	18
Soho 33 | **Madison**	19
☑ South City Grill | **multi. loc.**	23
Theater Sq. Grill | **Newark**	20
☑ 3 west | **Basking Ridge**	23
Tuckers | **Beach Haven**	18
Tun Tavern | **A.C.**	18
Ugly Mug | **Cape May**	16
Walpack Inn | **Wallpack**	19
☑ Washington Inn | **Cape May**	26
Yankee Doodle | **Princeton**	14

ARGENTINEAN

NEW Gaucho Steak | **Montclair**	–

ASIAN

Chez Elena Wu | **Voorhees**	24
Coconut Bay | **Voorhees**	21
Ginger & Spice | **Ramsey**	–
Metropolitan Cafe | **Freehold**	22
Ming | **Edison**	23
Posh | **Maple Shade**	23
Ritz Seafood | **Voorhees**	24
Sens Asian | **S Brunswick**	22
Taro | **Montclair**	21
Tina Louise | **Carlstadt**	24
Water Lily | **Collingswood**	24

BAKERIES

Ponzio's | **Cherry Hill**	16

BARBECUE

Big Ed's BBQ | **multi. loc.**	17
Corky's | **A.C.**	16
Cubby's BBQ | **Hackensack**	17
GRUB Hut | **Manville**	–
Indigo Smoke | **Montclair**	22
Memphis Pig Out | **Atlantic H.**	19
NEW Smokey's BBQ | **Montclair**	–

BRAZILIAN

Brasilia Grill | **Newark**	23

BRITISH

Elephant & Castle | **Cherry Hill**	11
Ship Inn | **Milford**	19

CAJUN

Bayou Cafe | **Manasquan**	23
Creole Cafe | **Sewell**	27
Luchento's | **Millstone**	20
Oddfellows | **Hoboken**	19
Old Bay | **New Bruns.**	17

CALIFORNIAN

Napa Valley | **Paramus**	22
Tomatoes | **Margate**	24

CARIBBEAN

Bahama Breeze | **Cherry Hill**	17
NEW Caneel Bay | **Harvey Cedars**	17
Sister Sue's | **Asbury Pk**	21

CHINESE
(* dim sum specialist)

Cathay 22 | **Springfield**	23
Chengdu 46 | **Clifton**	24
Crown Palace* | **multi. loc.**	22
Dim Sum Dynasty* | **Ridgewood**	21
Edo Sushi | **Pennington**	20
☑ Far East Taste | **Eatontown**	26
Hunan Chinese | **Morris Plains**	23
Hunan Spring | **Springfield**	19
Hunan Taste | **Denville**	23
Joe's Peking | **Marlton**	23
Look See | **Ramsey**	19
Lotus Cafe | **Hackensack**	24
Meemah | **Edison**	24
Mr. Chu | **E Hanover**	22
☑ P.F. Chang's | **multi. loc.**	21

Sakura Spring | **Cherry Hill** 23

Sally Ling | **Fort Lee** 19

Shanghai Jazz | **Madison** 21

Sunny Garden | **W Windsor** 22

West Lake | **Matawan** 25

Wonder Seafood* | **Edison** 24

Ya Ya Noodles | **Skillman** ‒

CHOPHOUSE

Chophouse, The | **Gibbsboro** 23

COFFEE SHOPS/DINERS

🛛 Baumgart's Café | **multi. loc.** 19

Fedora Cafe | **Lawrenceville** 19

Hard Grove | **Jersey City** 14

Mastoris | **Bordentown** 19

Ponzio's | **Cherry Hill** 16

NEW Skylark Diner | **Edison** 19

Tick Tock | **Clifton** 17

COLOMBIAN

El Familiar | **Toms River Twp** ‒

CONTINENTAL

NEW Alessio 426 | **Metuchen** 20

Beau Rivage | **Medford** 22

🛛 Black Forest Inn | **Stanhope** 23

Café Gallery | **Burlington** 21

Court Street | **Hoboken** 21

Farnsworth Hse. | **Bordentown** 21

Ho-Ho-Kus Inn | **Ho-Ho-Kus** 21

Inn at Millrace | **Hope** 21

Lincroft Inn | **Middletown** 18

Madeleine's | **Northvale** 24

Pheasants Land. | **Hillsborough** 17

NEW Restaurant L | **Allendale** ‒

Stony Hill Inn | **Hackensack** 23

Theater Sq. Grill | **Newark** 20

CREOLE

Bayou Cafe | **Manasquan** 23

Clementine's | **Avon-by-Sea** 24

Creole Cafe | **Sewell** 27

🛛 410 Bank St. | **Cape May** 27

Luchento's | **Millstone** 20

🛛 Mélange Cafe | **Cherry Hill** 26

Oddfellows | **Hoboken** 19

Old Bay | **New Bruns.** 17

CUBAN

Azúcar | **Jersey City** 19

NEW Casona | **Collingswood** 24

Cuba Libre | **A.C.** 21

NEW Cuban Pete's | **Montclair** 17

NEW Habana Latin | ‒
   Ridgefield Pk

Hard Grove | **Jersey City** 14

🛛 La Isla | **Hoboken** 26

Martino's | **Somerville** 21

Rebecca's | **Edgewater** 24

DELIS/SANDWICH SHOPS

Eppes Essen | **Livingston** 18

Jack Cooper's | **Edison** 19

Jerry & Harvey's | **Marlboro** 18

Kibitz Room | **Cherry Hill** 24

Olde Corner Deli | **Island Hts** 26

Richard's | **Long Branch** 20

DESSERT

🛛 Cheesecake Fact. | **multi. loc.** 19

🛛 Old Man Rafferty | **multi. loc.** 19

EASTERN EUROPEAN

Blue Danube | **Trenton** 22

NEW Underground Café | 13
   Princeton

ECLECTIC

Anthony David's | **Hoboken** 25

Bistro at Red Bank | **Red Bank** 21

🛛 Black Duck | **W Cape May** 26

Blue | **Surf City** 23

Brix 67 | **Summit** 18

Bula World Cuisine | **Newton** 23

🛛 Cafe Matisse | **Rutherford** 27

Cafe Metro | **Denville** 21

🛛 Cafe Panache | **Ramsey** 28

California Grill | **Flemington** 20

Echo | **Red Bank** 19

Eurasian Eatery | **Red Bank** 20

Fantasea Reef | **A.C.** 17

Fedora Cafe | **Lawrenceville** 19

NEW 503 Park | **Scotch Plains** 20

Frenchtown Inn | **Frenchtown** 23

Full Moon | **Lambertville** 17

🛛 Gables, The | **Beach Haven** 26

Garlic Rose | **multi. loc.** 21

Grand Colonial | **Union Twp** 25

Joel's Malibu | **Ridgewood** ⁻

Jonathan's | **A.C.** 22

Labrador | **Normandy Bch** 23

Laguna Grill | **Brigantine** 22

Lilly's on Canal | **Lambertville** 21

Little Café | **Voorhees** 25

NEW Market/Mid. | **Asbury Pk** 23

Mattar's | **Allamuchy** 24

Metropolitan Cafe | **Freehold** 22

Z Park & Orchard |
E Rutherford 22

Red Square | **A.C.** ⁻

NEW restaurant.mc | **Millburn** ⁻

Sails | **Somers Point** 18

Sallee Tee's | **Monmouth Bch** 21

NEW Savannah's | **Stockholm** ⁻

Shaker Cafe | **Flemington** ⁻

NEW Sonsie | **A.C.** ⁻

NEW Spice Cuisine |
Bloomfield ⁻

Terra | **Maplewood** 20

Tomatoes | **Margate** 24

Triumph Brewing | **Princeton** 18

Village Gourmet | **Rutherford** 21

ETHIOPIAN

Makeda | **New Bruns.** 23

FILIPINO

Bistro San Miguel | **Middletown** ⁻

FONDUE

Magic Pot | **Edgewater** 19

Melting Pot | **multi. loc.** 19

FRENCH

Alexander's | **Cape May** 24

Alisa Cafe | **Cherry Hill** 22

Andaman | **Morristown** 23

Z Aozora | **Montclair** 25

Beau Rivage | **Medford** 22

Bistro En | **Teaneck** 22

Champa Laos | **Cherry Hill** 23

Z Chez Catherine | **Westfield** 27

Chez Elena Wu | **Voorhees** 24

Claude's | **N Wildwood** 25

Z Ferry House | **Princeton** 25

Frenchtown Inn | **Frenchtown** 23

Z Grand Cafe | **Morristown** 25

Ixora | **Whitehouse Station** 25

La Campagne | **Cherry Hill** 24

Z Latour | **Ridgewood** 27

Le Petit Chateau | **Bernardsville** 25

Z Lorena's | **Maplewood** 27

Madeleine's | **Northvale** 24

Manon | **Lambertville** 25

NEW Passione | **Montclair** 23

Posh | **Maple Shade** 23

Z Saddle River Inn | **Saddle R.** 27

Silver Spring | **Flanders** 23

Siri's Thai French | **Cherry Hill** 25

Soufflé | **Summit** 23

Verjus | **Maplewood** 25

Verve | **Somerville** 23

Water Lily | **Collingswood** 24

Z Zoe's | **Sparta** 26

FRENCH (BISTRO)

Bienvenue | **Red Bank** 24

Bistro 44 | **Toms River** 25

Z Chef's Table | **Franklin Lakes** 28

Circa | **High Bridge** 20

Elysian Cafe | **Hoboken** 21

Epernay | **Montclair** 21

Harvest Bistro | **Closter** 22

Indigo Moon | **Atlantic H.** 26

NEW Kitchen 233 | **Westmont** 22

Le Fandy | **Fair Haven** 26

Z Le Rendez-Vous | **Kenilworth** 26

Madame Claude | **Jersey City** 23

Pierre's | **Morristown** 23

Sophie's Bistro | **Somerset** 22

FRENCH (BRASSERIE)

NEW Z Avenue | **Long Branch** 22

FRENCH (NEW)

Brothers Moon | **Hopewell** 22

Z Origin | **multi. loc.** 26

Z Rat's | **Hamilton** 24

Z Serenade | **Chatham** 27

Stage House | **Scotch Plains** 23

GERMAN

Black Forest | **Allentown** 19

Z Black Forest Inn | **Stanhope** 23

Cenzino | **Oakland**	24	La Pastaria | **multi. loc.**	19
Chef Vola's | **A.C.**	26	La Scala | N | **Somerville**	22
Christie's | **Howell**	24	La Spiaggia | **Ship Bottom**	26
Cinque Figlie | **Morristown**	21	La Strada | **Randolph**	22
NEW Z CoccoLa | **Hillsborough**	22	LouCás | **Edison**	24
Columbia Inn | **Montville**	20	Luchento's | **Millstone**	20
Corso 98 | **Montclair**	21	Luigi's | **E Hanover**	19
Cucina Rosa | **Cape May**	23	Luka's | **Ridgefield Pk**	22
da Filippo | **Somerville**	24	Lu Nello | **Totowa**	25
Dante's | **Mendham**	21	Mama Tucci | N | **Livingston**	–
E & V | **Paterson**	24	Margherita's | **Hoboken**	22
Eccola | **Parsippany**	23	Marra's | **Ridgewood**	20
Espo's | S | **Raritan**	21	Marsilio's | **Trenton**	22
Z Fascino | **Montclair**	26	Mia | **A.C.**	26
Federici's | **Freehold**	21	Michael's Cucina | **Manalapan**	19
Ferrari's | **Freehold Twp**	22	Nunzio | **Collingswood**	23
Filomena | S | **multi. loc.**	20	Z Ombra | **A.C.**	25
Fiorino | N | **Summit**	23	NEW One 53 | **Rocky Hill**	–
Frankie Fed's | **Freehold Twp**	20	Osteria Giotto | **Montclair**	25
Frescos | **Cape May**	24	Panico's | **New Bruns.**	24
Gaetano's | **Red Bank**	19	Pete & Elda's | **Neptune City**	–
Gaslight | **Hoboken**	20	Pino's La Forchetta | **Marlboro**	18
Gianna's | **Atlantic H.**	25	Pizzicato | **Marlton**	21
Girasole | S | **A.C.**	25	Portobello | **Oakland**	20
Girasole | **Bound Brook**	25	Portofino | **Tinton Falls**	25
Giumarello's | N | **Westmont**	25	Porto Leggero | **Jersey City**	23
GoodFellas | N | **Garfield**	–	Posillipo | **Asbury Pk**	22
Grissini | **Englewood Cliffs**	22	Primavera | **W Orange**	20
Ho-Ho-Kus Inn | **Ho-Ho-Kus**	21	Pronto Cena | **Newark**	22
Homestead Inn | **Trenton**	23	Radicchio | N | **Ridgewood**	23
I Cavallini | **Colts Neck**	25	Raimondo's | **Ship Bottom**	23
Il Capriccio | **Whippany**	26	Reservoir Tavern | **Boonton**	22
Il Forno Trattoria | S | **Montclair**	23	Richie Cecere's | **Montclair**	21
Il Michelangelo | **Boonton**	21	Rick's | **Lambertville**	–
Z Il Mondo | N | **Madison**	25	Ristorante Benito | **Union**	25
Il Tulipano | **Cedar Grove**	23	Roberto's Dolce | N | **Beach Haven**	22
Il Villaggio | **Carlstadt**	23		
Italian Bistro | **Cherry Hill**	17	Roberto's II | **Edgewater**	19
Jamie's Restaurant | **Clifton**	–	Rocca | **Glen Rock**	22
Jimmy's | S | **Asbury Pk**	24	Roman Cafe | **Harrington Pk**	19
Kinchley's Tavern | **Ramsey**	21	San Remo | **Shrewsbury**	22
La Campagna | N | **multi. loc.**	24	Sapori | **Collingswood**	24
Laceno Italian | **Voorhees**	25	Z Scalini Fedeli | N | **Chatham**	27
La Cipollina | **Freehold**	23	Settebello Cafe | N | **Morristown**	22
La Focaccia | N | **Summit**	24		
La Nonna/Piancone's | N | **multi. loc.**	18	NEW Z Sirena | **Long Branch**	23
		Sogno | **Red Bank**	23

Solaia | **Englewood**	20
Solari's | **Hackensack**	21
Solo Bella | **Jackson**	21
Specchio | **A.C.**	25
Squan Tavern | **Manasquan**	19
Stony Hill Inn | **Hackensack**	23
Teresa's Cafe | **Princeton**	21
Theresa's | **Westfield**	23
Tosca | N | **Kenilworth**	20
Tre Figlio | **Egg Harbor**	24
Tre Piani | **Plainsboro**	21
Tuzzio's | **Long Branch**	21
Ventura's | **Margate**	17
Vic's | **Bradley Bch**	20
Villa Vittoria | **Brick**	22

JAPANESE
(* sushi specialist)

Z Ajihei* | **Princeton**	26
NEW Akai Lounge* | **Englewood**	23
Aligado Asian* | **Hazlet**	23
Z Aozora | **Montclair**	25
Bistro En* | **Teaneck**	22
Brix 67* | **Summit**	18
Dai-Kichi* | **Upper Montclair**	22
East* | **Teaneck**	18
Edo Sushi* | **Pennington**	20
Elements Asia* | **Lawrenceville**	23
Ichiban* | **Princeton**	17
Ikko* | **Brick**	22
Ixora* | **Whitehouse Station**	25
Klein's Fish Market* | **Belmar**	20
K.O.B.E.* | **Holmdel**	25
Komegashi* | **Jersey City**	24
Konbu* | **Manalapan**	25
Mahzu* | **multi. loc.**	22
Megu Sushi* | **Cherry Hill**	22
Midori* | **Denville**	24
Mikado* | **multi. loc.**	22
Monster Sushi* | **Summit**	19
Nikko* | **Whippany**	24
Nobi* | **Toms River Twp**	25
Nori* | **multi. loc.**	22
Nouveau Sushi* | **Montclair**	25
Ota-Ya* | **Lambertville**	23
Oyako Tso's* | **Freehold**	21
Robongi | **Hoboken**	25

Z Sagami* | **Collingswood**	26
Sakura-Bana* | **Ridgewood**	25
Sakura Spring | **Cherry Hill**	23
Sawa Steak* | **multi. loc.**	22
Shogun* | **multi. loc.**	18
Shumi* | **Somerville**	25
Sono Sushi* | **Middletown**	26
NEW Sumo | **Wall**	-
Sushi by Kazu* | **Howell**	28
Sushi Lounge* | **multi. loc.**	24
Z Taka* | **Asbury Pk**	26
NEW Takara | **Ocean Twp**	25
Tomo's Cuisine | **Little Falls**	-
Tsuki* | **Bernardsville**	22
Wasabi* | **multi. loc.**	24
Wild Ginger* | **Englewood**	25
Yumi* | **Sea Bright**	26

JEWISH

Eppes Essen | **Livingston**	18
Kibitz Room | **Cherry Hill**	24

KOREAN
(* barbecue specialist)

Doo Rae Myun Ok | **Fort Lee**	21
So Moon Nan Jip* | **Palisades Pk**	23

MALAYSIAN

Meemah | **Edison**	24
Penang | **multi. loc.**	20
Taste of Asia | **Chatham**	21

MEDITERRANEAN

NEW Europa at Monroe | **Monroe Twp**	-
Frescos | **Cape May**	24
Hamilton's Grill | **Lambertville**	24
Lodos | **New Milford**	21
Mediterra | **Princeton**	20
Z Moonstruck | **Asbury Pk**	24
NEW Oceanos | **Fair Lawn**	-
Osteria Dante | **Red Bank**	19
Seven Hills | **Highland Pk**	21
Terrace Rest. | **Short Hills**	22
NEW Thyme Square | **Red Bank**	21
Tre Piani | **Plainsboro**	21
2Senza | **Red Bank**	20
Varka Fish House | **Ramsey**	25
NEW Verdigre | **New Bruns.**	22
Vine | **Basking Ridge**	22

CUISINES

MEXICAN

Aby's Mexican | **Matawan**	22
Baja | **multi. loc.**	20
Casa Maya | **multi. loc.**	20
Charrito's | **multi. loc.**	24
Chilangos | **Highlands**	21
El Azteca | **Mt Laurel**	21
El Familiar | **Toms River Twp**	–
Z El Meson | **Freehold**	24
NEW Habana Latin | **Ridgefield Pk**	–
Jose's | **Spring Lake Hts**	22
Jose's Mexican | **multi. loc.**	19
Juanito's | **multi. loc.**	23
La Esperanza | **Lindenwold**	24
La Tapatia | **Asbury Pk**	–
Los Amigos | **multi. loc.**	23
Mexican Food | **Marlton**	18
Mexico Lindo | **Brick**	28
NEW Sapo Verde | **Atlantic H.**	–
Senorita's | **Bloomfield**	20
Surf Taco | **multi. loc.**	20
Taqueria | **Jersey City**	20
Tortilla Press | **Collingswood**	23
Tortuga's | **multi. loc.**	21

MIDDLE EASTERN

NEW Addiwan | **Montclair**	18
Ali Baba | **Hoboken**	20
BoBo's 33 | **Atlantic H.**	22
Norma's Med. | **Cherry Hill**	21

MOROCCAN

Oasis Grill | **Cherry Hill**	25

NOODLE SHOPS

Noodle House | **N Brunswick**	19
Penang | **multi. loc.**	20

NUEVO LATINO

Sabor | **multi. loc.**	22

PACIFIC RIM

Pacific Grille | **Mt Laurel**	20

PAN-ASIAN

NEW Asia Star | **Tinton Falls**	–
Z Baumgart's Café | **multi. loc.**	19
NEW Buddakan | **A.C.**	–

Elements Asia | **Lawrenceville**	23
Grand Shanghai | **Edison**	21
Ming | **Morristown**	23
Nori | **multi. loc.**	22
Nouveau Sushi | **Montclair**	25
Teak | **Red Bank**	23
Yumi | **Sea Bright**	26

PAN-LATIN

Casa Solar | **Belmar**	25
NEW Casona | **Collingswood**	24
Lua | **Hoboken**	22
Nova Terra | **New Bruns.**	22
Zafra | **Hoboken**	24

PIZZA

Benny Tudino's | **Hoboken**	21
Brooklyn's Pizza | **multi. loc.**	22
Columbia Inn | **Montville**	20
Conte's | **Princeton**	–
Z DeLorenzo's | **Trenton**	28
Federici's | **Freehold**	21
Frankie Fed's | **Freehold Twp**	20
Grimaldi's Pizza | **Hoboken**	25
Il Forno Trattoria | **Montclair**	23
Kinchley's Tavern | **Ramsey**	21
Margherita's | **Hoboken**	22
Pete & Elda's | **Neptune City**	–
Pino's La Forchetta | **Marlboro**	18
Pizzicato | **Marlton**	21
Reservoir Tavern | **Boonton**	22
Tacconelli's | **Maple Shade**	20
Vic's | **Bradley Bch**	20

POLISH

Krakus | **Wallington**	–

PORTUGUESE

Adega Grill | **Newark**	24
Z Bistro Olé | **Asbury Pk**	25
Don Pepe | **multi. loc.**	21
Europa South | **Pt. Pleas. Bch**	20
Z Fernandes Steak | **Newark**	26
Iberia | **Newark**	21
Pearl of the Sea | **Long Branch**	18
NEW Pic-Nic | **E Newark**	–
Portuguese Manor | **Perth Amboy**	21
Segovia | **Moonachie**	22

| Spain | **Newark** | 21 |
| Tony Da Caneca | **Newark** | 24 |

PUB FOOD

Alchemist/Barrister	**Princeton**	16
Allendale B&G	**Allendale**	16
Black Horse	**Mendham**	19
Elephant & Castle	**Cherry Hill**	11
Inn/Hawke	**Lambertville**	18
Light Horse	**Jersey City**	22
Quiet Man	**Dover**	22
Rod's Olde Irish	**Sea Girt**	19
Ship Inn	**Milford**	19
NEW Tashmoo	**Morristown**	-
Ugly Mug	**Cape May**	16

RUSSIAN

| Red Square | **A.C.** | - |

SANDWICHES

Sallee Tee's	**Monmouth Bch**	21
NEW Tony Luke's	**A.C.**	-
Z White House	**A.C.**	27

SEAFOOD

Allen's Clam	**New Gretna**	-
Athenian Gdn.	**Galloway Twp**	23
Atlantic B&G	**S Seaside Pk**	24
Axelsson's	**Cape May**	22
Bahrs Landing	**Highlands**	15
Barnacle Ben's	**Moorestown**	19
Berkeley	**S Seaside Pk**	18
NEW Blue Fish	**Flemington**	20
Z Blue Point	**Princeton**	25
Blueside Grill	**Englewood**	18
NEW Blue Wave	**Westfield**	-
Bobby Chez	**multi. loc.**	25
Busch's Seafood	**Sea Isle City**	19
Capt'n Ed's	**Pt. Pleas.**	19
Z Chart House	**Weehawken**	20
Chophouse, The	**Gibbsboro**	23
Copper Fish	**Cape May**	20
Crab's Claw	**Lavallette**	17
Crab Trap	**Somers Point**	21
da Filippo	**Somerville**	24
Dock's Oyster	**A.C.**	26
Doris & Ed's	**Highlands**	25
Emerald Fish	**Cherry Hill**	23

Fantasea Reef	**A.C.**	17
Ferrari's	**Freehold Twp**	22
Fresco Steak	**Milltown**	23
Hamilton's Grill	**Lambertville**	24
Harry's Lobster	**Sea Bright**	22
Harvey Cedars	**multi. loc.**	22
Hunt Club	**Summit**	20
Inlet Café	**Highlands**	19
John Henry's	**Trenton**	21
Klein's Fish Market	**Belmar**	20
Kunkel's	**Haddon Hts**	20
Laceno Italian	**Voorhees**	25
Latitude 40N	**Pt. Pleas. Bch**	23
Z Legal Sea Foods	**multi. loc.**	20
Little Tuna	**Haddonfield**	20
Lobster House	**Cape May**	20
LouCás	**Edison**	24
Z McCormick/Schmick	**multi. loc.**	20
Milford Oyster House	**Milford**	-
Mill	**Spring Lake Hts**	20
Mud City	**Manahawkin**	21
Navesink Fishery	**Middletown**	24
NEW Neil's Original Oyster	**Highlands**	-
NEW Octopus's Gard.	**Stafford**	22
Opah Grille	**Gladstone**	24
Pacific Grille	**Mt Laurel**	20
Park	**Park Ridge**	24
Pearl of the Sea	**Long Branch**	18
NEW Phillips Seafood	**A.C.**	-
Ray's Little Silver	**Little Silver**	23
Red's Lobster	**Pt. Pleas. Bch**	24
Ritz Seafood	**Voorhees**	24
Rooney's	**Long Branch**	18
NEW Z SeaBlue	**A.C.**	27
Sea Shack	**Hackensack**	20
Shipwreck Grill	**Brielle**	25
Smoke Chophouse	**Englewood**	22
Solaia	**Englewood**	20
Z South City Grill	**multi. loc.**	23
Spike's	**Pt. Pleas. Bch**	22
Suez Canal	**Jersey City**	-
3 Forty Grill	**Hoboken**	21
Tucker's Steak	**Somers Point**	19
Two If By Sea	**Red Bank**	22

Varka Fish House | **Ramsey**	25
West Lake | **Matawan**	25
Windansea | **Highlands**	20
Wonder Seafood | **Edison**	24

SMALL PLATES

(See also Spanish tapas specialist)

Echo | Eclectic | **Red Bank**	19
Elements Café | Amer. | **Haddon Hts**	21
Grand Colonial | Eclectic | **Union Twp**	25
Lua | Pan-Latin | **Hoboken**	22
Marco & Pepe | Amer. | **Jersey City**	22

SOUL FOOD

Delta's | **New Bruns.**	22
Je's | **Newark**	26

SOUTH AMERICAN

☑ Cucharamama | **Hoboken**	26

SOUTHERN

Delta's | **New Bruns.**	22
House of Blues | **A.C.**	16
Indigo Smoke | **Montclair**	22
Je's | **Newark**	26
Niecy's | **S Orange**	20
Silver Oak Bistro | **Ridgewood**	23
NEW Smokey's BBQ | **Montclair**	–

SOUTHWESTERN

Copper Canyon | **Atlantic H.**	25
GRUB Hut | **Manville**	–
Los Amigos | **multi. loc.**	23
☑ Mojave Grille | **Westfield**	24
Rattlesnake Ranch | **Denville**	16

SPANISH

(* tapas specialist)

Adega Grill | **Newark**	24
☑ Bistro Olé | **Asbury Pk**	25
Casa Vasca* | **Newark**	24
Don Pepe | **multi. loc.**	21
El Cid | **Paramus**	21
Europa South | **Pt. Pleas. Bch**	20
☑ Fornos of Spain | **Newark**	23
Iberia | **Newark**	21
Lola's* | **Hoboken**	22

Mompou* | **Newark**	20
Portuguese Manor | **Perth Amboy**	21
Savanna* | **Red Bank**	20
Segovia | **Moonachie**	22
Spain | **Newark**	21
Spanish Tavern | **multi. loc.**	22
Tapas de Espana* | **multi. loc.**	20
Tony Da Caneca | **Newark**	24

STEAKHOUSES

☑ Arthur's Steak/Tavern | **multi. loc.**	18
Assembly Steak | **Englewood Cliffs**	16
BayPoint Prime | **Pt. Pleas. Bch**	24
Blue Eyes | **Sewell**	20
NEW Bobby Flay Steak | **A.C.**	24
Brennan's Steak | **Neptune City**	22
Capt'n Ed's | **Pt. Pleas.**	19
Don Pepe's Steak | **Pine Brook**	22
☑ Fernandes Steak | **Newark**	26
Fleming's | **Edgewater**	22
Frankie & Johnnie | **Hoboken**	23
Fresco Steak | **Milltown**	23
NEW Gallagher's Steak | **A.C.**	22
NEW Gaucho Steak | **Montclair**	–
Hunt Club | **Summit**	20
Kunkel's | **Haddon Hts**	20
Manhattan Steak | **Oakhurst**	22
Mignon Steak | **Rutherford**	23
Mill | **Spring Lake Hts**	20
Morton's Steak | **Hackensack**	24
Nero's Grille | **Livingston**	17
Old Homestead | **A.C.**	25
Palm | **A.C.**	24
Park | **Park Ridge**	24
Pub | **Pennsauken**	18
☑ River Palm | **multi. loc.**	25
Rod's Steak | **Convent Station**	21
NEW Roots Steak | **Summit**	–
☑ Ruth's Chris | **multi. loc.**	24
Sammy's Cider | **Mendham**	21
Shogun | **multi. loc.**	18
Smoke Chophouse | **Englewood**	22
Strip House | **Livingston**	23
Tucker's Steak | **Somers Point**	19
What's Your Beef? | **Rumson**	20

TAIWANESE

China Palace | **Middletown** ‗

THAI

Aligado Asian | **Hazlet** 23
Andaman | **Morristown** 23
Aroma Royal Thai | **Franklin Pk** 22
Bamboo Leaf | **multi. loc.** 24
Bangkok Garden | **Hackensack** 24
Champa Laos | **Cherry Hill** 23
Chao Phaya | **multi. loc.** 23
🛂 Far East Taste | **Eatontown** 26
Ginger Thai | **Freehold Twp** 15
Mie Thai | **Woodbridge** 25
New Main | **Chatham** 23
🛂 Origin | **multi. loc.** 26
Pad Thai | **Highland Pk** 22
Penang | **multi. loc.** 20
Siam | **Lambertville** 21
Siam Garden | **Red Bank** 23
Sirin | **Morristown** 22
Siri's Thai French | **Cherry Hill** 25
Somsak/Taan | **Voorhees** 23
NEW Spice Cuisine | ‗
  Bloomfield
Sri Thai | **Hoboken** 24
Thai Chef | **multi. loc.** 21

Thai Kitchen | **multi. loc.** 23
Thai Thai | **Stirling** 25
Tuptim | **Montclair** 22
Wondee's Thai | **Hackensack** ‗

TURKISH

Beyti Kebab | **Union City** 24
Bosphorus | **Lake Hiawatha** 22
Dayi'nin Yeri | **Cliffside Pk** ‗
Lalezar | **Montclair** ‗
Lodos | **New Milford** 21
NEW Nazmi's | **Cliffside Pk** ‗
Samdan | **Cresskill** 22
Seven Hills | **Highland Pk** 21
NEW Sultan's | **Hackettstown** ‗

VEGETARIAN

(* vegan)
Chand Palace | **Parsippany** 22
Kaya's Kitchen* | **Belmar** ‗
Tuptim | **Montclair** 22

VIETNAMESE

Bamboo Leaf | **multi. loc.** 24
Nha Trang Place | **Jersey City** 24
Pho Thang Long | **Jersey City** ‗
Saigon R./Mo' Pho' | **multi. loc.** 24

CUISINES

Locations

Includes restaurant names, cuisines and Food ratings. ◪ icon indicates places with the highest ratings, popularity and importance.

Metro New York Area

ALLENDALE

Allendale B&G | *Pub*	16
NEW Restaurant L | *Continental*	–

BELLEVILLE

Belmont Tavern | *Italian*	24

BERKELEY HEIGHTS

Trap Rock | *Amer.*	21

BLOOMFIELD

Senorita's | *Mex.*	20
NEW Spice Cuisine | *Eclectic*	–

CALDWELL

Nori | *Pan-Asian*	22

CARLSTADT

Il Villaggio | *Italian*	23
Tina Louise | *Asian*	24

CEDAR GROVE

Il Tulipano | *Italian*	23

CLIFFSIDE PARK

Dayi'nin Yeri | *Turkish*	–
◪ It's Greek To Me | *Greek*	18
NEW Nazmi's | *Turkish*	–

CLIFTON

Belvedere | *Italian*	19
Chengdu 46 | *Chinese*	24
Jamie's Restaurant | *Italian*	–
Tick Tock | *Diner*	17

CLOSTER

Harvest Bistro | *French*	22

CRANFORD

Garlic Rose | *Eclectic*	21

CRESSKILL

Samdan | *Turkish*	22

EAST NEWARK

NEW Pic-Nic | *Portug.*	–

EAST RUTHERFORD

◪ Park & Orchard | *Eclectic*	22

EDGEWATER

◪ Baumgart's Café | *Amer./Pan-Asian*	19
Brooklyn's Pizza | *Pizza*	22
Fleming's | *Steak*	22
Magic Pot | *Fondue*	19
Rebecca's | *Cuban*	24
◪ River Palm | *Steak*	25
Roberto's II | *Italian*	19

EMERSON

◪ Arthur's Steak/Tavern | *Steak*	18

ENGLEWOOD

NEW Akai Lounge | *Jap.*	23
◪ Baumgart's Café | *Amer./Pan-Asian*	19
Blueside Grill | *Amer./Seafood*	18
◪ It's Greek To Me | *Greek*	18
Saigon R./Mo' Pho' | *Viet.*	24
Smoke Chophouse | *Seafood/Steak*	22
Solaia | *Italian*	20
Tapas de Espana | *Spanish*	20
Wild Ginger | *Jap.*	25

ENGLEWOOD CLIFFS

Assembly Steak | *Steak*	16
Cafe Italiano | *Italian*	18
Grissini | *Italian*	22

FAIRFIELD

Aria Ristorante | *Italian*	21

FAIR LAWN

NEW Oceanos | *Greek/Med.*	–
◪ River Palm | *Steak*	25

FORT LEE

Doo Rae Myun Ok | *Korean* — 21
🅩 It's Greek To Me | *Greek* — 18
Saigon R./Mo' Pho' | *Viet.* — 24
Sally Ling | *Chinese* — 19

FRANKLIN LAKES

🅩 Chef's Table | *French* — 28

GARFIELD

GoodFellas | *Italian* — -

GLEN ROCK

Rocca | *Italian* — 22

HACKENSACK

Bangkok Garden | *Thai* — 24
Brooklyn's Pizza | *Pizza* — 22
🅩 Cheesecake Fact. | *Amer.* — 19
Cubby's BBQ | *BBQ* — 17
Lotus Cafe | *Chinese* — 24
🅩 McCormick/Schmick | *Seafood* — 20
Morton's Steak | *Steak* — 24
Restaurant | *Amer.* — 21
Sea Shack | *Seafood* — 20
Solari's | *Italian* — 21
Stony Hill Inn | *Continental/Italian* — 23
Thai Chef | *Thai* — 21
Wondee's Thai | *Thai* — -

HARRINGTON PARK

Roman Cafe | *Italian* — 19

HAWTHORNE

Sabor | *Nuevo Latino* — 22

HOBOKEN

Ali Baba | *Mideast.* — 20
🅩 Amanda's | *Amer.* — 26
Anthony David's | *Eclectic/Italian* — 25
🅩 Arthur's Steak/Tavern | *Steak* — 18
🅩 Augustino's | *Italian* — 26
Baja | *Mex.* — 20
Benny Tudino's | *Pizza* — 21
Brass Rail | *Amer.* — 19
Charrito's | *Mex.* — 24

City Bistro | *Amer.* — 19
Court Street | *Continental* — 21
🅩 Cucharamama | *S Amer.* — 26
Cup Joint | *Amer.* — 20
Elysian Cafe | *French* — 21
Frankie & Johnnie | *Steak* — 23
Gaslight | *Amer./Italian* — 20
Grimaldi's Pizza | *Pizza* — 25
India on Hudson | *Indian* — 19
🅩 It's Greek To Me | *Greek* — 18
🅩 Karma Kafe | *Indian* — 25
🅩 La Isla | *Cuban* — 26
Lola's | *Spanish* — 22
Lua | *Pan-Latin* — 22
Madison B&G | *Amer.* — 21
Margherita's | *Italian* — 22
NEW Mercy Grill | *Amer.* — -
Oddfellows | *Cajun/Creole* — 19
Onieal's | *Amer.* — 19
Robongi | *Jap.* — 25
Sri Thai | *Thai* — 24
Sushi Lounge | *Jap.* — 24
3 Forty Grill | *Amer.* — 21
Zafra | *Pan-Latin* — 24

HO-HO-KUS

Ho-Ho-Kus Inn | *Continental/Italian* — 21

JERSEY CITY

Amiya | *Indian* — 21
Azúcar | *Cuban* — 19
Baja | *Mex.* — 20
Casa Dante | *Italian* — 22
Hard Grove | *Amer./Cuban* — 14
🅩 It's Greek To Me | *Greek* — 18
Komegashi | *Jap.* — 24
Liberty House | *Amer.* — 20
Light Horse | *Amer.* — 22
Madame Claude | *French* — 23
Marco & Pepe | *Amer.* — 22
Nha Trang Place | *Viet.* — 24
Pho Thang Long | *Viet.* — -
Porto Leggero | *Italian* — 23
🅩 South City Grill | *Amer.* — 23
Suez Canal | *Seafood* — -
Taqueria | *Mex.* — 20

KENILWORTH

☑ Le Rendez-Vous | *French* — 26
Tosca | *Italian* — 20

LITTLE FALLS

Bellissimo's | *Italian* — 24
Tomo's Cuisine | *Jap.* — –

LITTLE FERRY

Fat Kat | *Amer.* — 24

LIVINGSTON

Eppes Essen | *Deli* — 18
Lulu's Bistro | *Amer.* — 21
Mama Tucci | *Italian* — –
Nero's Grille | *Steak* — 17
Strip House | *Steak* — 23

MAHWAH

Boulevard Grille | *Amer.* — 18
☑ River Palm | *Steak* — 25

MAPLEWOOD

☑ Lorena's | *French* — 27
Terra | *Eclectic* — 20
Verjus | *French* — 25

MIDLAND PARK

Arturo's | *Italian* — 22

MILLBURN

☑ Basilico | *Italian* — 23
La Campagna | *Italian* — 24
NEW restaurant.mc | *Eclectic* — –

MONTCLAIR

NEW Addiwan | *Mideast.* — 18
☑ Aozora | *French/Jap.* — 25
Blu | *Amer.* — 25
Corso 98 | *Italian* — 21
NEW Cuban Pete's | *Cuban* — 17
NEW ☑ CulinAriane | *Amer.* — 27
Egan & Sons | *Irish* — 17
Epernay | *French* — 21
☑ Fascino | *Italian* — 26
NEW Gaucho Steak | Argent./Steak — –
Il Forno Trattoria | *Italian* — 23
Indigo Smoke | *BBQ* — 22
Lalezar | *Turkish* — –

Nori | *Pan-Asian* — 22
Nouveau Sushi | *Pan-Asian* — 25
Osteria Giotto | *Italian* — 25
NEW Passione | *French* — 23
Raymond's | *Amer.* — 21
Richie Cecere's | *Italian* — 21
NEW Smokey's BBQ | BBQ/Southern — –
Table 8 | *Amer.* — 23
Taro | *Pan-Asian* — 21
Thai Chef | *Thai* — 21
Tuptim | *Thai* — 22

MONTVALE

Aldo & Gianni | *Italian* — 21

MOONACHIE

Bazzarelli | *Italian* — 22
Segovia | *Portug./Spanish* — 22

MOUNTAINSIDE

Raagini | *Indian* — 22
Spanish Tavern | *Spanish* — 22

NEWARK

Adega Grill | *Portug./Spanish* — 24
Brasilia Grill | *Brazilian* — 23
Casa Vasca | *Spanish* — 24
Don Pepe | *Portug./Spanish* — 21
☑ Fernandes Steak | *Steak* — 26
☑ Fornos of Spain | *Spanish* — 23
Iberia | *Portug./Spanish* — 21
Je's | *Soul Food* — 26
Maize | *Amer.* — 21
Mompou | *Spanish* — 20
Pronto Cena | *Italian* — 22
Spain | *Portug./Spanish* — 21
Spanish Tavern | *Spanish* — 22
Theater Sq. Grill | Amer./Continental — 20
Tony Da Caneca | Portug./Spanish — 24

NEW MILFORD

Lodos | *Med./Turkish* — 21

NEW PROVIDENCE

Aquila Cucina | *Italian* — 21
Jose's Mexican | *Mex.* — 19

NORTH BERGEN

Sabor | *Nuevo Latino* — 22
Tapas de Espana | *Spanish* — 20

NORTHVALE

Madeleine's | *Continental/French* — 24

OAKLAND

Cenzino | *Italian* — 24
Portobello | *Italian* — 20
Ruga | *Amer.* — 20

PALISADES PARK

So Moon Nan Jip | *Korean* — 23

PARAMUS

🄩 Chakra | *Amer.* — 21
El Cid | *Spanish* — 21
🄩 Legal Sea Foods | *Seafood* — 20
Napa Valley | *Amer.* — 22

PARK RIDGE

Esty Street | *Amer.* — 23
Park | *Seafood/Steak* — 24

PATERSON

E & V | *Italian* — 24

RAHWAY

🄩 David Drake | *Amer.* — 27

RAMSEY

🄩 Cafe Panache | *Eclectic* — 28
Ginger & Spice | *Asian* — −
Kinchley's Tavern | *Pizza* — 21
Look See | *Chinese* — 19
Varka Fish House | *Greek/Seafood* — 25

RIDGEFIELD PARK

NEW Habana Latin | *Cuban/Mex.* — −
Luka's | *Italian* — 22

RIDGEWOOD

🄩 Baumgart's Café | *Amer./Pan-Asian* — 19
Bazzini | *Amer.* — 21
Brooklyn's Pizza | *Pizza* — 22
Country Pancake | *Amer.* — 19

Dim Sum Dynasty | *Chinese* — 21
Gazelle Café | *Amer.* — −
🄩 It's Greek To Me | *Greek* — 18
Joel's Malibu | *Eclectic* — −
🄩 Latour | *French* — 27
Marra's | *Italian* — 20
Radicchio | *Italian* — 23
Sakura-Bana | *Jap.* — 25
Silver Oak Bistro | *Amer./Southern* — 23
Village Green | *Amer.* — 25

ROCHELLE PARK

🄩 South City Grill | *Amer.* — 23

RUTHERFORD

🄩 Cafe Matisse | *Eclectic* — 27
Mignon Steak | *Steak* — 23
Village Gourmet | *Eclectic* — 21

SADDLE RIVER

🄩 Saddle River Inn | *Amer./French* — 27

SCOTCH PLAINS

NEW 503 Park | *Eclectic* — 20
Stage House | *French* — 23

SECAUCUS

Bareli's | *Italian* — 23

SHORT HILLS

🄩 Dining Room | *Amer.* — 26
🄩 Legal Sea Foods | *Seafood* — 20
Terrace Rest. | *Med.* — 22

SOUTH HACKENSACK

Aldo & Gianni | *Italian* — 21

SOUTH ORANGE

Cafe Arugula | *Italian* — 20
Neelam | *Indian* — 18
Niecy's | *Southern* — 20

SPRINGFIELD

Cathay 22 | *Chinese* — 23
Hunan Spring | *Chinese* — 19

SUMMIT

Brix 67 | *Eclectic/Jap.* — 18
NEW DabbaWalla | *Indian* — 19

LOCATIONS

Fiorino | Italian | 23
Hunt Club | Seafood/Steak | 20
Z Huntley Taverne | Amer. | 22
La Focaccia | Italian | 24
La Pastaria | Italian | 19
Monster Sushi | Jap. | 19
NEW Roots Steak | Steak | -
Soufflé | French | 23

TEANECK

Amarone | Italian | 21
Bistro En | French | 22
East | Jap. | 18

TENAFLY

NEW Axia Taverna | Greek | 21

TOTOWA

Lu Nello | Italian | 25

UNION

Ristorante Benito | Italian | 25

UNION CITY

Beyti Kebab | Turkish | 24
Charrito's | Mex. | 24

UPPER MONTCLAIR

Alan@594 | Italian | 20
Dai-Kichi | Jap. | 22
Orbis Bistro | Amer. | 22

VERONA

NEW Amazing Hot Dog | Hot Dogs | 22

WALLINGTON

Krakus | Polish | -

WANAQUE

Berta's Chateau | Italian | 22

WASHINGTON TOWNSHIP

Bacari Grill | Amer. | 21

WAYNE

Z Cheesecake Fact. | Amer. | 19

WEEHAWKEN

Arthur's Landing | Amer. | 20
Z Chart House | Amer./Seafood | 20
Z Ruth's Chris | Steak | 24

WESTFIELD

Acquaviva | Italian | 23
NEW Blue Wave | Seafood | -
Z Chez Catherine | French | 27
NEW Isabella's | Amer. | 22
Z Mojave Grille | SW | 24
Theresa's | Italian | 23

WEST NEW YORK

Z P.F. Chang's | Chinese | 21

WEST ORANGE

Z Highlawn Pavil. | Amer. | 24
Z Manor | Amer. | 23
Primavera | Italian | 20

WESTWOOD

Z It's Greek To Me | Greek | 18
Melting Pot | Fondue | 19

Central

BASKING RIDGE

NEW Bombay Curry | Indian | -
Z 3 west | Amer. | 23
Vine | Amer./Med. | 22

BEDMINSTER

Z Pluckemin Inn | Amer. | 25

BERNARDSVILLE

Z Bernards Inn | Amer. | 26
Grill 73 | Amer. | 22
Le Petit Chateau | French | 25
Tsuki | Jap. | 22

BOONTON

Il Michelangelo | Italian | 21
Reservoir Tavern | Pizza | 22

BOUND BROOK

Girasole | Italian | 25

BRANCHBURG

Cafe Cucina | Italian | 23

BRIDGEWATER

Cafe Emilia | Italian | 22
Z McCormick/Schmick | Seafood | 20
Thai Kitchen | Thai | 23

CHATHAM

New Main | *Thai*	23
☑ Scalini Fedeli | *Italian*	27
☑ Serenade | *French*	27
Taste of Asia | *Malaysian*	21

CHESTER

Benito's | *Italian*	24

CONVENT STATION

Rod's Steak | *Steak*	21

CRANBURY

Cranbury Inn | *Amer.*	17

DENVILLE

Cafe Metro | *Eclectic*	21
Hunan Taste | *Chinese*	23
Midori | *Jap.*	24
Rattlesnake Ranch | *SW*	16

DOVER

Quiet Man | *Pub*	22

EAST BRUNSWICK

Bombay Gardens | *Indian*	22
NEW Gusto Grill | *Amer.*	–
Shogun | *Jap./Steak*	18
Wasabi | *Jap.*	24

EAST HANOVER

Luigi's | *Italian*	19
Mr. Chu | *Chinese*	22
Penang | *Malaysian*	20
Saffron | *Indian*	23

EDISON

Akbar | *Indian*	18
☑ Cheesecake Fact. | *Amer.*	19
Grand Shanghai | *Pan-Asian*	21
Jack Cooper's | *Deli*	19
Java Moon | *Amer.*	19
LouCás | *Italian/Seafood*	24
Meemah | *Chinese/Malaysian*	24
Ming | *Asian*	23
Moghul | *Indian*	24
NEW Moksha | *Indian*	22
Penang | *Malaysian*	20
NEW Skylark Diner | *Amer.*	19
Wonder Seafood | *Chinese*	24

FLANDERS

Silver Spring | *French*	23

FRANKLIN PARK

Aroma Royal Thai | *Thai*	22

GLADSTONE

Opah Grille | *Seafood*	24

GREEN BROOK

Shogun | *Jap./Steak*	18

HIGHLAND PARK

Pad Thai | *Thai*	22
NEW Pithari Taverna | *Greek*	–
Seven Hills | *Med./Turkish*	21

HILLSBOROUGH

Cafe Graziella | *Italian*	22
NEW ☑ CoccoLa | *Amer./Italian*	22
☑ Old Man Rafferty | *Amer.*	19
Pheasants Land. | *Continental*	17
Thai Kitchen | *Thai*	23

ISELIN

Casa Giuseppe | *Italian*	24
Chowpatty | *Indian*	–

LAKE HIAWATHA

Bosphorus | *Turkish*	22

MADISON

Garlic Rose | *Eclectic*	21
☑ Il Mondo | *Italian*	25
Shanghai Jazz | *Chinese*	21
Soho 33 | *Amer.*	19

MANVILLE

GRUB Hut | *BBQ*	–

MENDHAM

Black Horse | *Pub*	19
Dante's | *Italian*	21
Sammy's Cider | *Steak*	21

METUCHEN

NEW Alessio 426 | *Continental*	20
Metuchen Inn | *Amer.*	22

MEYERSVILLE

Casa Maya | *Mex.*	20
NEW Meyersville Inn | *Amer.*	–

LOCATIONS

MILLTOWN

Fresco Steak | *Seafood/Steak* 23

MONROE TOWNSHIP

NEW Europa at Monroe | *Med.* –

MONTVILLE

Columbia Inn | *Pizza* 20

MORRIS PLAINS

☑ Arthur's Steak/Tavern | *Steak* 18

Hunan Chinese | *Chinese* 23

MORRISTOWN

Andaman | *French/Thai* 23
Cinque Figlie | *Italian* 21
Copeland | *Amer.* 25
☑ Grand Cafe | *French* 25
La Campagna | *Italian* 24
NEW Mehndi | *Indian* –
Ming | *Asian* 23
Ora | *Amer.* 20
☑ Origin | *French/Thai* 26
Pamir | *Afghan* 21
Pierre's | *French* 23
Settebello Cafe | *Italian* 22
Sirin | *Thai* 22
Sushi Lounge | *Jap.* 24
NEW Tashmoo | *Pub* –
Tim Schafer's | *Amer.* 25

MOUNTAIN LAKES

☑ South City Grill | *Amer.* 23

NEW BRUNSWICK

NEW ☑ Catherine Lombardi | *Italian* 21
Clydz | *Amer.* 23
Delta's | *Southern* 22
☑ Frog & Peach | *Amer.* 26
Makeda | *Ethiopian* 23
Nova Terra | *Pan-Latin* 22
Old Bay | *Cajun/Creole* 17
☑ Old Man Rafferty | *Amer.* 19
Panico's | *Italian* 24
NEW Piquant Bread B&G | *Indian* –
SoHo on George | *Amer.* 23

☑ Stage Left | *Amer.* 26
NEW Verdigre | *Amer.* 22

NORTH BRUNSWICK

☑ Arthur's Steak/Tavern | *Steak* 18
Noodle House | *Asian* 19

OLD BRIDGE

A Tavola | *Italian* 23
Big Ed's BBQ | *BBQ* 17
Pine Tavern | *Amer.* 22

PARSIPPANY

Chand Palace | *Indian* 22
Eccola | *Italian* 23
☑ Ruth's Chris | *Steak* 24

PEAPACK

Limestone Cafe | *Amer.* 22

PERTH AMBOY

Portuguese Manor | *Portug./Spanish* 21

PINE BROOK

Don Pepe | *Portug./Spanish* 21
Don Pepe's Steak | *Steak* 22

PISCATAWAY

Al Dente | *Italian* 23
Malabar House | *Indian* –

PLAINSBORO

Tre Piani | *Italian/Med.* 21

RANDOLPH

An American Grill | *Amer.* 21
La Strada | *Italian* 22

RARITAN

Acqua | *Italian* 21
Espo's | *Italian* 21

RIVERDALE

Rosemary & Sage | *Amer.* 26

ROCKY HILL

NEW One 53 | *Italian* –

SKILLMAN

Ya Ya Noodles | *Chinese* –

SOMERSET

Chao Phaya | *Thai* — 23
Sophie's Bistro | *French* — 22

SOMERVILLE

Chao Phaya | *Thai* — 23
da Filippo | *Italian/Seafood* — 24
La Scala | *Italian* — 22
Martino's | *Cuban* — 21
Melting Pot | *Fondue* — 19
☑ Origin | *French/Thai* — 26
Shumi | *Jap.* — 25
Thai Chef | *Thai* — 21
Verve | *Amer./French* — 23
Wasabi | *Jap.* — 24

SOUTH BRUNSWICK

Sens Asian | *Asian* — 22

STIRLING

Thai Thai | *Thai* — 25

WARREN

Jose's Mexican | *Mex.* — 19

WHIPPANY

Il Capriccio | *Italian* — 26
Melting Pot | *Fondue* — 19
Nikko | *Jap.* — 24

WOODBRIDGE

Mie Thai | *Thai* — 25

North Shore

ABERDEEN

Mahzu | *Jap.* — 22

ALLENTOWN

Black Forest | *German* — 19

ASBURY PARK

☑ Bistro Olé | *Portug./Spanish* — 25
NEW Brickwall Tav. | *Amer.* — 19
Harrison | *Amer.* — 24
Jimmy's | *Italian* — 24
La Tapatia | *Mex.* — –
NEW Market/Mid. | *Eclectic* — 23
☑ Moonstruck | *Med.* — 24
Posillipo | *Italian* — 22
Sister Sue's | *Carib.* — 21
☑ Taka | *Jap.* — 26

ATLANTIC HIGHLANDS

BoBo's 33 | *Mideast.* — 22
Copper Canyon | *SW* — 25
Gianna's | *Italian* — 25
Indigo Moon | *French* — 26
Memphis Pig Out | *BBQ* — 19
NEW Sapo Verde | *Mex.* — –

AVON-BY-THE-SEA

Avon Pavilion | *Amer.* — 18
Clementine's | *Creole* — 24

BARNEGAT

Brannon's Hurricane | *Amer.* — 21

BAY HEAD

NEW Bay Head Bistro | *Amer.* — 21
Grenville | *Amer.* — 21

BEACH HAVEN

☑ Gables, The | *Eclectic* — 26
Harvey Cedars | *Seafood* — 22
Roberto's Dolce | *Italian* — 22
Tuckers | *Amer.* — 18

BELMAR

Brandl. | *Amer.* — 24
Casa Solar | *Pan-Latin* — 25
Kaya's Kitchen | *Veg.* — –
Klein's Fish Market | *Seafood* — 20
Matisse | *Amer.* — 22

BRADLEY BEACH

Bamboo Leaf | *Thai/Viet.* — 24
Bella Sogno | *Italian* — 21
La Nonna/Piancone's | *Italian* — 18
Vic's | *Pizza* — 20

BRICK

Ikko | *Jap.* — 22
Java Moon | *Amer.* — 19
Mexico Lindo | *Mex.* — 28
Villa Vittoria | *Italian* — 22

BRIELLE

La Nonna/Piancone's | *Italian* — 18
Shipwreck Grill | *Amer.* — 25

COLTS NECK

Christopher's | *Amer.* — 21
I Cavallini | *Italian* — 25

EATONTOWN

☑ Far East Taste | *Chinese/Thai* 26
Sawa Steak | *Jap.* 22

FAIR HAVEN

Le Fandy | *French* 26
☑ Nauvoo Grill | *Amer.* 16
Raven & Peach | *Amer.* 24

FREEHOLD

☑ El Meson | *Mex.* 24
Federici's | *Pizza* 21
La Cipollina | *Italian* 23
Main St. Bistro | *Amer.* 21
Metropolitan Cafe | *Asian/Eclectic* 22
Oyako Tso's | *Jap.* 21

FREEHOLD TOWNSHIP

Aangan | *Indian* 23
Cafe Coloré | *Italian* 21
Ferrari's | *Italian* 22
Frankie Fed's | *Italian* 20
Ginger Thai | *Thai* 15
Mahzu | *Jap.* 22

HARVEY CEDARS

NEW Caneel Bay | *Carib.* 17
Harvey Cedars | *Seafood* 22
Plantation | *Amer.* 19

HAZLET

Aligado Asian | *Jap./Thai* 23

HIGHLANDS

Bahrs Landing | *Seafood* 15
☑ Bay Ave. Trattoria | *Amer./Italian* 28
Chilangos | *Mex.* 21
Doris & Ed's | *Amer.* 25
Inlet Café | *Seafood* 19
NEW Neil's Original Oyster | *Amer./Seafood* –
Windansea | *Seafood* 20

HOLMDEL

☑ It's Greek To Me | *Greek* 18
K.O.B.E. | *Jap.* 25

HOWELL

Bamboo Leaf | *Thai/Viet.* 24
Cabin | *Amer.* 18

Christie's | *Italian* 24
Juanito's | *Mex.* 23
Sushi by Kazu | *Jap.* 28

ISLAND HEIGHTS

Olde Corner Deli | *Deli* 26

JACKSON

Java Moon | *Amer.* 19
Solo Bella | *Italian* 21

KEYPORT

Drew's Bayshore | *Amer.* 28

LAVALLETTE

Crab's Claw | *Seafood* 17

LITTLE SILVER

Ray's Little Silver | *Seafood* 23
NEW Table | *Amer.* –

LONG BEACH TOWNSHIP

NEW daddy O | *Amer.* 18

LONG BRANCH

NEW ☑ Avenue | *French* 22
Charley's | *Amer.* 19
☑ It's Greek To Me | *Greek* 18
McLoone's | *Amer.* 17
Pearl of the Sea | *Portug.* 18
Richard's | *Deli* 20
Rooney's | *Seafood* 18
Sawa Steak | *Jap.* 22
NEW ☑ Sirena | *Italian* 23
Tuzzio's | *Italian* 21

MANAHAWKIN

Mud City | *Seafood* 21

MANALAPAN

Java Moon | *Amer.* 19
Konbu | *Jap.* 25
Michael's Cucina | *Italian* 19
Spargo's Grille | *Amer.* 25

MANASQUAN

Bayou Cafe | *Cajun/Creole* 23
Mahogany Grille | *Amer.* 23
Squan Tavern | *Italian* 19
Surf Taco | *Mex.* 20

MARLBORO

Brioso	*Italian*	23
Crown Palace	*Chinese*	22
Jerry & Harvey's	*Deli*	18
Pino's La Forchetta	*Italian*	18

MATAWAN

Aby's Mexican	*Mex.*	22
Buttonwood Manor	*Amer.*	18
West Lake	*Chinese*	25

MIDDLETOWN

Anna's Italian	*Italian*	22
Bistro San Miguel	*Filipino*	-
China Palace	*Taiwanese*	-
Crown Palace	*Chinese*	22
Lincroft Inn	*Continental*	18
Navesink Fishery	*Seafood*	24
Neelam	*Indian*	18
☑ Nicholas	*Amer.*	29
Sono Sushi	*Jap.*	26

MILLSTONE

Luchento's	*Italian*	20

MONMOUTH BEACH

Sallee Tee's	*Amer./Eclectic*	21

NEPTUNE CITY

Brennan's Steak	*Steak*	22
Pete & Elda's	*Pizza*	-

NORMANDY BEACH

Labrador	*Eclectic*	23

OAKHURST/OCEAN TOWNSHIP

Manhattan Steak	*Steak*	22
NEW Takara	*Jap.*	25

POINT PLEASANT

Capt'n Ed's	*Seafood/Steak*	19
Clark's Landing	*Amer.*	17

POINT PLEASANT BEACH

BayPoint Prime	*Steak*	24
Europa South	*Portug./Spanish*	20
Latitude 40N	*Seafood*	23
Red's Lobster	*Seafood*	24
Spike's	*Seafood*	22
Surf Taco	*Mex.*	20

RED BANK

Basil T's	*Amer./Italian*	20
Bienvenue	*French*	24
Bistro at Red Bank	*Eclectic*	21
Dish	*Amer.*	22
Echo	*Eclectic*	19
Eurasian Eatery	*Eclectic*	20
Gaetano's	*Italian*	19
Juanito's	*Mex.*	23
La Pastaria	*Italian*	19
Melting Pot	*Fondue*	19
Molly Pitcher	*Amer.*	22
Osteria Dante	*Med.*	19
Red	*Amer.*	20
Savanna	*Spanish*	20
Siam Garden	*Thai*	23
Sogno	*Italian*	23
Teak	*Pan-Asian*	23
NEW Thyme Square	*Med.*	21
Two If By Sea	*Amer.*	22
2Senza	*Med.*	20

RUMSON

Barnacle Bill's	*Hamburgers*	21
NEW ☑ David Burke	*Amer.*	26
Salt Creek	*Amer.*	20
What's Your Beef?	*Steak*	20

SEA BRIGHT

Anjelica's	*Italian*	25
Harry's Lobster	*Seafood*	22
McLoone's	*Amer.*	17
Yumi	*Pan-Asian*	26

SEA GIRT

Rod's Olde Irish	*Pub*	19

SHIP BOTTOM

La Spiaggia	*Italian*	26
Raimondo's	*Italian*	23

SHREWSBURY

Java Moon	*Amer.*	19
Pasta Fresca Café	*Amer.*	22
San Remo	*Italian*	22

SOUTH SEASIDE PARK

Atlantic B&G	*Amer./Seafood*	24
Berkeley	*Seafood*	18
Surf Taco	*Mex.*	20

LOCATIONS

SPRING LAKE

Black Trumpet	*Amer.*	23
Island Palm Grill	*Amer.*	18
Z Whispers	*Amer.*	27

SPRING LAKE HEIGHTS

Jose's	*Mex.*	22
Mill	*Amer.*	20

STAFFORD

NEW Octopus's Gard.	*Seafood*	22

SURF CITY

Blue	*Amer./Eclectic*	23
Yellow Fin	*Amer.*	25

TINTON FALLS

NEW Asia Star	*Pan-Asian*	–
Portofino	*Italian*	25

TOMS RIVER

Bistro 44	*Amer./French*	25
Slowly	*Amer.*	23

TOMS RIVER TOWNSHIP

Aamantran	*Indian*	23
El Familiar	*Colombian/Mex.*	–
Java Moon	*Amer.*	19
Nobi	*Jap.*	25
Shogun	*Jap./Steak*	18

WALL

Java Moon	*Amer.*	19
Scarborough Fair	*Amer.*	20
NEW Sumo	*Jap.*	–

South Shore

ATLANTIC CITY

Angelo's	*Italian*	20
NEW Bobby Flay Steak	*Steak*	24
NEW Buddakan	*Pan-Asian*	–
Capriccio	*Italian*	25
Carmine's	*Italian*	20
Chef Vola's	*Italian*	26
NEW Continental	*Amer.*	–
Corky's	*BBQ*	16
Cuba Libre	*Cuban*	21
Dock's Oyster	*Seafood*	26
Fantasea Reef	*Eclectic*	17

NEW Gallagher's Steak	*Steak*	22
Girasole	*Italian*	25
House of Blues	*Southern*	16
Irish Pub	*Irish*	18
Jonathan's	*Eclectic*	22
Los Amigos	*Mex.*	23
Mia	*Italian*	26
Old Homestead	*Steak*	25
Z Ombra	*Italian*	25
Palm	*Steak*	24
Z P.F. Chang's	*Chinese*	21
NEW Phillips Seafood	*Seafood*	–
Red Square	*Eclectic/Russian*	–
NEW Z SeaBlue	*Seafood*	27
NEW Sonsie	*Eclectic*	–
Specchio	*Italian*	25
NEW Tony Luke's	*Sandwiches*	–
Tun Tavern	*Amer.*	18
Z White House	*Sandwiches*	27
NEW Wolfgang Puck	*Amer.*	23

AVALON

Cafe Loren	*Amer.*	25

BRIGANTINE

Laguna Grill	*Amer./Eclectic*	22

CAPE MAY

Alexander's	*French*	24
Axelsson's	*Seafood*	22
Blue Pig Tavern	*Amer.*	20
Copper Fish	*Amer./Seafood*	20
Cucina Rosa	*Italian*	23
Z Ebbitt Room	*Amer.*	27
Z 410 Bank St.	*Creole*	27
Frescos	*Italian/Med.*	24
Lobster House	*Seafood*	20
NEW Lucky Bones	*Amer.*	18
Mad Batter	*Amer.*	21
Merion Inn	*Amer.*	20
Z Peter Shields	*Amer.*	26
Tisha's	*Amer.*	25
Ugly Mug	*Amer.*	16
Z Union Park	*Amer.*	26
Z Washington Inn	*Amer.*	26

CLERMONT

Karen & Rei's	*Amer.*	27

EGG HARBOR

Renault Winery | *Amer.* 22
Tre Figlio | *Italian* 24

GALLOWAY

☑ Ram's Head Inn | *Amer.* 26

GALLOWAY TOWNSHIP

Athenian Gdn. | *Greek* 23

LINWOOD

Barrel's | *Italian* 19

MARGATE

Barrel's | *Italian* 19
Bobby Chez | *Seafood* 25
LoBianco | *Amer.* 25
Steve & Cookie's | *Amer.* 25
Tomatoes | *Calif./Eclectic* 24
Ventura's | *Italian* 17

NORTH WILDWOOD

Claude's | *French* 25

OCEAN CITY

Nag's Head | *Amer.* 26

SEA ISLE CITY

Busch's Seafood | *Seafood* 19

SMITHVILLE

Smithville Inn | *Amer.* 18

SOMERS POINT

Crab Trap | *Seafood* 21
Sails | *Eclectic* 18
Tucker's Steak | *Seafood/Steak* 19

WEST CAPE MAY

☑ Black Duck | *Eclectic* 26

WILDWOOD

Marie Nicole's | *Amer.* 23

Delaware Valley

ALLAMUCHY

Mattar's | *Amer./Eclectic* 24

FLEMINGTON

NEW Blue Fish | *Seafood* 20
California Grill | *Eclectic* 20

Matt's Red Roost. | *Amer.* 25
Shaker Cafe | *Amer./Eclectic* ‒

FRENCHTOWN

Frenchtown Inn | *Eclectic/French* 23

HACKETTSTOWN

NEW Sultan's | *Turkish* ‒

HAMBURG

Restaurant Latour | *Amer.* ‒

HAMILTON

☑ Rat's | *French* 24

HIGH BRIDGE

Casa Maya | *Mex.* 20
Circa | *French* 20

HOPE

Inn at Millrace | 21
    Amer./Continental

HOPEWELL

NEW ☑ Blue Bottle | *Amer.* 27
Brothers Moon | *French* 22

LAMBERTVILLE

Anton's/Swan | *Amer.* 22
Bell's | *Amer./Italian* 19
Full Moon | *Eclectic* 17
Hamilton's Grill | *Med.* 24
Inn/Hawke | *Amer.* 18
Lambertville Stat. | *Amer.* 17
Lilly's on Canal | *Eclectic* 21
Manon | *French* 25
No. 9 | *Amer.* 24
Ota-Ya | *Jap.* 23
Rick's | *Italian* ‒
Siam | *Thai* 21
Tortuga's | *Mex.* 21

LAWRENCE

Lawrenceville Inn | *Amer.* 22

LAWRENCEVILLE

Acacia | *Amer.* 25
Elements Asia | *Pan-Asian* 23
Fedora Cafe | *Eclectic* 19
Java Moon | *Amer.* 19
Passage to India | *Indian* 23
Simply Radish. | *Amer.* 18

MILFORD

Milford Oyster House | *Seafood* –
Ship Inn | *Pub* 19

NEWTON

☑ André's | *Amer.* 27
Bula World Cuisine | *Eclectic* 23

OLDWICK

Tewksbury Inn | *Amer.* 22

PENNINGTON

Edo Sushi | *Chinese/Jap.* 20

PRINCETON

☑ Ajihei | *Jap.* 26
Alchemist/Barrister | *Amer.* 16
☑ Blue Point | *Seafood* 25
Conte's | *Pizza* –
☑ Ferry House | *Amer./French* 25
Ichiban | *Jap.* 17
Lahiere's | *Amer.* 21
Main St. Euro-Amer. | *Amer.* 18
Mediterra | *Med.* 20
Teresa's Cafe | *Italian* 21
Tortuga's | *Mex.* 21
Triumph Brewing | *Eclectic* 18
NEW Underground Café | 13
  E Euro.
Yankee Doodle | *Amer.* 14

RINGOES

Harvest Moon | *Amer.* 24

ROSEMONT

Cafe at Rosemont | *Amer.* 22

SERGEANTSVILLE

Sergeantsville Inn | *Amer.* 23

SPARTA

☑ Zoe's | *French* 26

STANHOPE

Bell's Mansion | *Amer.* 18
☑ Black Forest Inn | 23
  Continental/German

STOCKHOLM

NEW Savannah's | *Eclectic* –

STOCKTON

Meil's | *Amer.* 23

TRENTON

Amici Milano | *Italian* 22
Blue Danube | *E Euro.* 22
☑ DeLorenzo's | *Pizza* 28
Homestead Inn | *Italian* 23
John Henry's | *Seafood* 21
Marsilio's | *Italian* 22

UNION TOWNSHIP

Grand Colonial | *Eclectic* 25
☑ Perryville Inn | *Amer.* 26

WALLPACK CENTER

Walpack Inn | *Amer.* 19

WEST WINDSOR

Penang | *Malaysian* 20
Sunny Garden | *Chinese* 22

WHITEHOUSE STATION

Ixora | *French/Jap.* 25

Suburban Philly Area

AUDUBON

NEW Alphabet Soup | *Amer.* –

BERLIN

Filomena | *Italian* 20

BORDENTOWN

Farnsworth Hse. | *Continental* 21
Mastoris | *Diner* 19

BURLINGTON

Big Ed's BBQ | *BBQ* 17
Café Gallery | *Continental* 21

CHERRY HILL

Alisa Cafe | *French* 22
Athens Café | *Greek* 19
Bahama Breeze | *Carib.* 17
Barone's | *Italian* 20
Bobby Chez | *Seafood* 25
Caffe Aldo | *Italian* 23
Champa Laos | *French/Thai* 23
☑ Cheesecake Fact. | *Amer.* 19

Elephant & Castle	*Pub*	11
Emerald Fish	*Seafood*	23
Italian Bistro	*Italian*	17
Kibitz Room	*Deli*	24
La Campagne	*French*	24
Megu Sushi	*Jap.*	22
☑ Mélange Cafe	*Creole*	26
Mikado	*Jap.*	22
Norma's Med.	*Mideast.*	21
Oasis Grill	*Moroccan*	25
P.J. Whelihan's	*Amer.*	17
Ponzio's	*Diner*	16
Sakura Spring	*Chinese/Jap.*	23
Siri's Thai French	*French/Thai*	25

CLEMENTON

| Filomena | *Italian* | 20 |

COLLINGSWOOD

Barone's	*Italian*	20
Bobby Chez	*Seafood*	25
NEW Casona	*Cuban*	24
Nunzio	*Italian*	23
Pop Shop	*Amer.*	18
☑ Sagami	*Jap.*	26
Sapori	*Italian*	24
Tortilla Press	*Mex.*	23
Water Lily	*Asian/French*	24
Word of Mouth	*Amer.*	24

DEPTFORD

| Filomena | *Italian* | 20 |

GIBBSBORO

| Chophouse, The | *Chops/Seafood* | 23 |

HADDONFIELD

| Little Tuna | *Seafood* | 20 |
| P.J. Whelihan's | *Amer.* | 17 |

HADDON HEIGHTS

NEW Anthony's	*Italian*	23
Elements Café	*Amer.*	21
Kunkel's	*Seafood/Steak*	20

LINDENWOLD

| La Esperanza | *Mex.* | 24 |

MAPLE SHADE

Mikado	*Jap.*	22
P.J. Whelihan's	*Amer.*	17
Posh	*Asian/French*	23
Tacconelli's	*Pizza*	20

MARLTON

Food for Thought	*Amer.*	24
Gagan Bistro	*Indian*	-
Joe's Peking	*Chinese*	23
Mexican Food	*Mex.*	18
Mikado	*Jap.*	22
☑ P.F. Chang's	*Chinese*	21
Pizzicato	*Italian*	21

MEDFORD

| Beau Rivage | *Continental/French* | 22 |
| Braddock's | *Amer.* | 22 |

MEDFORD LAKES

| P.J. Whelihan's | *Amer.* | 17 |

MOORESTOWN

| Barnacle Ben's | *Seafood* | 19 |
| Barone's | *Italian* | 20 |

MOUNT HOLLY

| High Street Grill | *Amer.* | 23 |
| Robin's Nest | *Amer.* | 22 |

MOUNT LAUREL

Bobby Chez	*Seafood*	25
El Azteca	*Mex.*	21
Pacific Grille	*Pac. Rim*	20

NEW GRETNA

| Allen's Clam | *Seafood* | - |

PENNSAUKEN

| Pub | *Steak* | 18 |

SEWELL

Blue Eyes	*Steak*	20
Creole Cafe	*Cajun/Creole*	27
P.J. Whelihan's	*Amer.*	17

VOORHEES

| Bobby Chez | *Seafood* | 25 |
| Catelli | *Italian* | 24 |

Chez Elena Wu	*Asian/French*	24
Coconut Bay	*Asian*	21
Laceno Italian	*Italian/Seafood*	25
Little Café	*Eclectic*	25
Ritz Seafood	*Seafood*	24
Somsak/Taan	*Thai*	23

WEST BERLIN

Los Amigos	*Mex.*	23

WESTMONT

Cork	*Amer.*	21
Giumarello's	*Italian*	25
NEW Kitchen 233	*Amer./French*	22

Special Features

Listings cover the best in each category and include restaurant names, locations and Food ratings. Multi-location restaurants' features may vary by branch. ⊠ indicates places with the highest ratings, popularity and importance.

BREAKFAST

(See also Hotel Dining)

Avon Pavilion | **Avon-by-Sea**	18
Brannon's Hurricane | **Barnegat**	21
Christopher's | **Colts Neck**	21
Country Pancake | **Ridgewood**	19
Eppes Essen | **Livingston**	18
Full Moon | **Lambertville**	17
Java Moon | **multi. loc.**	19
Je's | **Newark**	26
Meil's | **Stockton**	23
Ponzio's | **Cherry Hill**	16
Zafra | **Hoboken**	24

BRUNCH

⊠ Amanda's | **Hoboken**	26
Anthony David's | **Hoboken**	25
Braddock's | **Medford**	22
Brothers Moon | **Hopewell**	22
Cafe at Rosemont | **Rosemont**	22
Café Gallery | **Burlington**	21
⊠ Chart House | **Weehawken**	20
Court Street | **Hoboken**	21
Crown Palace | **multi. loc.**	22
Frenchtown Inn | **Frenchtown**	23
Grenville | **Bay Hd.**	21
Grill 73 | **Bernardsville**	22
Harvest Bistro | **Closter**	22
Labrador | **Normandy Bch**	23
La Campagne | **Cherry Hill**	24
Lambertville Stat. | **Lambertville**	17
Madame Claude | **Jersey City**	23
Marco & Pepe | **Jersey City**	22
Molly Pitcher | **Red Bank**	22
Napa Valley | **Paramus**	22
⊠ Rat's | **Hamilton**	24
Restaurant | **Hackensack**	21
Taqueria | **Jersey City**	20
Terrace Rest. | **Short Hills**	22
Tortilla Press | **Collingswood**	23

Verjus | **Maplewood**	25
Zafra | **Hoboken**	24

BUFFET SERVED

(Check availability)

Aamantran | **Toms River Twp**	23
Aangan | **Freehold Twp**	23
Akbar | **Edison**	18
NEW Alessio 426 | **Metuchen**	20
Allendale B&G | **Allendale**	16
Amiya | **Jersey City**	21
Assembly Steak | **Englewood Cliffs**	16
Bistro San Miguel | **Middletown**	-
⊠ Black Forest Inn | **Stanhope**	23
NEW Bombay Curry | **Basking Ridge**	-
Bombay Gardens | **E Brunswick**	22
Café Gallery | **Burlington**	21
Chand Palace | **Parsippany**	22
Copeland | **Morristown**	25
Fantasea Reef | **A.C.**	17
Gagan Bistro | **Marlton**	-
House of Blues | **A.C.**	16
Hunt Club | **Summit**	20
India on Hudson | **Hoboken**	19
⊠ Karma Kafe | **Hoboken**	25
Kaya's Kitchen | **Belmar**	-
Lambertville Stat. | **Lambertville**	17
Madeleine's | **Northvale**	24
Madison B&G | **Hoboken**	21
⊠ Manor | **W Orange**	23
Matisse | **Belmar**	22
McLoone's | **multi. loc.**	17
NEW Mehndi | **Morristown**	-
Mill | **Spring Lake Hts**	20
Moghul | **Edison**	24
NEW Moksha | **Edison**	22
Molly Pitcher | **Red Bank**	22
Neelam | **multi. loc.**	18
Noodle House | **N Brunswick**	19

Old Man Rafferty	**New Bruns.**	19
Passage to India	**Lawrenceville**	23
Pierre's	**Morristown**	23
Raagini	**Mountainside**	22
Rod's Steak	**Convent Station**	21
Saffron	**E Hanover**	23
Salt Creek	**Rumson**	20
NEW Savannah's	**Stockholm**	–
Shanghai Jazz	**Madison**	21
Smithville Inn	**Smithville**	18
Strip House	**Livingston**	23
Terrace Rest.	**Short Hills**	22

BUSINESS DINING

Assembly Steak	**Englewood Cliffs**	16
Z Chez Catherine	**Westfield**	27
Copeland	**Morristown**	25
NEW Z David Burke	**Rumson**	26
Z Dining Room	**Short Hills**	26
Z Fascino	**Montclair**	26
Fiorino	**Summit**	23
NEW Gallagher's Steak	**A.C.**	22
Z Highlawn Pavil.	**W Orange**	24
Ho-Ho-Kus Inn	**Ho-Ho-Kus**	21
I Cavallini	**Colts Neck**	25
Il Tulipano	**Cedar Grove**	23
Jamie's Restaurant	**Clifton**	–
NEW Kitchen 233	**Westmont**	22
K.O.B.E.	**Holmdel**	25
Lawrenceville Inn	**Lawrence Twp**	22
Lu Nello	**Totowa**	25
Manhattan Steak	**Oakhurst**	22
Mill	**Spring Lake Hts**	20
NEW Moksha	**Edison**	22
Morton's Steak	**Hackensack**	24
Old Homestead	**A.C.**	25
Ora	**Morristown**	20
Panico's	**New Bruns.**	24
Passage to India	**Lawrenceville**	23
NEW Phillips Seafood	**A.C.**	–
Pierre's	**Morristown**	23
Z Pluckemin Inn	**Bedminster**	25
Portofino	**Tinton Falls**	25
Raven & Peach	**Fair Haven**	24
Z River Palm	**multi. loc.**	25

NEW Roots Steak	**Summit**	–
NEW Z Sirena	**Long Branch**	23
Smoke Chophouse	**Englewood**	22
Specchio	**A.C.**	25
Stony Hill Inn	**Hackensack**	23
Vine	**Basking Ridge**	22
Wasabi	**Somerville**	24

BYO

Aamantran	**Toms River Twp**	23
Aangan	**Freehold Twp**	23
Aby's Mexican	**Matawan**	22
Acacia	**Lawrenceville**	25
NEW Addiwan	**Montclair**	18
Z Ajihei	**Princeton**	26
Alan@594	**Upper Montclair**	20
Aldo & Gianni	**S Hackensack**	21
NEW Alessio 426	**Metuchen**	20
Alexander's	**Cape May**	24
Ali Baba	**Hoboken**	20
Aligado Asian	**Hazlet**	23
Alisa Cafe	**Cherry Hill**	22
Allen's Clam	**New Gretna**	–
NEW Alphabet Soup	**Audubon**	–
NEW Amazing Hot Dog	**Verona**	22
Andaman	**Morristown**	23
Anjelica's	**Sea Bright**	25
Anna's Italian	**Middletown**	22
Anthony David's	**Hoboken**	25
NEW Anthony's	**Haddon Hts**	23
Z Aozora	**Montclair**	25
Aquila Cucina	**New Providence**	21
NEW Asia Star	**Tinton Falls**	–
A Tavola	**Old Bridge**	23
Athenian Gdn.	**Galloway Twp**	23
Athens Café	**Cherry Hill**	19
Avon Pavilion	**Avon-by-Sea**	18
Bamboo Leaf	**multi. loc.**	24
Barnacle Ben's	**Moorestown**	19
Barone's	**multi. loc.**	20
Barrel's	**multi. loc.**	19
Z Basilico	**Millburn**	23
Z Baumgart's Café	**multi. loc.**	19
Z Bay Ave. Trattoria	**Highlands**	28
NEW Bay Head Bistro	**Bay Hd.**	21
Bayou Cafe	**Manasquan**	23

BayPoint Prime | **Pt. Pleas. Bch**	24
Bazzini | **Ridgewood**	21
Bella Sogno | **Bradley Bch**	21
Benito's | **Chester**	24
Bienvenue | **Red Bank**	24
Bistro at Red Bank | **Red Bank**	21
Bistro 44 | **Toms River**	25
☑ Bistro Olé | **Asbury Pk**	25
Bistro San Miguel | **Middletown**	–
☑ Black Duck | **W Cape May**	26
Black Forest | **Allentown**	19
Black Trumpet | **Spring Lake**	23
Blu | **Montclair**	25
Blue | **Surf City**	23
NEW ☑ Blue Bottle | **Hopewell**	27
NEW Blue Fish | **Flemington**	20
☑ Blue Point | **Princeton**	25
NEW Blue Wave | **Westfield**	–
Bobby Chez | **multi. loc.**	25
BoBo's 33 | **Atlantic H.**	22
NEW Bombay Curry | **Basking Ridge**	–
Bombay Gardens | **E Brunswick**	22
Bosphorus | **Lake Hiawatha**	22
Boulevard Grille | **Mahwah**	18
Brandl. | **Belmar**	24
Brannon's Hurricane | **Barnegat**	21
Brioso | **Marlboro**	23
Brix 67 | **Summit**	18
Brooklyn's Pizza | **multi. loc.**	22
Brothers Moon | **Hopewell**	22
Bula World Cuisine | **Newton**	23
Cafe Arugula | **S Orange**	20
Cafe at Rosemont | **Rosemont**	22
Cafe Coloré | **Freehold Twp**	21
Cafe Graziella | **Hillsborough**	22
Cafe Loren | **Avalon**	25
☑ Cafe Matisse | **Rutherford**	27
Cafe Metro | **Denville**	21
☑ Cafe Panache | **Ramsey**	28
California Grill | **Flemington**	20
NEW Caneel Bay | **Harvey Cedars**	17
Capt'n Ed's | **Pt. Pleas.**	19
Casa Maya | **multi. loc.**	20
Casa Solar | **Belmar**	25
NEW Casona | **Collingswood**	24
Champa Laos | **Cherry Hill**	23
Chand Palace | **Parsippany**	22
Chao Phaya | **multi. loc.**	23
Charrito's | **multi. loc.**	24
☑ Chef's Table | **Franklin Lakes**	28
Chef Vola's | **A.C.**	26
Chez Elena Wu | **Voorhees**	24
Chophouse, The | **Gibbsboro**	23
Chowpatty | **Iselin**	–
Christie's | **Howell**	24
Christopher's | **Colts Neck**	21
Claude's | **N Wildwood**	25
Clementine's | **Avon-by-Sea**	24
Coconut Bay | **Voorhees**	21
Copeland | **Morristown**	25
Copper Canyon | **Atlantic H.**	25
Cork | **Westmont**	21
Corso 98 | **Montclair**	21
Creole Cafe | **Sewell**	27
NEW Cuban Pete's | **Montclair**	17
Cucina Rosa | **Cape May**	23
NEW ☑ CulinAriane | **Montclair**	27
Cup Joint | **Hoboken**	20
NEW DabbaWalla | **Summit**	19
da Filippo | **Somerville**	24
Dai-Kichi | **Upper Montclair**	22
Dante's | **Mendham**	21
Dayi'nin Yeri | **Cliffside Pk**	–
☑ DeLorenzo's | **Trenton**	28
Dim Sum Dynasty | **Ridgewood**	21
Doo Rae Myun Ok | **Fort Lee**	21
Drew's Bayshore | **Keyport**	28
Edo Sushi | **Pennington**	20
El Azteca | **Mt Laurel**	21
Elements Asia | **Lawrenceville**	23
Elements Café | **Haddon Hts**	21
El Familiar | **Toms River Twp**	–
☑ El Meson | **Freehold**	24
Emerald Fish | **Cherry Hill**	23
Epernay | **Montclair**	21
Eppes Essen | **Livingston**	18
Eurasian Eatery | **Red Bank**	20
☑ Far East Taste | **Eatontown**	26
☑ Fascino | **Montclair**	26
Fat Kat | **Little Ferry**	24
Fedora Cafe | **Lawrenceville**	19
Ferrari's | **Freehold Twp**	22

◨ Ferry House	**Princeton**	25
NEW 503 Park	**Scotch Plains**	20
Food for Thought	**Marlton**	24
◨ 410 Bank St.	**Cape May**	27
Frankie Fed's	**Freehold Twp**	20
Frescos	**Cape May**	24
Fresco Steak	**Milltown**	23
Full Moon	**Lambertville**	17
◨ Gables, The	**Beach Haven**	26
Gaetano's	**Red Bank**	19
Gagan Bistro	**Marlton**	–
NEW Gallagher's Steak	**A.C.**	22
Garlic Rose	**Madison**	21
NEW Gaucho Steak	**Montclair**	–
Gazelle Café	**Ridgewood**	–
Gianna's	**Atlantic H.**	25
Ginger & Spice	**Ramsey**	–
Ginger Thai	**Freehold Twp**	15
Girasole	**Bound Brook**	25
Grill 73	**Bernardsville**	22
GRUB Hut	**Manville**	–
NEW Habana Latin	**Ridgefield Pk**	–
Hamilton's Grill	**Lambertville**	24
Harvey Cedars	**multi. loc.**	22
Hunan Spring	**Springfield**	19
Ichiban	**Princeton**	17
Ikko	**Brick**	22
Il Forno Trattoria	**Montclair**	23
◨ Il Mondo	**Madison**	25
Indigo Moon	**Atlantic H.**	26
Indigo Smoke	**Montclair**	22
NEW Isabella's	**Westfield**	22
Island Palm Grill	**Spring Lake**	18
◨ It's Greek To Me	**multi. loc.**	18
Ixora	**Whitehouse Station**	25
Jack Cooper's	**Edison**	19
Java Moon	**multi. loc.**	19
Jerry & Harvey's	**Marlboro**	18
Joel's Malibu	**Ridgewood**	–
Joe's Peking	**Marlton**	23
Jose's	**Spring Lake Hts**	22
Jose's Mexican	**multi. loc.**	19
Juanito's	**multi. loc.**	23
Karen & Rei's	**Clermont**	27
Kaya's Kitchen	**Belmar**	–
Kibitz Room	**Cherry Hill**	24

K.O.B.E.	**Holmdel**	25
Konbu	**Manalapan**	25
Kunkel's	**Haddon Hts**	20
Labrador	**Normandy Bch**	23
La Campagna	**multi. loc.**	24
La Campagne	**Cherry Hill**	24
Laceno Italian	**Voorhees**	25
La Cipollina	**Freehold**	23
La Focaccia	**Summit**	24
◨ La Isla	**Hoboken**	26
La Pastaria	**multi. loc.**	19
La Scala	**Somerville**	22
La Spiaggia	**Ship Bottom**	26
La Tapatia	**Asbury Pk**	–
Latitude 40N	**Pt. Pleas. Bch**	23
◨ Latour	**Ridgewood**	27
Lawrenceville Inn	**Lawrence Twp**	22
Le Fandy	**Fair Haven**	26
◨ Le Rendez-Vous	**Kenilworth**	26
Lilly's on Canal	**Lambertville**	21
Limestone Cafe	**Peapack**	22
Little Café	**Voorhees**	25
Little Tuna	**Haddonfield**	20
LoBianco	**Margate**	25
Lodos	**New Milford**	21
Look See	**Ramsey**	19
◨ Lorena's	**Maplewood**	27
Lotus Cafe	**Hackensack**	24
LouCás	**Edison**	24
Luchento's	**Millstone**	20
Luka's	**Ridgefield Pk**	22
Lulu's Bistro	**Livingston**	21
Madame Claude	**Jersey City**	23
Mad Batter	**Cape May**	21
Magic Pot	**Edgewater**	19
Mahzu	**multi. loc.**	22
Main St. Bistro	**Freehold**	21
Malabar House	**Piscataway**	–
Mama Tucci	**Livingston**	–
Manon	**Lambertville**	25
Margherita's	**Hoboken**	22
Marra's	**Ridgewood**	20
Martino's	**Somerville**	21
Matisse	**Belmar**	22
Matt's Red Roost.	**Flemington**	25
Meemah	**Edison**	24

Megu Sushi | **Cherry Hill**	22	
Meil's | **Stockton**	23	
☑ Mélange Cafe | **Cherry Hill**	26	
Mexico Lindo | **Brick**	28	
NEW Meyersville Inn | **Meyersville**	–	
Michael's Cucina | **Manalapan**	19	
Midori | **Denville**	24	
Mie Thai | **Woodbridge**	25	
Mignon Steak | **Rutherford**	23	
Mikado | **multi. loc.**	22	
Ming | **Edison**	23	
Moghul | **Edison**	24	
☑ Mojave Grille | **Westfield**	24	
NEW Moksha | **Edison**	22	
Monster Sushi | **Summit**	19	
Mr. Chu | **E Hanover**	22	
Mud City | **Manahawkin**	21	
Navesink Fishery | **Middletown**	24	
NEW Nazmi's | **Cliffside Pk**	–	
Neelam | **multi. loc.**	18	
New Main | **Chatham**	23	
Nha Trang Place | **Jersey City**	24	
Niecy's | **S Orange**	20	
Nobi | **Toms River Twp**	25	
No. 9 | **Lambertville**	24	
Noodle House | **N Brunswick**	19	
Nori | **multi. loc.**	22	
Norma's Med. | **Cherry Hill**	21	
Nouveau Sushi | **Montclair**	25	
Nunzio | **Collingswood**	23	
Oasis Grill | **Cherry Hill**	25	
NEW Octopus's Gard. | **Stafford**	22	
Olde Corner Deli | **Island Hts**	26	
Ora | **Morristown**	20	
Orbis Bistro | **Upper Montclair**	22	
☑ Origin | **multi. loc.**	26	
Osteria Dante | **Red Bank**	19	
Osteria Giotto | **Montclair**	25	
Ota-Ya | **Lambertville**	23	
Oyako Tso's | **Freehold**	21	
Pacific Grille | **Mt Laurel**	20	
Pamir | **Morristown**	21	
NEW Passione | **Montclair**	23	
Pasta Fresca Café | **Shrewsbury**	22	
Penang | **multi. loc.**	20	
Peter Shields | **Cape May**	26	
Pho Thang Long | **Jersey City**	–	
NEW Piquant Bread B&G | **New Bruns.**	–	
NEW Pithari Taverna | **Highland Pk**	–	
Pizzicato | **Marlton**	21	
Pop Shop | **Collingswood**	18	
Raagini | **Mountainside**	22	
Radicchio | **Ridgewood**	23	
Raimondo's | **Ship Bottom**	23	
Raymond's | **Montclair**	21	
Ray's Little Silver | **Little Silver**	23	
Rebecca's | **Edgewater**	24	
Red's Lobster | **Pt. Pleas. Bch**	24	
NEW Restaurant L | **Allendale**	–	
Richard's | **Long Branch**	20	
Rick's | **Lambertville**	–	
Ritz Seafood | **Voorhees**	24	
Roberto's Dolce | **Beach Haven**	22	
Robongi | **Hoboken**	25	
Rocca | **Glen Rock**	22	
NEW Roots Steak | **Summit**	–	
Rosemary & Sage | **Riverdale**	26	
Ruga | **Oakland**	20	
☑ Ruth's Chris | **Weehawken**	24	
Sabor | **N Bergen**	22	
☑ Saddle River Inn | **Saddle R.**	27	
Saffron | **E Hanover**	23	
☑ Sagami | **Collingswood**	26	
Saigon R./Mo' Pho' | **multi. loc.**	24	
Sakura-Bana | **Ridgewood**	25	
Sakura Spring | **Cherry Hill**	23	
San Remo | **Shrewsbury**	22	
Sapori | **Collingswood**	24	
NEW Sapo Verde | **Atlantic H.**	–	
Savanna | **Red Bank**	20	
Sawa Steak | **multi. loc.**	22	
Sens Asian | **S Brunswick**	22	
☑ Serenade | **Chatham**	27	
Settebello Cafe | **Morristown**	22	
Seven Hills | **Highland Pk**	21	
Shaker Cafe | **Flemington**	–	
Shanghai Jazz | **Madison**	21	
Shumi | **Somerville**	25	
Siam | **Lambertville**	21	
Siam Garden | **Red Bank**	23	

SPECIAL FEATURES

Silver Oak Bistro | **Ridgewood**	23
Simply Radish. | **Lawrenceville**	18
NEW Z Sirena | **Long Branch**	23
Sirin | **Morristown**	22
Siri's Thai French | **Cherry Hill**	25
Sister Sue's | **Asbury Pk**	21
Slowly | **Toms River**	23
Smoke Chophouse | **Englewood**	22
Sogno | **Red Bank**	23
Soho 33 | **Madison**	19
Solo Bella | **Jackson**	21
Somsak/Taan | **Voorhees**	23
Sono Sushi | **Middletown**	26
Sophie's Bistro | **Somerset**	22
Soufflé | **Summit**	23
Spargo's Grille | **Manalapan**	25
Spike's | **Pt. Pleas. Bch**	22
Sri Thai | **Hoboken**	24
NEW Sultan's | **Hackettstown**	-
NEW Sumo | **Wall**	-
Sunny Garden | **W Windsor**	22
Surf Taco | **multi. loc.**	20
Sushi by Kazu | **Howell**	28
Table 8 | **Montclair**	23
Tacconelli's | **Maple Shade**	20
Z Taka | **Asbury Pk**	26
NEW Takara | **Ocean Twp**	25
Taqueria | **Jersey City**	20
Taro | **Montclair**	21
Taste of Asia | **Chatham**	21
Terra | **Maplewood**	20
Thai Chef | **multi. loc.**	21
Thai Kitchen | **multi. loc.**	23
Thai Thai | **Stirling**	25
Theresa's | **Westfield**	23
NEW Thyme Square | **Red Bank**	21
Tim Schafer's | **Morristown**	25
Tina Louise | **Carlstadt**	24
Tisha's | **Cape May**	25
Tomo's Cuisine | **Little Falls**	-
Tortilla Press | **Collingswood**	23
Tortuga's | **Princeton**	21
Tsuki | **Bernardsville**	22
Tuptim | **Montclair**	22
NEW Underground Café | **Princeton**	13
Z Union Park | **Cape May**	26

Village Gourmet | **Rutherford**	21
Village Green | **Ridgewood**	25
Wasabi | **E Brunswick**	24
Water Lily | **Collingswood**	24
West Lake | **Matawan**	25
Z Whispers | **Spring Lake**	27
Wild Ginger | **Englewood**	25
Wondee's Thai | **Hackensack**	-
Wonder Seafood | **Edison**	24
Word of Mouth | **Collingswood**	24
Ya Ya Noodles | **Skillman**	-
Yellow Fin | **Surf City**	25
Yumi | **Sea Bright**	26
Zafra | **Hoboken**	24

CATERING

Aamantran | **Toms River Twp**	23
Aangan | **Freehold Twp**	23
Z Amanda's | **Hoboken**	26
Andaman | **Morristown**	23
Z André's | **Newton**	27
Anjelica's | **Sea Bright**	25
Anthony David's | **Hoboken**	25
Athenian Gdn. | **Galloway Twp**	23
Athens Café | **Cherry Hill**	19
Z Augustino's | **Hoboken**	26
Barone's | **multi. loc.**	20
Z Bernards Inn | **Bernardsville**	26
Bombay Gardens | **E Brunswick**	22
Brannon's Hurricane | **Barnegat**	21
Brioso | **Marlboro**	23
Brothers Moon | **Hopewell**	22
Cafe Loren | **Avalon**	25
Z Cafe Matisse | **Rutherford**	27
Z Cafe Panache | **Ramsey**	28
Caffe Aldo | **Cherry Hill**	23
Casa Dante | **Jersey City**	22
Catelli | **Voorhees**	24
Chowpatty | **Iselin**	-
Z Cucharamama | **Hoboken**	26
da Filippo | **Somerville**	24
Dock's Oyster | **A.C.**	26
Doris & Ed's | **Highlands**	25
Eppes Essen | **Livingston**	18
Esty Street | **Park Ridge**	23
Z Far East Taste | **Eatontown**	26
Z Ferry House | **Princeton**	25

SPECIAL FEATURES

Porto Leggero | *M. Cetrulo, A. Stella* | **Jersey City**	23
☑ Scalini Fedeli | *Michael Cetrulo* | **Chatham**	27
NEW ☑ SeaBlue | *Michael Mina* | **A.C.**	27
☑ Serenade | *James Laird* | **Chatham**	27
Silver Oak Bistro | *Gary Needham* | **Ridgewood**	23
Specchio | *Luke Palladino* | **A.C.**	25
NEW Wolfgang Puck | *Wolfgang Puck* | **A.C.**	23
Zafra | *Maricel Presilla* | **Hoboken**	24

CHILD-FRIENDLY

(Alternatives to the usual fast-food places; * children's menu available)

Aby's Mexican* | **Matawan**	22
Alisa Cafe | **Cherry Hill**	22
☑ Amanda's | **Hoboken**	26
☑ André's | **Newton**	27
Anjelica's | **Sea Bright**	25
Athens Café | **Cherry Hill**	19
Axelsson's* | **Cape May**	22
Bahama Breeze* | **Cherry Hill**	17
Bamboo Leaf | **Bradley Bch**	24
Bareli's | **Secaucus**	23
Barone's* | **multi. loc.**	20
☑ Baumgart's Café* | **multi. loc.**	19
Bazzini* | **Ridgewood**	21
Bellissimo's | **Little Falls**	24
Bell's | **Lambertville**	19
Bell's Mansion* | **Stanhope**	18
Beyti Kebab | **Union City**	24
Big Ed's BBQ* | **multi. loc.**	17
☑ Black Duck | **W Cape May**	26
☑ Black Forest Inn | **Stanhope**	23
Blue | **Surf City**	23
☑ Blue Point* | **Princeton**	25
Bobby Chez | **multi. loc.**	25
Bombay Gardens | **E Brunswick**	22
Braddock's* | **Medford**	22
Brannon's Hurricane* | **Barnegat**	21
Brioso | **Marlboro**	23
Cabin* | **Howell**	18

Cafe Loren | **Avalon**	25
Caffe Aldo | **Cherry Hill**	23
Capriccio | **A.C.**	25
Casa Dante | **Jersey City**	22
Casa Giuseppe | **Iselin**	24
Casa Vasca | **Newark**	24
Catelli | **Voorhees**	24
Cenzino | **Oakland**	24
Chao Phaya | **Somerville**	23
☑ Cheesecake Fact. | **multi. loc.**	19
Chengdu 46 | **Clifton**	24
Christie's* | **Howell**	24
Clydz | **New Bruns.**	23
Copper Fish* | **Cape May**	20
☑ Cucharamama | **Hoboken**	26
da Filippo | **Somerville**	24
Dock's Oyster* | **A.C.**	26
E & V | **Paterson**	24
El Azteca* | **Mt Laurel**	21
Elements Café | **Haddon Hts**	21
Elephant & Castle* | **Cherry Hill**	11
☑ El Meson* | **Freehold**	24
Espo's* | **Raritan**	21
Esty Street | **Park Ridge**	23
☑ Far East Taste | **Eatontown**	26
Fat Kat* | **Little Ferry**	24
Filomena* | **multi. loc.**	20
Food for Thought | **Marlton**	24
☑ Fornos of Spain | **Newark**	23
☑ 410 Bank St. | **Cape May**	27
Frankie Fed's* | **Freehold Twp**	20
Frenchtown Inn | **Frenchtown**	23
☑ Grand Cafe | **Morristown**	25
Harvest Moon | **Ringoes**	24
Homestead Inn | **Trenton**	23
Ikko* | **Brick**	22
Indigo Moon | **Atlantic H.**	26
Inn/Hawke* | **Lambertville**	18
Italian Bistro* | **Cherry Hill**	17
☑ It's Greek To Me* | **multi. loc.**	18
Ixora | **Whitehouse Station**	25
Java Moon* | **multi. loc.**	19
Jonathan's* | **A.C.**	22
Kibitz Room* | **Cherry Hill**	24
La Campagne | **Cherry Hill**	24
Laceno Italian | **Voorhees**	25
La Esperanza* | **Lindenwold**	24

La Scala | **Somerville**	22
☑ Legal Sea Foods* | **multi. loc.**	20
Little Tuna | **Haddonfield**	20
Lu Nello | **Totowa**	25
☑ Manor | **W Orange**	23
Margherita's | **Hoboken**	22
Meil's | **Stockton**	23
☑ Mélange Cafe | **Cherry Hill**	26
Mexican Food* | **Marlton**	18
Mexico Lindo* | **Brick**	28
Midori | **Denville**	24
Mie Thai | **Woodbridge**	25
Mikado | **Cherry Hill**	22
Ming | **Edison**	23
Moghul | **Edison**	24
Mud City* | **Manahawkin**	21
Nag's Head* | **Ocean City**	26
Navesink Fishery | **Middletown**	24
New Main | **Chatham**	23
No. 9 | **Lambertville**	24
Norma's Med.* | **Cherry Hill**	21
Nunzio | **Collingswood**	23
Opah Grille* | **Gladstone**	24
Ota-Ya | **Lambertville**	23
Pacific Grille* | **Mt Laurel**	20
Panico's | **New Bruns.**	24
☑ Park & Orchard* | **E Rutherford**	22
Passage to India | **Lawrenceville**	23
☑ P.F. Chang's | **Marlton**	21
Pierre's | **Morristown**	23
Pizzicato | **Marlton**	21
Ponzio's* | **Cherry Hill**	16
Pop Shop* | **Collingswood**	18
Pub* | **Pennsauken**	18
Raimondo's* | **Ship Bottom**	23
☑ Ram's Head Inn* | **Galloway**	26
☑ Rat's | **Hamilton**	24
Rebecca's | **Edgewater**	24
Reservoir Tavern | **Boonton**	22
Ristorante Benito | **Union**	25
Ritz Seafood | **Voorhees**	24
Robongi | **Hoboken**	25
Rosemary & Sage | **Riverdale**	26
Ruga | **Oakland**	20
Sabor | **N Bergen**	22
Saffron | **E Hanover**	23

☑ Sagami | **Collingswood**	26
Saigon R./Mo' Pho' | **Englewood**	24
Sawa Steak* | **Eatontown**	22
Shipwreck Grill | **Brielle**	25
Shumi | **Somerville**	25
Siri's Thai French | **Cherry Hill**	25
Sister Sue's | **Asbury Pk**	21
Sogno | **Red Bank**	23
SoHo on George | **New Bruns.**	23
Somsak/Taan | **Voorhees**	23
Sono Sushi* | **Middletown**	26
Steve & Cookie's | **Margate**	25
Surf Taco* | **multi. loc.**	20
Sushi by Kazu | **Howell**	28
Thai Kitchen | **multi. loc.**	23
Thai Thai | **Stirling**	25
Theresa's* | **Westfield**	23
Tina Louise | **Carlstadt**	24
Tomatoes | **Margate**	24
Tortilla Press* | **Collingswood**	23
Tre Figlio* | **Egg Harbor**	24
Tuckers* | **Beach Haven**	18
Verjus | **Maplewood**	25
Wasabi | **multi. loc.**	24
West Lake | **Matawan**	25
☑ White House | **A.C.**	27
Wild Ginger | **Englewood**	25
Word of Mouth | **Collingswood**	24
Zafra | **Hoboken**	24
☑ Zoe's | **Sparta**	26

DANCING

Acqua | **Raritan**	21
Azúcar | **Jersey City**	19
Baja | **Jersey City**	20
Blueside Grill | **Englewood**	18
NEW Brickwall Tav. | **Asbury Pk**	19
Busch's Seafood | **Sea Isle City**	19
Cabin | **Howell**	18
Casa Dante | **Jersey City**	22
NEW ☑ CoccoLa | **Hillsborough**	22
Cuba Libre | **A.C.**	21
Delta's | **New Bruns.**	22
Echo | **Red Bank**	19
Filomena | **Berlin**	20
Hunt Club | **Summit**	20
Laguna Grill | **Brigantine**	22

SPECIAL FEATURES

Madeleine's | **Northvale**	24
🅩 Manor | **W Orange**	23
Mill | **Spring Lake Hts**	20
Mompou | **Newark**	20
P.J. Whelihan's | **Sewell**	17
Portuguese Manor | **Perth Amboy**	21
🅩 Rat's | **Hamilton**	24
Restaurant | **Hackensack**	21
Sabor | **N Bergen**	22
🆕 Savannah's | **Stockholm**	-
🅩 South City Grill | **multi. loc.**	23
🆕 Verdigre | **New Bruns.**	22
Windansea | **Highlands**	20

DELIVERY/TAKEOUT

(D=delivery, T=takeout)

Aamantran | D, T | **Toms River Twp**	23
Aby's Mexican | D, T | **Matawan**	22
Alisa Cafe | T | **Cherry Hill**	22
Athenian Gdn. | T | **Galloway Twp**	23
Bahama Breeze | T | **Cherry Hill**	17
🅩 Baumgart's Café | T | **multi. loc.**	19
Bayou Cafe | D | **Manasquan**	23
Bell's | T | **Lambertville**	19
Belmont Tavern | T | **Belleville**	24
Beyti Kebab | T | **Union City**	24
Big Ed's BBQ | T | **multi. loc.**	17
Blue Danube | T | **Trenton**	22
Bobby Chez | T | **multi. loc.**	25
Brannon's Hurricane | T | **Barnegat**	21
Brooklyn's Pizza | T | **multi. loc.**	22
Cafe at Rosemont | T | **Rosemont**	22
California Grill | T | **Flemington**	20
Casa Maya | T | **Meyersville**	20
Chao Phaya | T | **Somerville**	23
Chilangos | T | **Highlands**	21
Crown Palace | T | **multi. loc.**	22
🅩 DeLorenzo's | T | **Trenton**	28
El Familiar | T | **Toms River Twp**	-
🅩 El Meson | T | **Freehold**	24
Eppes Essen | T | **Livingston**	18
🅩 Far East Taste | T | **Eatontown**	26

Federici's | T | **Freehold**	21
Filomena | T | **multi. loc.**	20
Frankie Fed's | T | **Freehold Twp**	20
Full Moon | T | **Lambertville**	17
Grimaldi's Pizza | D | **Hoboken**	25
Harvey Cedars | T | **Beach Haven**	22
Hunan Chinese | T | **Morris Plains**	23
India on Hudson | D | **Hoboken**	19
Indigo Smoke | T | **Montclair**	22
🅩 It's Greek To Me | T | **multi. loc.**	18
Java Moon | T | **multi. loc.**	19
Je's | D, T | **Newark**	26
Joe's Peking | T | **Marlton**	23
Juanito's | T | **multi. loc.**	23
🅩 Karma Kafe | D | **Hoboken**	25
Komegashi | D, T | **Jersey City**	24
Limestone Cafe | T | **Peapack**	22
Los Amigos | T | **multi. loc.**	23
Lotus Cafe | D | **Hackensack**	24
Madison B&G | T | **Hoboken**	21
Mahzu | T | **Aberdeen**	22
Margherita's | D | **Hoboken**	22
Mastoris | T | **Bordentown**	19
Meemah | T | **Edison**	24
Meil's | T | **Stockton**	23
Memphis Pig Out | T | **Atlantic H.**	19
Mexico Lindo | T | **Brick**	28
Mie Thai | T | **Woodbridge**	25
Mikado | T | **Cherry Hill**	22
Moghul | T | **Edison**	24
New Main | T | **Chatham**	23
Niecy's | T | **S Orange**	20
Nobi | T | **Toms River Twp**	25
Noodle House | T | **N Brunswick**	19
Norma's Med. | T | **Cherry Hill**	21
🅩 Old Man Rafferty | T | **multi. loc.**	19
Ota-Ya | T | **Lambertville**	23
Pad Thai | T | **Highland Pk**	22
Passage to India | T | **Lawrenceville**	23
Penang | D, T | **multi. loc.**	20
🅩 P.F. Chang's | T | **multi. loc.**	21
Raagini | T | **Mountainside**	22

Reservoir Tavern | T | **Boonton** 22
Richard's | T | **Long Branch** 20
Robongi | D, T | **Hoboken** 25
Saffron | D | **E Hanover** 23
Saigon R./Mo' Pho' | T | 24
Englewood
Sakura-Bana | T | **Ridgewood** 25
Seven Hills | T | **Highland Pk** 21
Shogun | T | **multi. loc.** 18
Shumi | T | **Somerville** 25
Siam | T | **Lambertville** 21
Sono Sushi | T | **Middletown** 26
Spike's | T | **Pt. Pleas. Bch** 22
Sri Thai | D | **Hoboken** 24
Sunny Garden | T | **W Windsor** 22
Sushi Lounge | D, T | **Hoboken** 24
Taste of Asia | T | **Chatham** 21
Thai Chef | T | **multi. loc.** 21
Thai Kitchen | T | **multi. loc.** 23
Tina Louise | T | **Carlstadt** 24
Tortuga's | T | **multi. loc.** 21
Tuzzio's | T | **Long Branch** 21
Vic's | T | **Bradley Bch** 20
Wasabi | D, T | **multi. loc.** 24
West Lake | T | **Matawan** 25
☑ White House | T | **A.C.** 27
Wonder Seafood | T | **Edison** 24

DESSERT

Aquila Cucina | **New Providence** 21
☑ Baumgart's Café | **multi. loc.** 19
☑ Chakra | **Paramus** 21
☑ Cheesecake Fact. | **multi. loc.** 19
Copeland | **Morristown** 25
☑ Fascino | **Montclair** 26
Fedora Cafe | **Lawrenceville** 19
Karen & Rei's | **Clermont** 27
☑ Old Man Rafferty | **multi. loc.** 19
Raymond's | **Montclair** 21
Robin's Nest | **Mt Holly** 22

ENTERTAINMENT

(Call for days and times of performances)

Atlantic B&G | jazz | 24
S Seaside Pk
Bahama Breeze | Caribbean | 17
Cherry Hill

☑ Bernards Inn | piano | 26
Bernardsville
Beyti Kebab | belly dancing | 24
Union City
Blue Eyes | singer | **Sewell** 20
☑ Blue Point | jazz | **Princeton** 25
Bula World Cuisine | jazz | 23
Newton
Caffe Aldo | accordion | 23
Cherry Hill
Catelli | band | **Voorhees** 24
da Filippo | piano | **Somerville** 24
☑ Dining Room | guitar/jazz | 26
Short Hills
Dock's Oyster | piano | **A.C.** 26
☑ Ebbitt Room | jazz | 27
Cape May
Filomena | varies | **multi. loc.** 20
Food for Thought | piano | 24
Marlton
☑ Grand Cafe | piano | 25
Morristown
Harvest Moon | piano | **Ringoes** 24
Il Capriccio | piano | **Whippany** 26
Indigo Smoke | jazz/R&B | 22
Montclair
Lalezar | belly dancing | –
Montclair
Le Petit Chateau | varies | 25
Bernardsville
Makeda | funk/jazz | 23
New Bruns.
Matisse | jazz | **Belmar** 22
Mattar's | piano | **Allamuchy** 24
McLoone's | jazz/rock | 17
Sea Bright
Molly Pitcher | piano | **Red Bank** 22
Mompou | varies | **Newark** 20
☑ Moonstruck | jazz/piano | 24
Asbury Pk
Norma's Med. | belly dancing | 21
Cherry Hill
Nova Terra | Latin | **New Bruns.** 22
☑ Peter Shields | piano | 26
Cape May
Pub | jazz | **Pennsauken** 18
☑ Ram's Head Inn | piano | 26
Galloway
☑ Rat's | varies | **Hamilton** 24

Raven & Peach | guitar/piano | **Fair Haven** `24`

Sabor | DJ | **multi. loc.** `22`

Shanghai Jazz | jazz | **Madison** `21`

Shipwreck Grill | jazz | **Brielle** `25`

Steve & Cookie's | varies | **Margate** `25`

Tortilla Press | guitar | **Collingswood** `23`

Tre Figlio | varies | **Egg Harbor** `24`

Verve | varies | **Somerville** `23`

Windansea | varies | **Highlands** `20`

FAMILY-STYLE

Adega Grill | **Newark** `24`

Carmine's | **A.C.** `20`

Chef Vola's | **A.C.** `26`

Cinque Figlie | **Morristown** `21`

Italian Bistro | **Cherry Hill** `17`

Michael's Cucina | **Manalapan** `19`

Pad Thai | **Highland Pk** `22`

Pearl of the Sea | **Long Branch** `18`

Z P.F. Chang's | **multi. loc.** `21`

Spanish Tavern | **Mountainside** `22`

FIREPLACES

Acqua | **Raritan** `21`

NEW Addiwan | **Montclair** `18`

Adega Grill | **Newark** `24`

Z Amanda's | **Hoboken** `26`

Anna's Italian | **Middletown** `22`

Anton's/Swan | **Lambertville** `22`

Aria Ristorante | **Fairfield** `21`

Z Arthur's Steak/Tavern | **N Brunswick** `18`

NEW Z Avenue | **Long Branch** `22`

NEW Axia Taverna | **Tenafly** `21`

Bareli's | **Secaucus** `23`

Beau Rivage | **Medford** `22`

Z Bernards Inn | **Bernardsville** `26`

Berta's Chateau | **Wanaque** `22`

Z Black Forest Inn | **Stanhope** `23`

Black Horse | **Mendham** `19`

Black Trumpet | **Spring Lake** `23`

Blue Pig Tavern | **Cape May** `20`

Blueside Grill | **Englewood** `18`

Braddock's | **Medford** `22`

Cabin | **Howell** `18`

NEW Casona | **Collingswood** `24`

NEW Z Catherine Lombardi | **New Bruns.** `21`

Chophouse, The | **Gibbsboro** `23`

Christopher's | **Colts Neck** `21`

Clark's Landing | **Pt. Pleas.** `17`

Clydz | **New Bruns.** `23`

Cork | **Westmont** `21`

Crab's Claw | **Lavallette** `17`

Cranbury Inn | **Cranbury** `17`

Z Ebbitt Room | **Cape May** `27`

Eccola | **Parsippany** `23`

Elephant & Castle | **Cherry Hill** `11`

NEW Europa at Monroe | **Monroe Twp** `-`

Fat Kat | **Little Ferry** `24`

Filomena | **Deptford** `20`

Z Gables, The | **Beach Haven** `26`

Giumarello's | **Westmont** `25`

Z Grand Cafe | **Morristown** `25`

Grenville | **Bay Hd.** `21`

Harry's Lobster | **Sea Bright** `22`

Harvest Bistro | **Closter** `22`

Harvest Moon | **Ringoes** `24`

Z Huntley Taverne | **Summit** `22`

Il Michelangelo | **Boonton** `21`

Inlet Café | **Highlands** `19`

Inn at Millrace | **Hope** `21`

Inn/Hawke | **Lambertville** `18`

Jamie's Restaurant | **Clifton** `-`

Jonathan's | **A.C.** `22`

Karen & Rei's | **Clermont** `27`

Kunkel's | **Haddon Hts** `20`

La Campagne | **Cherry Hill** `24`

Laguna Grill | **Brigantine** `22`

La Nonna/Piancone's | **Brielle** `18`

Mad Batter | **Cape May** `21`

Mahogany Grille | **Manasquan** `23`

Main St. Euro-Amer. | **Princeton** `18`

Mama Tucci | **Livingston** `-`

McLoone's | **Sea Bright** `17`

Metuchen Inn | **Metuchen** `22`

NEW Meyersville Inn | **Meyersville** `-`

Molly Pitcher | **Red Bank** `22`

Nag's Head | **Ocean City** `26`

Z Nauvoo Grill | **Fair Haven** `16`

NEW Neil's Original Oyster | **Highlands** `-`

subscribe to zagat.com

Nero's Grille | **Livingston**	17
⦿ Perryville Inn | **Union Twp**	26
⦿ Peter Shields | **Cape May**	26
Pheasants Land. | **Hillsborough**	17
P.J. Whelihan's | **Medford Lakes**	17
Plantation | **Harvey Cedars**	19
⦿ Pluckemin Inn | **Bedminster**	25
Portobello | **Oakland**	20
Posillipo | **Asbury Pk**	22
Pub | **Pennsauken**	18
⦿ Ram's Head Inn | **Galloway**	26
⦿ Rat's | **Hamilton**	24
Restaurant | **Hackensack**	21
Richie Cecere's | **Montclair**	21
Roberto's Dolce | **Beach Haven**	22
Roman Cafe | **Harrington Pk**	19
NEW Savannah's | **Stockholm**	-
Scarborough Fair | **Wall**	20
⦿ Serenade | **Chatham**	27
Sergeantsville Inn | **Sergeantsville**	23
Settebello Cafe | **Morristown**	22
Seven Hills | **Highland Pk**	21
Shanghai Jazz | **Madison**	21
Smithville Inn | **Smithville**	18
Solaia | **Englewood**	20
Stage House | **Scotch Plains**	23
⦿ Stage Left | **New Bruns.**	26
Steve & Cookie's | **Margate**	25
⦿ 3 west | **Basking Ridge**	23
Tosca | **Kenilworth**	20
Trap Rock | **Berkeley Hts**	21
Tuckers | **Beach Haven**	18
⦿ Union Park | **Cape May**	26
Walpack Inn | **Wallpack**	19
⦿ Washington Inn | **Cape May**	26
⦿ Whispers | **Spring Lake**	27
NEW Wolfgang Puck | **A.C.**	23
Yankee Doodle | **Princeton**	14

HISTORIC PLACES

(Year opened; * building)

1697 | Lincroft Inn* | **Middletown**	18
1682 | Farnsworth Hse.* | **Bordentown**	21
1685 | Grand Colonial* | **Union Twp**	25

1734 | Sergeantsville Inn* | **Sergeantsville**	23
1737 | Stage House* | **Scotch Plains**	23
1742 | Black Horse* | **Mendham**	19
1750 | Cranbury Inn* | **Cranbury**	17
1785 | Meyersville Inn* | **Meyersville**	-
1787 | Smithville Inn* | **Smithville**	18
1790 | Ho-Ho-Kus Inn* | **Ho-Ho-Kus**	21
1800 | Bell's Mansion* | **Stanhope**	18
1800 | Cafe at Rosemont* | **Rosemont**	22
1800 | Tewksbury Inn* | **Oldwick**	22
1805 | Frenchtown Inn* | **Frenchtown**	23
1818 | Stony Hill Inn* | **Hackensack**	23
1823 | Braddock's* | **Medford**	22
1840 | David Drake* | **Rahway**	27
1840 | Milford Oyster House* | **Milford**	-
1840 | Washington Inn* | **Cape May**	26
1843 | Metuchen Inn* | **Metuchen**	22
1850 | Delta's* | **New Bruns.**	22
1850 | Light Horse* | **Jersey City**	22
1856 | High Street Grill* | **Mt Holly**	23
1856 | Il Michelangelo* | **Boonton**	21
1860 | Inn/Hawke* | **Lambertville**	18
1863 | Lambertville Stat.* | **Lambertville**	17
1864 | Renault Winery* | **Egg Harbor**	22
1868 | Rick's* | **Lambertville**	-
1870 | Silver Spring* | **Flanders**	23
1874 | Saddle River Inn* | **Saddle R.**	27
1879 | Ebbitt Room* | **Cape May**	27
1880 | Claude's* | **N Wildwood**	25
1880 | 410 Bank St.* | **Cape May**	27

1880 | Moonstruck* | **Asbury Pk** 24

1882 | Busch's Seafood | 19
Sea Isle City

1882 | Mad Batter* | **Cape May** 21

1883 | Alexander's* | **Cape May** 24

1890 | Gables, The* | 26
Beach Haven

1890 | Grenville* | **Bay Hd.** 21

1890 | Matt's Red Roost.* | 25
Flemington

1890 | Red* | **Red Bank** 20

1890 | Whispers* | **Spring Lake** 27

1892 | Lawrenceville Inn* | 22
Lawrence Twp

1895 | Amanda's* | **Hoboken** 26

1895 | Elysian Cafe* | **Hoboken** 21

1895 | Limestone Cafe* | 22
Peapack

1897 | Dock's Oyster | **A.C.** 26

1900 | Athenian Gdn.* | 23
Galloway Twp

1900 | Doris & Ed's* | **Highlands** 25

1900 | Robin's Nest* | **Mt Holly** 22

1900 | Scarborough Fair* | **Wall** 20

1903 | Columbia Inn* | 20
Montville

1905 | Casona* | **Collingswood** 24

1906 | Onieal's* | **Hoboken** 19

1909 | Highlawn Pavil.* | 24
W Orange

1910 | Stage Left* | **New Bruns.** 26

1912 | Grill 73* | **Bernardsville** 22

1917 | Bahrs Landing | **Highlands** 15

1919 | Lahiere's | **Princeton** 21

1920 | Brannon's Hurricane* | 21
Barnegat

1920 | Ugly Mug* | **Cape May** 16

1921 | Chef Vola's | **A.C.** 26

1921 | Federici's | **Freehold** 21

1926 | Iberia | **Newark** 21

1926 | Spike's | **Pt. Pleas. Bch** 22

1927 | Berta's Chateau* | 22
Wanaque

1928 | Molly Pitcher* | **Red Bank** 22

1929 | Hunt Club | **Summit** 20

1929 | Posillipo* | **Asbury Pk** 22

1930 | Anthony's* | **Haddon Hts** 23

1930 | Pheasants Land.* | 17
Hillsborough

1932 | Lobster House | 20
Cape May

1932 | Spanish Tavern | **Newark** 22

1933 | Harry's Lobster | 22
Sea Bright

1933 | Sammy's Cider | 21
Mendham

1935 | Allendale B&G | **Allendale** 16

1935 | Angelo's | **A.C.** 20

1936 | Reservoir Tavern | 22
Boonton

1936 | Steve & Cookie's* | 25
Margate

1937 | Kinchley's Tavern | 21
Ramsey

1937 | Yankee Doodle | 14
Princeton

1938 | Mill | **Spring Lake Hts** 20

1939 | Bell's | **Lambertville** 19

1939 | Homestead Inn | **Trenton** 23

1939 | Solari's | **Hackensack** 21

1940 | La Spiaggia* | 26
Ship Bottom

1941 | Conte's | **Princeton** –

1941 | Walpack Inn* | **Wallpack** 19

1942 | Tuzzio's* | **Long Branch** 21

1945 | Berkeley | **S Seaside Pk** 18

1946 | White House* | **A.C.** 27

1947 | DeLorenzo's | **Trenton** 28

1947 | Vic's | **Bradley Bch** 20

1948 | Tick Tock* | **Clifton** 17

1950 | Fat Kat* | **Little Ferry** 24

1950 | Main St. Euro-Amer.* | 18
Princeton

1951 | Marsilio's | **Trenton** 22

1951 | Pub | **Pennsauken** 18

1951 | Rod's Steak | 21
Convent Station

1956 | Arthur's Steak/Tavern | 18
Morris Plains

1956 | Manor | **W Orange** 23

1957 | Eppes Essen | **Livingston** 18

HOTEL DINING

Alexander's Inn
   Alexander's | **Cape May** 24

Blue Bay Inn
   Copper Canyon | **Atlantic H.** 25

Borgata Hotel, Casino & Spa
NEW Bobby Flay Steak | A.C. 24
Old Homestead | A.C. 25
Z Ombra | A.C. 25
NEW Z SeaBlue | A.C. 27
Specchio | A.C. 25
NEW Tony Luke's | A.C. –
NEW Wolfgang Puck | A.C. 23

Caesars on the Boardwalk
Mia | A.C. 26

Carroll Villa Hotel
Mad Batter | Cape May 21

Clarion Hotel
Elephant & Castle |
Cherry Hill 11

Congress Hall Hotel
Blue Pig Tavern | Cape May 20

Crystal Spring Resort
Restaurant Latour | Hamburg –

daddy O
NEW daddy O | Long Beach 18

Grand Summit Hotel
Hunt Club | Summit 20

Green Gables Inn
Z Gables, The | Beach Haven 26

Grenville Hotel
Grenville | Bay Hd. 21

Hewitt Wellington Hotel
Z Whispers | Spring Lake 27

Hilton at Short Hills
Z Dining Room | Short Hills 26
Terrace Rest. | Short Hills 22

Hilton Hotel
Z Ruth's Chris | Parsippany 24

Ho-Ho-Kus Inn
Ho-Ho-Kus Inn | Ho-Ho-Kus 21

Madison Hotel
Rod's Steak | Convent Station 21

Molly Pitcher Inn
Molly Pitcher | Red Bank 22

Nassau Inn
Yankee Doodle | Princeton 14

Ocean Club Condos
Girasole | A.C. 25

Resorts Atlantic City Casino
Capriccio | A.C. 25

NEW Gallagher's Steak | A.C. 22

Robert Treat Hotel
Maize | Newark 21

Sandpiper Inn
Black Trumpet | Spring Lake 23

Sheraton Hotel
Tun Tavern | A.C. 18

Swan Hotel
Anton's/Swan | Lambertville 22

Quarter at the Tropicana
Carmine's | A.C. 20
Cuba Libre | A.C. 21

Virginia Hotel
Z Ebbitt Room | Cape May 27

Westin Governor Morris
Copeland | Morristown 25

Westminster Hotel
Strip House | Livingston 23

Wilshire Grand
Primavera | W Orange 20

JACKET REQUIRED

Z Bernards Inn | Bernardsville 26
Z Dining Room | Short Hills 26
Z Highlawn Pavil. | W Orange 24
Z Manor | W Orange 23
Molly Pitcher | Red Bank 22

LATE DINING

(Weekday closing hour)
NEW Addiwan | 12 AM |
Montclair 18
Allendale B&G | 1 AM |
Allendale 16
Basil T's | 12 AM | Red Bank 20
Benny Tudino's | 12:45 AM |
Hoboken 21
NEW Brickwall Tav. | 1 AM |
Asbury Pk 19
Carmine's | 12 AM | A.C. 20
Clydz | 1:30 AM | New Bruns. 23
NEW Cuban Pete's | 12 AM |
Montclair 17
Elephant & Castle | varies |
Cherry Hill 11
House of Blues | 12 AM | A.C. 16
Iberia | 1:30 AM | Newark 21
Irish Pub | 24 hrs. | A.C. 18

Kinchley's Tavern | 12 AM | **Ramsey** — 21

NEW Lucky Bones | 1 AM | **Cape May** — 18

Marie Nicole's | 12 AM | **Wildwood** — 23

Mastoris | 1 AM | **Bordentown** — 19

Pete & Elda's | 12 AM | **Neptune City** — –

Z P.F. Chang's | varies | **A.C.** — 21

P.J. Whelihan's | 2 AM | **multi. loc.** — 17

Ponzio's | 1 AM | **Cherry Hill** — 16

NEW Skylark Diner | 1 AM | **Edison** — 19

So Moon Nan Jip | 3 AM | **Palisades Pk** — 23

Tick Tock | 24 hrs. | **Clifton** — 17

Tun Tavern | varies | **A.C.** — 18

MEET FOR A DRINK

Acqua | **Raritan** — 21
Adega Grill | **Newark** — 24
Arturo's | **Midland Pk** — 22
Atlantic B&G | **S Seaside Pk** — 24
NEW Z Avenue | **Long Branch** — 22
Barnacle Bill's | **Rumson** — 21
Basil T's | **Red Bank** — 20
Bell's | **Lambertville** — 19
Black Horse | **Mendham** — 19
Blue Pig Tavern | **Cape May** — 20
BoBo's 33 | **Atlantic H.** — 22
NEW Brickwall Tav. | **Asbury Pk** — 19
Cenzino | **Oakland** — 24
Charley's | **Long Branch** — 19
Chilangos | **Highlands** — 21
Circa | **High Bridge** — 20
Clark's Landing | **Pt. Pleas.** — 17
NEW Continental | **A.C.** — –
Copper Canyon | **Atlantic H.** — 25
Crab's Claw | **Lavallette** — 17
Cuba Libre | **A.C.** — 21
Z Cucharamama | **Hoboken** — 26
NEW daddy O | **Long Beach** — 18
NEW Z David Burke | **Rumson** — 26
Z David Drake | **Rahway** — 27
Echo | **Red Bank** — 19
Espo's | **Raritan** — 21

Frankie & Johnnie | **Hoboken** — 23
Gaslight | **Hoboken** — 20
House of Blues | **A.C.** — 16
Hunt Club | **Summit** — 20
Z Huntley Taverne | **Summit** — 22
Inlet Café | **Highlands** — 19
Inn/Hawke | **Lambertville** — 18
Irish Pub | **A.C.** — 18
NEW Kitchen 233 | **Westmont** — 22
Los Amigos | **multi. loc.** — 23
Lua | **Hoboken** — 22
Marco & Pepe | **Jersey City** — 22
NEW Market/Mid. | **Asbury Pk** — 23
McLoone's | **Sea Bright** — 17
Mediterra | **Princeton** — 20
Metropolitan Cafe | **Freehold** — 22
Mia | **A.C.** — 26
Mompou | **Newark** — 20
NEW Neil's Original Oyster | **Highlands** — –
Oddfellows | **Hoboken** — 19
Old Bay | **New Bruns.** — 17
Z Old Man Rafferty | **multi. loc.** — 19
Onieal's | **Hoboken** — 19
Opah Grille | **Gladstone** — 24
Pine Tavern | **Old Bridge** — 22
Plantation | **Harvey Cedars** — 19
Quiet Man | **Dover** — 22
Restaurant | **Hackensack** — 21
Rod's Olde Irish | **Sea Girt** — 19
Sails | **Somers Point** — 18
Sallee Tee's | **Monmouth Bch** — 21
Salt Creek | **Rumson** — 20
Ship Inn | **Milford** — 19
Z South City Grill | **multi. loc.** — 23
Z Stage Left | **New Bruns.** — 26
Sushi Lounge | **Hoboken** — 24
Teak | **Red Bank** — 23
Tewksbury Inn | **Oldwick** — 22
Trap Rock | **Berkeley Hts** — 21
Triumph Brewing | **Princeton** — 18
Tuckers | **Beach Haven** — 18
Tun Tavern | **A.C.** — 18
Two If By Sea | **Red Bank** — 22
Ugly Mug | **Cape May** — 16
Vine | **Basking Ridge** — 22
Windansea | **Highlands** — 20

SPECIAL FEATURES

Bangkok Garden | **Hackensack**	24
⚡ Baumgart's Café | **multi. loc.**	19
Bayou Cafe | **Manasquan**	23
Beyti Kebab | **Union City**	24
Bistro San Miguel | **Middletown**	–
Blue | **Surf City**	23
Blue Danube | **Trenton**	22
NEW Bombay Curry | **Basking Ridge**	–
Casa Solar | **Belmar**	25
Champa Laos | **Cherry Hill**	23
Chand Palace | **Parsippany**	22
Chao Phaya | **Somerville**	23
Chef Vola's | **A.C.**	26
Chilangos | **Highlands**	21
China Palace | **Middletown**	–
⚡ Cucharamama | **Hoboken**	26
NEW DabbaWalla | **Summit**	19
Dayi'nin Yeri | **Cliffside Pk**	–
Doo Rae Myun Ok | **Fort Lee**	21
Elements Asia | **Lawrenceville**	23
⚡ El Meson | **Freehold**	24
⚡ Far East Taste | **Eatontown**	26
Fedora Cafe | **Lawrenceville**	19
Garlic Rose | **multi. loc.**	21
Ginger & Spice | **Ramsey**	–
Grand Shanghai | **Edison**	21
Hard Grove | **Jersey City**	14
⚡ It's Greek To Me | **multi. loc.**	18
Je's | **Newark**	26
⚡ Karma Kafe | **Hoboken**	25
K.O.B.E. | **Holmdel**	25
Krakus | **Wallington**	–
La Esperanza | **Lindenwold**	24
⚡ La Isla | **Hoboken**	26
Little Café | **Voorhees**	25
Madame Claude | **Jersey City**	23
Mad Batter | **Cape May**	21
Makeda | **New Bruns.**	23
Malabar House | **Piscataway**	–
Manon | **Lambertville**	25
Martino's | **Somerville**	21
Meemah | **Edison**	24
Meil's | **Stockton**	23
Mexico Lindo | **Brick**	28
Mie Thai | **Woodbridge**	25
Ming | **Edison**	23
Moghul | **Edison**	24
NEW Moksha | **Edison**	22
Mompou | **Newark**	20
Navesink Fishery | **Middletown**	24
NEW Nazmi's | **Cliffside Pk**	–
New Main | **Chatham**	23
Nha Trang Place | **Jersey City**	24
Niecy's | **S Orange**	20
Norma's Med. | **Cherry Hill**	21
Old Bay | **New Bruns.**	17
Ota-Ya | **Lambertville**	23
Pamir | **Morristown**	21
⚡ Park & Orchard | **E Rutherford**	22
Passage to India | **Lawrenceville**	23
Penang | **Edison**	20
NEW Piquant Bread B&G | **New Bruns.**	–
Pop Shop | **Collingswood**	18
Raagini | **Mountainside**	22
⚡ Rat's | **Hamilton**	24
Saffron | **E Hanover**	23
Saigon R./Mo' Pho' | **Englewood**	24
Sens Asian | **S Brunswick**	22
Seven Hills | **Highland Pk**	21
Shaker Cafe | **Flemington**	–
Siam | **Lambertville**	21
Siam Garden | **Red Bank**	23
Siri's Thai French | **Cherry Hill**	25
Sister Sue's | **Asbury Pk**	21
NEW Smokey's BBQ | **Montclair**	–
Somsak/Taan | **Voorhees**	23
Suez Canal | **Jersey City**	–
NEW Sultan's | **Hackettstown**	–
Sunny Garden | **W Windsor**	22
⚡ Taka | **Asbury Pk**	26
Taro | **Montclair**	21
Taste of Asia | **Chatham**	21
Teak | **Red Bank**	23
Tina Louise | **Carlstadt**	24
Water Lily | **Collingswood**	24
West Lake | **Matawan**	25
Wild Ginger | **Englewood**	25
Ya Ya Noodles | **Skillman**	–
Yumi | **Sea Bright**	26

OUTDOOR DINING

(G=garden; P=patio; S=sidewalk; T=terrace)

Anthony David's | S | **Hoboken**	25
Anton's/Swan | P | **Lambertville**	22
Arthur's Landing | T | **Weehawken**	20
Atlantic B&G | P | **S Seaside Pk**	24
Avon Pavilion | T | **Avon-by-Sea**	18
Axelsson's | G | **Cape May**	22
Bahama Breeze | T | **Cherry Hill**	17
Bamboo Leaf | S | **Bradley Bch**	24
Barone's | P, S | **multi. loc.**	20
☑ Bernards Inn | T | **Bernardsville**	26
Blue | P | **Surf City**	23
☑ Blue Point | P | **Princeton**	25
Bobby Chez | P | **Margate**	25
Brothers Moon | S | **Hopewell**	22
Café Gallery | T | **Burlington**	21
☑ Cafe Matisse | G | **Rutherford**	27
Caffe Aldo | P | **Cherry Hill**	23
☑ Cucharamama | S | **Hoboken**	26
Elysian Cafe | P, S | **Hoboken**	21
Filomena | P | **Berlin**	20
Frenchtown Inn | P | **Frenchtown**	23
☑ Frog & Peach | P | **New Bruns.**	26
☑ Gables, The | P | **Beach Haven**	26
Girasole | P | **A.C.**	25
Girasole | P | **Bound Brook**	25
Giumarello's | P | **Westmont**	25
☑ Grand Cafe | P | **Morristown**	25
Hamilton's Grill | P | **Lambertville**	24
Harvest Moon | G | **Ringoes**	24
India on Hudson | S | **Hoboken**	19
Inn/Hawke | P | **Lambertville**	18
Jonathan's | T | **A.C.**	22
Klein's Fish Market | P, T | **Belmar**	20
La Campagne | G, T | **Cherry Hill**	24
☑ Latour | S | **Ridgewood**	27
☑ Le Rendez-Vous | S | **Kenilworth**	26
Lilly's on Canal | P | **Lambertville**	21
Matisse | T | **Belmar**	22
☑ Mélange Cafe | P | **Cherry Hill**	26
Mexican Food | P | **Marlton**	18
Mill | T | **Spring Lake Hts**	20
☑ Moonstruck | T | **Asbury Pk**	24
Nag's Head | P | **Ocean City**	26
☑ Perryville Inn | P | **Union Twp**	26
☑ Peter Shields | T | **Cape May**	26
☑ Rat's | T | **Hamilton**	24
Raven & Peach | P | **Fair Haven**	24
Rebecca's | P | **Edgewater**	24
Robin's Nest | T | **Mt Holly**	22
Robongi | S | **Hoboken**	25
☑ Ruth's Chris | S | **Weehawken**	24
Ship Inn | S | **Milford**	19
Shipwreck Grill | T | **Brielle**	25
Stage House | G | **Scotch Plains**	23
☑ Stage Left | P | **New Bruns.**	26
Tisha's | P | **Cape May**	25
Tuckers | P | **Beach Haven**	18
Village Green | S | **Ridgewood**	25
Windansea | T | **Highlands**	20
Word of Mouth | P | **Collingswood**	24
Zafra | P | **Hoboken**	24
☑ Zoe's | P | **Sparta**	26

PEOPLE-WATCHING

NEW Alphabet Soup | **Audubon**	-
☑ Bernards Inn | **Bernardsville**	26
NEW Bobby Flay Steak | **A.C.**	24
Brix 67 | **Summit**	18
NEW Buddakan | **A.C.**	-
Caffe Aldo | **Cherry Hill**	23
Catelli | **Voorhees**	24
☑ Chart House | **Weehawken**	20
Clark's Landing | **Pt. Pleas.**	17
Clydz | **New Bruns.**	23
NEW Continental | **A.C.**	-
Copeland | **Morristown**	25
Cuba Libre | **A.C.**	21
☑ Cucharamama | **Hoboken**	26
NEW daddy O | **Long Beach**	18
☑ David Drake | **Rahway**	27
Delta's | **New Bruns.**	22
Eccola | **Parsippany**	23
Echo | **Red Bank**	19

SPECIAL FEATURES

Restaurant	Rating
☑ Huntley Taverne | **Summit**	22
Ixora | **Whitehouse Station**	25
NEW Kitchen 233 | **Westmont**	22
Limestone Cafe | **Peapack**	22
Lua | **Hoboken**	22
Makeda | **New Bruns.**	23
Mia | **A.C.**	26
Molly Pitcher | **Red Bank**	22
Mompou | **Newark**	20
☑ Pluckemin Inn | **Bedminster**	25
Ponzio's | **Cherry Hill**	16
Pop Shop | **Collingswood**	18
Sails | **Somers Point**	18
Salt Creek | **Rumson**	20
Sammy's Cider | **Mendham**	21
☑ South City Grill | **Jersey City**	23
Tapas de Espana | **N Bergen**	20
Teak | **Red Bank**	23
☑ 3 west | **Basking Ridge**	23
NEW Wolfgang Puck | **A.C.**	23
☑ Zoe's | **Sparta**	26

POWER SCENES

Restaurant	Rating
☑ Basilico | **Millburn**	23
BayPoint Prime | **Pt. Pleas. Bch**	24
☑ Bernards Inn | **Bernardsville**	26
NEW Bobby Flay Steak | **A.C.**	24
☑ Cafe Panache | **Ramsey**	28
Caffe Aldo | **Cherry Hill**	23
Casa Dante | **Jersey City**	22
Catelli | **Voorhees**	24
NEW ☑ Catherine Lombardi | **New Bruns.**	21
☑ Chakra | **Paramus**	21
☑ Chez Catherine | **Westfield**	27
Cuba Libre | **A.C.**	21
NEW ☑ David Burke | **Rumson**	26
☑ Fascino | **Montclair**	26
☑ 410 Bank St. | **Cape May**	27
NEW Gallagher's Steak | **A.C.**	22
NEW Gaucho Steak | **Montclair**	–
Hunt Club | **Summit**	20
☑ Il Mondo | **Madison**	25
Lawrenceville Inn | **Lawrence Twp**	22
Marsilio's | **Trenton**	22
McLoone's | **Sea Bright**	17
Morton's Steak | **Hackensack**	24

Restaurant	Rating
Old Homestead | **A.C.**	25
Opah Grille | **Gladstone**	24
NEW Phillips Seafood | **A.C.**	–
Pierre's | **Morristown**	23
Ponzio's | **Cherry Hill**	16
☑ Saddle River Inn | **Saddle R.**	27
NEW ☑ SeaBlue | **A.C.**	27
☑ Serenade | **Chatham**	27
Solari's | **Hackensack**	21
NEW Table | **Little Silver**	–
☑ Washington Inn | **Cape May**	26
NEW Wolfgang Puck | **A.C.**	23

PRE-THEATER DINING

(Call for prices and times)

Restaurant	Rating
Arthur's Landing | **Weehawken**	20
Maize | **Newark**	21
Theater Sq. Grill | **Newark**	20
2Senza | **Red Bank**	20

PRIVATE ROOMS

(Restaurants charge less at off times; call for capacity)

Restaurant	Rating
☑ Amanda's | **Hoboken**	26
☑ André's | **Newton**	27
Barone's | **Moorestown**	20
☑ Bernards Inn | **Bernardsville**	26
☑ Bistro Olé | **Asbury Pk**	25
☑ Black Duck | **W Cape May**	26
☑ Cafe Matisse | **Rutherford**	27
Caffe Aldo | **Cherry Hill**	23
Catelli | **Voorhees**	24
☑ Chakra | **Paramus**	21
☑ Chez Catherine | **Westfield**	27
Chez Elena Wu | **Voorhees**	24
☑ Dining Room | **Short Hills**	26
☑ Ebbitt Room | **Cape May**	27
☑ Fascino | **Montclair**	26
Food for Thought | **Marlton**	24
☑ Gables, The | **Beach Haven**	26
Girasole | **Bound Brook**	25
Giumarello's | **Westmont**	25
Hamilton's Grill | **Lambertville**	24
Harvest Bistro | **Closter**	22
Karen & Rei's | **Clermont**	27
Mattar's | **Allamuchy**	24
☑ Nauvoo Grill | **Fair Haven**	16
☑ Nicholas | **Middletown**	29

Pacific Grille | **Mt Laurel**	20
☒ Perryville Inn | **Union Twp**	26
Porto Leggero | **Jersey City**	23
Pub | **Pennsauken**	18
☒ Serenade | **Chatham**	27
Stage House | **Scotch Plains**	23
☒ Stage Left | **New Bruns.**	26
Tomatoes | **Margate**	24
☒ Washington Inn | **Cape May**	26
☒ Zoe's | **Sparta**	26

PRIX FIXE MENUS

(Call for prices and times)

☒ André's | **Newton**	27
Anthony David's | **Hoboken**	25
☒ Bernards Inn | **Bernardsville**	26
Cafe at Rosemont | **Rosemont**	22
Café Gallery | **Burlington**	21
☒ Cafe Matisse | **Rutherford**	27
☒ Cafe Panache | **Ramsey**	28
☒ Chez Catherine | **Westfield**	27
☒ David Drake | **Rahway**	27
☒ Dining Room | **Short Hills**	26
☒ Ebbitt Room | **Cape May**	27
☒ Fascino | **Montclair**	26
Frenchtown Inn | **Frenchtown**	23
☒ Frog & Peach | **New Bruns.**	26
☒ Gables, The | **Beach Haven**	26
Ixora | **Whitehouse Station**	25
La Campagne | **Cherry Hill**	24
☒ Latour | **Ridgewood**	27
Manon | **Lambertville**	25
Mattar's | **Allamuchy**	24
☒ Nicholas | **Middletown**	29
Norma's Med. | **Cherry Hill**	21
Nunzio | **Collingswood**	23
☒ Perryville Inn | **Union Twp**	26
☒ Rat's | **Hamilton**	24
Rosemary & Sage | **Riverdale**	26
☒ Scalini Fedeli | **Chatham**	27
☒ Serenade | **Chatham**	27
Sono Sushi | **Middletown**	26
Stage House | **Scotch Plains**	23
☒ Stage Left | **New Bruns.**	26
Verjus | **Maplewood**	25
Village Green | **Ridgewood**	25
☒ Zoe's | **Sparta**	26

QUICK BITES

Aby's Mexican | **Matawan**	22
Alchemist/Barrister | **Princeton**	16
NEW Amazing Hot Dog | **Verona**	22
Buttonwood Manor | **Matawan**	18
NEW Continental | **A.C.**	-
Cubby's BBQ | **Hackensack**	17
Doo Rae Myun Ok | **Fort Lee**	21
Full Moon | **Lambertville**	17
GRUB Hut | **Manville**	-
Irish Pub | **A.C.**	18
Jack Cooper's | **Edison**	19
Jerry & Harvey's | **Marlboro**	18
La Tapatia | **Asbury Pk**	-
Mastoris | **Bordentown**	19
NEW Neil's Original Oyster | **Highlands**	-
Nha Trang Place | **Jersey City**	24
Noodle House | **N Brunswick**	19
NEW Pic-Nic | **E Newark**	-
Ponzio's | **Cherry Hill**	16
Pop Shop | **Collingswood**	18
Shaker Cafe | **Flemington**	-
Simply Radish. | **Lawrenceville**	18
NEW Takara | **Ocean Twp**	25
NEW Tashmoo | **Morristown**	-
Tick Tock | **Clifton**	17
NEW Tony Luke's | **A.C.**	-
Windansea | **Highlands**	20

QUIET CONVERSATION

Braddock's | **Medford**	22
☒ Chez Catherine | **Westfield**	27
Farnsworth Hse. | **Bordentown**	21
Fiorino | **Summit**	23
Food for Thought | **Marlton**	24
Frenchtown Inn | **Frenchtown**	23
Lawrenceville Inn | **Lawrence Twp**	22
Melting Pot | **Westwood**	19
NEW Meyersville Inn | **Meyersville**	-
Molly Pitcher | **Red Bank**	22
☒ Pluckemin Inn | **Bedminster**	25
☒ Rat's | **Hamilton**	24
Slowly | **Toms River**	23
Soufflé | **Summit**	23

| Village Green | **Ridgewood** | 25 |
| EZ Whispers | **Spring Lake** | 27 |

RAW BARS

NEW EZ Avenue	**Long Branch**	22
Bahrs Landing	**Highlands**	15
BayPoint Prime	**Pt. Pleas. Bch**	24
Berkeley	**S Seaside Pk**	18
Blue Eyes	**Sewell**	20
EZ Blue Point	**Princeton**	25
Blueside Grill	**Englewood**	18
Cafe Arugula	**S Orange**	20
Caffe Aldo	**Cherry Hill**	23
Catelli	**Voorhees**	24
Circa	**High Bridge**	20
Clark's Landing	**Pt. Pleas.**	17
NEW EZ CoccoLa	**Hillsborough**	22
Copeland	**Morristown**	25
Dock's Oyster	**A.C.**	26
Fresco Steak	**Milltown**	23
Grand Colonial	**Union Twp**	25
Grill 73	**Bernardsville**	22
Harvey Cedars	**multi. loc.**	22
Klein's Fish Market	**Belmar**	20
Kunkel's	**Haddon Hts**	20
La Focaccia	**Summit**	24
EZ Legal Sea Foods	**multi. loc.**	20
Liberty House	**Jersey City**	20
Little Tuna	**Haddonfield**	20
Lobster House	**Cape May**	20
EZ McCormick/Schmick	**Hackensack**	20
McLoone's	**multi. loc.**	17
Milford Oyster House	**Milford**	–
NEW Neil's Original Oyster	**Highlands**	–
Nero's Grille	**Livingston**	17
Old Homestead	**A.C.**	25
Plantation	**Harvey Cedars**	19
Red's Lobster	**Pt. Pleas. Bch**	24
Sallee Tee's	**Monmouth Bch**	21
Shipwreck Grill	**Brielle**	25
Solaia	**Englewood**	20
EZ South City Grill	**multi. loc.**	23
Spike's	**Pt. Pleas. Bch**	22
Steve & Cookie's	**Margate**	25
Varka Fish House	**Ramsey**	25

ROMANTIC PLACES

Acquaviva	**Westfield**	23
NEW Alphabet Soup	**Audubon**	–
EZ Amanda's	**Hoboken**	26
Anton's/Swan	**Lambertville**	22
Atlantic B&G	**S Seaside Pk**	24
Beau Rivage	**Medford**	22
EZ Cafe Matisse	**Rutherford**	27
Catelli	**Voorhees**	24
NEW EZ Catherine Lombardi	**New Bruns.**	21
Creole Cafe	**Sewell**	27
NEW EZ CulinAriane	**Montclair**	27
NEW EZ David Burke	**Rumson**	26
EZ Dining Room	**Short Hills**	26
EZ Ebbitt Room	**Cape May**	27
Fat Kat	**Little Ferry**	24
Frenchman Inn	**Frenchtown**	23
EZ Gables, The	**Beach Haven**	26
Gaslight	**Hoboken**	20
Giumarello's	**Westmont**	25
EZ Grand Cafe	**Morristown**	25
Grenville	**Bay Hd.**	21
Harvest Moon	**Ringoes**	24
I Cavallini	**Colts Neck**	25
Il Capriccio	**Whippany**	26
Inn at Millrace	**Hope**	21
Jose's Mexican	**multi. loc.**	19
K.O.B.E.	**Holmdel**	25
La Cipollina	**Freehold**	23
Lawrenceville Inn	**Lawrence Twp**	22
EZ Le Rendez-Vous	**Kenilworth**	26
Lilly's on Canal	**Lambertville**	21
Melting Pot	**Westwood**	19
Metuchen Inn	**Metuchen**	22
Mia	**A.C.**	26
Molly Pitcher	**Red Bank**	22
EZ Perryville Inn	**Union Twp**	26
EZ Peter Shields	**Cape May**	26
Pino's La Forchetta	**Marlboro**	18
Plantation	**Harvey Cedars**	19
EZ Ram's Head Inn	**Galloway**	26
EZ Rat's	**Hamilton**	24
Raven & Peach	**Fair Haven**	24
Rebecca's	**Edgewater**	24
Rod's Steak	**Convent Station**	21

Savanna	**Red Bank**	20
☑ Scalini Fedeli	**Chatham**	27
Scarborough Fair	**Wall**	20
NEW ☑ SeaBlue	**A.C.**	27
Sergeantsville Inn	**Sergeantsville**	23
Slowly	**Toms River**	23
Stony Hill Inn	**Hackensack**	23
☑ Taka	**Asbury Pk**	26
Tewksbury Inn	**Oldwick**	22
☑ Washington Inn	**Cape May**	26
Water Lily	**Collingswood**	24
☑ Whispers	**Spring Lake**	27

SENIOR APPEAL

NEW Alphabet Soup	**Audubon**	–
NEW Asia Star	**Tinton Falls**	–
Athenian Gdn.	**Galloway Twp**	23
Bahrs Landing	**Highlands**	15
Berkeley	**S Seaside Pk**	18
Buttonwood Manor	**Matawan**	18
California Grill	**Flemington**	20
Capt'n Ed's	**Pt. Pleas.**	19
Carmine's	**A.C.**	20
NEW ☑ Catherine Lombardi	**New Bruns.**	21
Chophouse, The	**Gibbsboro**	23
Christopher's	**Colts Neck**	21
Crab Trap	**Somers Point**	21
Don Pepe	**multi. loc.**	21
Don Pepe's Steak	**Pine Brook**	22
E & V	**Paterson**	24
El Cid	**Paramus**	21
Fantasea Reef	**A.C.**	17
☑ Fornos of Spain	**Newark**	23
Gagan Bistro	**Marlton**	–
NEW Gallagher's Steak	**A.C.**	22
Grenville	**Bay Hd.**	21
Iberia	**Newark**	21
Italian Bistro	**Cherry Hill**	17
Jack Cooper's	**Edison**	19
Java Moon	**multi. loc.**	19
NEW Kitchen 233	**Westmont**	22
Klein's Fish Market	**Belmar**	20
Lahiere's	**Princeton**	21
La Nonna/Piancone's	**Brielle**	18
☑ Legal Sea Foods	**Short Hills**	20
Little Tuna	**Haddonfield**	20

Lobster House	**Cape May**	20
LouCás	**Edison**	24
Mama Tucci	**Livingston**	–
☑ McCormick/Schmick	**Bridgewater**	20
NEW Meyersville Inn	**Meyersville**	–
Mill	**Spring Lake Hts**	20
NEW Oceanos	**Fair Lawn**	–
NEW Octopus's Gard.	**Stafford**	22
Pete & Elda's	**Neptune City**	–
Pop Shop	**Collingswood**	18
Portobello	**Oakland**	20
Portuguese Manor	**Perth Amboy**	21
NEW ☑ SeaBlue	**A.C.**	27
Sea Shack	**Hackensack**	20
Smithville Inn	**Smithville**	18
Tucker's Steak	**Somers Point**	19
Varka Fish House	**Ramsey**	25
Villa Vittoria	**Brick**	22
Water Lily	**Collingswood**	24
NEW Wolfgang Puck	**A.C.**	23

SINGLES SCENES

Acqua	**Raritan**	21
Atlantic B&G	**S Seaside Pk**	24
Big Ed's BBQ	**Burlington**	17
Blue Pig Tavern	**Cape May**	20
BoBo's 33	**Atlantic H.**	22
NEW Brickwall Tav.	**Asbury Pk**	19
Brooklyn's Pizza	**Ridgewood**	22
NEW Buddakan	**A.C.**	–
Cenzino	**Oakland**	24
Circa	**High Bridge**	20
City Bistro	**Hoboken**	19
Clark's Landing	**Pt. Pleas.**	17
Clydz	**New Bruns.**	23
NEW Continental	**A.C.**	–
Copper Canyon	**Atlantic H.**	25
Corky's	**A.C.**	16
Cuba Libre	**A.C.**	21
☑ Cucharamama	**Hoboken**	26
Grissini	**Englewood Cliffs**	22
NEW Gusto Grill	**E Brunswick**	–
House of Blues	**A.C.**	16
Inlet Café	**Highlands**	19

La Nonna/Piancone's | **Bradley Bch**	18
Lua | **Hoboken**	22
McLoone's | **Sea Bright**	17
NEW Mercy Grill | **Hoboken**	–
Metropolitan Cafe | **Freehold**	22
Mia | **A.C.**	26
Mompou | **Newark**	20
Nova Terra | **New Bruns.**	22
Z Old Man Rafferty | **multi. loc.**	19
NEW Piquant Bread B&G | **New Bruns.**	–
Plantation | **Harvey Cedars**	19
Quiet Man | **Dover**	22
Red | **Red Bank**	20
Restaurant | **Hackensack**	21
Rooney's | **Long Branch**	18
Sails | **Somers Point**	18
Sallee Tee's | **Monmouth Bch**	21
NEW Savannah's | **Stockholm**	–
Shipwreck Grill | **Brielle**	25
Sister Sue's | **Asbury Pk**	21
Z South City Grill | **Jersey City**	23
Sushi Lounge | **multi. loc.**	24
Teak | **Red Bank**	23
Tomatoes | **Margate**	24
Trap Rock | **Berkeley Hts**	21
Verve | **Somerville**	23
Windansea | **Highlands**	20

SLEEPERS

(Good to excellent food, but little known)

Aamantran | **Toms River Twp**	23
Aby's Mexican | **Matawan**	22
NEW Alessio 426 | **Metuchen**	20
Alexander's | **Cape May**	24
Aligado Asian | **Hazlet**	23
Anna's Italian | **Middletown**	22
NEW Bay Head Bistro | **Bay Hd.**	21
Bayou Cafe | **Manasquan**	23
BayPoint Prime | **Pt. Pleas. Bch**	24
Bella Sogno | **Bradley Bch**	21
Bistro 44 | **Toms River**	25
Blue Danube | **Trenton**	22
NEW Blue Fish | **Flemington**	20
BoBo's 33 | **Atlantic H.**	22
Bosphorus | **Lake Hiawatha**	22

Brannon's Hurricane | **Barnegat**	21
Bula World Cuisine | **Newton**	23
Cafe Loren | **Avalon**	25
Champa Laos | **Cherry Hill**	23
Chilangos | **Highlands**	21
Circa | **High Bridge**	20
Claude's | **N Wildwood**	25
Clementine's | **Avon-by-Sea**	24
Copper Fish | **Cape May**	20
Creole Cafe | **Sewell**	27
Cup Joint | **Hoboken**	20
Doo Rae Myun Ok | **Fort Lee**	21
Drew's Bayshore | **Keyport**	28
NEW 503 Park | **Scotch Plains**	20
Gianna's | **Atlantic H.**	25
Grand Shanghai | **Edison**	21
Harrison | **Asbury Pk**	24
Harry's Lobster | **Sea Bright**	22
High Street Grill | **Mt Holly**	23
Homestead Inn | **Trenton**	23
Ikko | **Brick**	22
Je's | **Newark**	26
Jose's | **Spring Lake Hts**	22
Karen & Rei's | **Clermont**	27
NEW Kitchen 233 | **Westmont**	22
K.O.B.E. | **Holmdel**	25
Konbu | **Manalapan**	25
Kunkel's | **Haddon Hts**	20
La Esperanza | **Lindenwold**	24
Laguna Grill | **Brigantine**	22
La Spiaggia | **Ship Bottom**	26
LoBianco | **Margate**	25
Lodos | **New Milford**	21
Marie Nicole's | **Wildwood**	23
Mattar's | **Allamuchy**	24
Megu Sushi | **Cherry Hill**	22
Mexico Lindo | **Brick**	28
NEW Moksha | **Edison**	22
Mompou | **Newark**	20
Nag's Head | **Ocean City**	26
Nha Trang Place | **Jersey City**	24
Niecy's | **S Orange**	20
Nobi | **Toms River Twp**	25
Oasis Grill | **Cherry Hill**	25
NEW Octopus's Gard. | **Stafford**	22
Olde Corner Deli | **Island Hts**	26

NEW Passione | **Montclair**	23
Pasta Fresca Café | **Shrewsbury**	22
Posh | **Maple Shade**	23
Sakura Spring | **Cherry Hill**	23
Sens Asian | **S Brunswick**	22
Silver Spring | **Flanders**	23
Sister Sue's | **Asbury Pk**	21
Solo Bella | **Jackson**	21
So Moon Nan Jip | **Palisades Pk**	23
Sushi by Kazu | **Howell**	28
NEW Takara | **Ocean Twp**	25
Taqueria | **Jersey City**	20
NEW Thyme Square | **Red Bank**	21
NEW Verdigre | **New Bruns.**	22
West Lake | **Matawan**	25
Wonder Seafood | **Edison**	24

SPECIAL OCCASIONS

Bacari Grill | **Washington Twp**	21
Beau Rivage | **Medford**	22
NEW Z Blue Bottle | **Hopewell**	27
NEW Bobby Flay Steak | **A.C.**	24
Z Cafe Matisse | **Rutherford**	27
Z Cafe Panache | **Ramsey**	28
Catelli | **Voorhees**	24
Z Chakra | **Paramus**	21
Z Chart House | **Weehawken**	20
Z Chef's Table | **Franklin Lakes**	28
Chengdu 46 | **Clifton**	24
Z Chez Catherine | **Westfield**	27
Z Cucharamama | **Hoboken**	26
Doris & Ed's | **Highlands**	25
Fat Kat | **Little Ferry**	24
Z Ferry House | **Princeton**	25
Food for Thought | **Marlton**	24
Frenchtown Inn | **Frenchtown**	23
NEW Gallagher's Steak | **A.C.**	22
Giumarello's | **Westmont**	25
Z Grand Cafe | **Morristown**	25
Harvest Moon | **Ringoes**	24
Z Highlawn Pavil. | **W Orange**	24
Il Capriccio | **Whippany**	26
Indigo Moon | **Atlantic H.**	26
Ixora | **Whitehouse Station**	25
Karen & Rei's | **Clermont**	27
K.O.B.E. | **Holmdel**	25
Z Latour | **Ridgewood**	27

Lawrenceville Inn | **Lawrence Twp**	22
Madeleine's | **Northvale**	24
Maize | **Newark**	21
Z Manor | **W Orange**	23
Mattar's | **Allamuchy**	24
Napa Valley | **Paramus**	22
Z Nicholas | **Middletown**	29
No. 9 | **Lambertville**	24
Nunzio | **Collingswood**	23
Z Peter Shields | **Cape May**	26
Posillipo | **Asbury Pk**	22
Pronto Cena | **Newark**	22
Z Ram's Head Inn | **Galloway**	26
Z Rat's | **Hamilton**	24
Raven & Peach | **Fair Haven**	24
Rebecca's | **Edgewater**	24
Robin's Nest | **Mt Holly**	22
Rod's Steak | **Convent Station**	21
Z Saddle River Inn | **Saddle R.**	27
NEW Z SeaBlue | **A.C.**	27
Z Serenade | **Chatham**	27
Shanghai Jazz | **Madison**	21
Slowly | **Toms River**	23
Specchio | **A.C.**	25
Stage House | **Scotch Plains**	23
Stony Hill Inn | **Hackensack**	23
Taro | **Montclair**	21
Z 3 west | **Basking Ridge**	23
Z Washington Inn | **Cape May**	26
Wild Ginger | **Englewood**	25
NEW Wolfgang Puck | **A.C.**	23
Z Zoe's | **Sparta**	26

TASTING MENUS

Anthony David's | **Hoboken**	25
Bella Sogno | **Bradley Bch**	21
Z Bernards Inn | **Bernardsville**	26
Bienvenue | **Red Bank**	24
Black Trumpet | **Spring Lake**	23
Z Cafe Panache | **Ramsey**	28
Z Chez Catherine | **Westfield**	27
Clementine's | **Avon-by-Sea**	24
Copeland | **Morristown**	25
Z David Drake | **Rahway**	27
Z Dining Room | **Short Hills**	26
Z Ebbitt Room | **Cape May**	27

Fascino | **Montclair**	26
Island Palm Grill | **Spring Lake**	18
La Campagne | **Cherry Hill**	24
Latour | **Ridgewood**	27
Lawrenceville Inn | **Lawrence Twp**	22
Le Petit Chateau | **Bernardsville**	25
Le Rendez-Vous | **Kenilworth**	26
LoBianco | **Margate**	25
Lorena's | **Maplewood**	27
Mélange Cafe | **Cherry Hill**	26
Nicholas | **Middletown**	29
Norma's Med. | **Cherry Hill**	21
Nouveau Sushi | **Montclair**	25
Nunzio | **Collingswood**	23
Ombra | **A.C.**	25
Ora | **Morristown**	20
NEW Passione | **Montclair**	23
Perryville Inn | **Union Twp**	26
Rat's | **Hamilton**	24
Renault Winery | **Egg Harbor**	22
Restaurant Latour | **Hamburg**	-
Rosemary & Sage | **Riverdale**	26
Serenade | **Chatham**	27
Slowly | **Toms River**	23
Spargo's Grille | **Manalapan**	25
Stage House | **Scotch Plains**	23
Stage Left | **New Bruns.**	26
Terra | **Maplewood**	20
Village Green | **Ridgewood**	25
Vine | **Basking Ridge**	22
Zoe's | **Sparta**	26

TRANSPORTING EXPERIENCES

Anton's/Swan | **Lambertville**	22
Avon Pavilion | **Avon-by-Sea**	18
Blue Danube | **Trenton**	22
Chakra | **Paramus**	21
Chao Phaya | **Somerville**	23
Cucharamama | **Hoboken**	26
Dining Room | **Short Hills**	26
Ebbitt Room | **Cape May**	27
Epernay | **Montclair**	21
Fascino | **Montclair**	26
Hamilton's Grill | **Lambertville**	24
Ixora | **Whitehouse Station**	25
K.O.B.E. | **Holmdel**	25

La Campagne | **Cherry Hill**	24
Lorena's | **Maplewood**	27
Makeda | **New Bruns.**	23
Manon | **Lambertville**	25
Ming | **Edison**	23
NEW Moksha | **Edison**	22
Pamir | **Morristown**	21
Perryville Inn | **Union Twp**	26
Pluckemin Inn | **Bedminster**	25
Rat's | **Hamilton**	24
Saddle River Inn | **Saddle R.**	27
Seven Hills | **Highland Pk**	21
Shanghai Jazz | **Madison**	21
Silver Oak Bistro | **Ridgewood**	23
Siri's Thai French | **Cherry Hill**	25
Sister Sue's | **Asbury Pk**	21
Taro | **Montclair**	21
Walpack Inn | **Wallpack**	19

TRENDY

Anna's Italian | **Middletown**	22
Axelsson's | **Cape May**	22
Basilico | **Millburn**	23
Bistro Olé | **Asbury Pk**	25
Blu | **Montclair**	25
Blue | **Surf City**	23
NEW Blue Bottle | **Hopewell**	27
Blueside Grill | **Englewood**	18
NEW Bobby Flay Steak | **A.C.**	24
BoBo's 33 | **Atlantic H.**	22
Brannon's Hurricane | **Barnegat**	21
NEW Brickwall Tav. | **Asbury Pk**	19
NEW Buddakan | **A.C.**	-
Cafe Matisse | **Rutherford**	27
NEW Casona | **Collingswood**	24
Chakra | **Paramus**	21
Chef Vola's | **A.C.**	26
Conte's | **Princeton**	-
NEW Continental | **A.C.**	-
Cuba Libre | **A.C.**	21
Cucharamama | **Hoboken**	26
NEW daddy O | **Long Beach**	18
NEW David Burke | **Rumson**	26
DeLorenzo's | **Trenton**	28
Delta's | **New Bruns.**	22
Dock's Oyster | **A.C.**	26
Doris & Ed's | **Highlands**	25

SPECIAL FEATURES

House of Blues	**A.C.**	16
Inlet Café	**Highlands**	19
Los Amigos	**multi. loc.**	23
Mexican Food	**Marlton**	18
Mia	**A.C.**	26
Mompou	**Newark**	20
Oddfellows	**Hoboken**	19
Old Bay	**New Bruns.**	17
☑ Old Man Rafferty	**multi. loc.**	19
Pine Tavern	**Old Bridge**	22
NEW Pithari Taverna	**Highland Pk**	–
☑ Pluckemin Inn	**Bedminster**	25
Rattlesnake Ranch	**Denville**	16
Red	**Red Bank**	20
☑ South City Grill	**multi. loc.**	23
Squan Tavern	**Manasquan**	19
Surf Taco	**multi. loc.**	20
Sushi Lounge	**Hoboken**	24
Tacconelli's	**Maple Shade**	20
Tapas de Espana	**N Bergen**	20
Teresa's Cafe	**Princeton**	21
Triumph Brewing	**Princeton**	18
NEW Wolfgang Puck	**A.C.**	23
Yankee Doodle	**Princeton**	14

VIEWS

Arthur's Landing	**Weehawken**	20
Atlantic B&G	**S Seaside Pk**	24
NEW ☑ Avenue	**Long Branch**	22
Avon Pavilion	**Avon-by-Sea**	18
Bahrs Landing	**Highlands**	15
Barnacle Bill's	**Rumson**	21
☑ Baumgart's Café	**Edgewater**	19
Berkeley	**S Seaside Pk**	18
NEW Buddakan	**A.C.**	–
Buttonwood Manor	**Matawan**	18
Café Gallery	**Burlington**	21
☑ Cafe Matisse	**Rutherford**	27
Capriccio	**A.C.**	25
☑ Chart House	**Weehawken**	20
Chophouse, The	**Gibbsboro**	23
City Bistro	**Hoboken**	19
Clark's Landing	**Pt. Pleas.**	17
Claude's	**N Wildwood**	25
NEW Continental	**A.C.**	–
Crab Trap	**Somers Point**	21
Doris & Ed's	**Highlands**	25
Hamilton's Grill	**Lambertville**	24
☑ Highlawn Pavil.	**W Orange**	24
House of Blues	**A.C.**	16
Il Forno Trattoria	**Montclair**	23
Inlet Café	**Highlands**	19
Jonathan's	**A.C.**	22
Komegashi	**Jersey City**	24
Labrador	**Normandy Bch**	23
Lambertville Stat.	**Lambertville**	17
Liberty House	**Jersey City**	20
Lilly's on Canal	**Lambertville**	21
LoBianco	**Margate**	25
Lua	**Hoboken**	22
Matisse	**Belmar**	22
McLoone's	**multi. loc.**	17
Milford Oyster House	**Milford**	–
Mill	**Spring Lake Hts**	20
Molly Pitcher	**Red Bank**	22
☑ Moonstruck	**Asbury Pk**	24
NEW Neil's Original Oyster	**Highlands**	–
NEW Phillips Seafood	**A.C.**	–
P.J. Whelihan's	**Medford Lakes**	17
Plantation	**Harvey Cedars**	19
Porto Leggero	**Jersey City**	23
☑ Rat's	**Hamilton**	24
Red	**Red Bank**	20
Restaurant Latour	**Hamburg**	–
Robin's Nest	**Mt Holly**	22
Rooney's	**Long Branch**	18
☑ Saddle River Inn	**Saddle R.**	27
Sallee Tee's	**Monmouth Bch**	21
Ship Inn	**Milford**	19
Smithville Inn	**Smithville**	18
NEW Sonsie	**A.C.**	–
3 Forty Grill	**Hoboken**	21
Tisha's	**Cape May**	25
Tuckers	**Beach Haven**	18
☑ Union Park	**Cape May**	26
Ventura's	**Margate**	17
Walpack Inn	**Wallpack**	19
Windansea	**Highlands**	20
☑ Zoe's	**Sparta**	26

SPECIAL FEATURES

Liberty House	**Jersey City**	20	☑ Manor	**W Orange**	23
Lilly's on Canal	**Lambertville**	21	Mediterra	**Princeton**	20
Lua	**Hoboken**	22	Mia	**A.C.**	26
Matisse	**Belmar**	22	Napa Valley	**Paramus**	22
McLoone's	**multi. loc.**	17	☑ Nicholas	**Middletown**	29
Mill	**Spring Lake Hts**	20	☑ Ombra	**A.C.**	25
Molly Pitcher	**Red Bank**	22	☑ Park & Orchard		22
NEW Neil's Original Oyster	**Highlands**	–	**E Rutherford**	
☑ Peter Shields	**Cape May**	26	☑ Pluckemin Inn	**Bedminster**	25
Pronto Cena	**Newark**	22	☑ Rat's	**Hamilton**	24
☑ Rat's	**Hamilton**	24	Restaurant Latour	**Hamburg**	–
Red's Lobster	**Pt. Pleas. Bch**	24	Salt Creek	**Rumson**	20
Robin's Nest	**Mt Holly**	22	☑ Scalini Fedeli	**Chatham**	27
Rooney's	**Long Branch**	18	NEW ☑ SeaBlue	**A.C.**	27
Sallee Tee's	**Monmouth Bch**	21	☑ Serenade	**Chatham**	27
NEW ☑ Sirena	**Long Branch**	23	Specchio	**A.C.**	25
3 Forty Grill	**Hoboken**	21	Stage House	**Scotch Plains**	23
Tisha's	**Cape May**	25	☑ Stage Left	**New Bruns.**	26
Tuckers	**Beach Haven**	18	☑ 3 west	**Basking Ridge**	23
☑ Union Park	**Cape May**	26	Tre Figlio	**Egg Harbor**	24
Ventura's	**Margate**	17	Tre Piani	**Plainsboro**	21
Windansea	**Highlands**	20	Two If By Sea	**Red Bank**	22
☑ Zoe's	**Sparta**	26	☑ Washington Inn	**Cape May**	26
			NEW Wolfgang Puck	**A.C.**	23

WINNING WINE LISTS

Beau Rivage	**Medford**	22
☑ Bernards Inn	**Bernardsville**	26
Berta's Chateau	**Wanaque**	22
☑ Black Forest Inn	**Stanhope**	23
NEW Bobby Flay Steak	**A.C.**	24
Brass Rail	**Hoboken**	19
NEW ☑ Catherine Lombardi	**New Bruns.**	21
☑ Chakra	**Paramus**	21
Chengdu 46	**Clifton**	24
Court Street	**Hoboken**	21
Crab's Claw	**Lavallette**	17
☑ Cucharamama	**Hoboken**	26
NEW ☑ David Burke	**Rumson**	26
☑ David Drake	**Rahway**	27
Doris & Ed's	**Highlands**	25
Esty Street	**Park Ridge**	23
☑ Frog & Peach	**New Bruns.**	26
Harvest Moon	**Ringoes**	24
NEW Kitchen 233	**Westmont**	22
Le Petit Chateau	**Bernardsville**	25

WORTH A TRIP

Atlantic City	
Dock's Oyster	26
NEW ☑ SeaBlue	27
☑ White House	27
Basking Ridge	
☑ 3 west	23
Bedminster	
☑ Pluckemin Inn	25
Bernardsville	
☑ Bernards Inn	26
Brant Beach	
NEW daddy O	18
Cape May	
☑ Ebbitt Room	27
☑ 410 Bank St.	27
Frescos	24
☑ Peter Shields	26
Chatham	
☑ Scalini Fedeli	27
☑ Serenade	27

SPECIAL FEATURES

Wine Vintage Chart

This chart, based on our 0 to 30 scale, is designed to help you select wine. The ratings (by **Howard Stravitz,** a law professor at the University of South Carolina) reflect the vintage quality and the wine's readiness to drink. We exclude the 1987, 1991–1993 vintages because they are not that good. A dash indicates the wine is either past its peak or too young to rate.

Whites	86	88	89	90	94	95	96	97	98	99	00	01	02	03	04	05
French:																
Alsace	–	–	26	26	25	24	24	23	26	24	26	27	25	22	24	25
Burgundy	25	–	23	22	–	28	27	24	23	26	25	24	27	23	25	26
Loire Valley	–	–	–	–	–	–	–	–	–	–	24	25	26	23	24	25
Champagne	25	24	26	29	–	26	27	24	23	24	24	22	26	–	–	–
Sauternes	28	29	25	28	–	21	23	25	23	24	24	28	25	26	21	26
California:																
Chardonnay	–	–	–	–	–	–	–	–	–	24	23	26	26	27	28	29
Sauvignon Blanc	–	–	–	–	–	–	–	–	–	–	–	27	28	26	27	26
Austrian:																
Grüner Velt./Riesling	–	–	–	–	–	25	21	28	28	27	22	23	24	26	26	26
German:	–	25	26	27	24	23	26	25	26	23	21	29	27	25	26	26

Reds	86	88	89	90	94	95	96	97	98	99	00	01	02	03	04	05
French:																
Bordeaux	25	23	25	29	22	26	25	23	25	24	29	26	24	25	23	27
Burgundy	–	–	24	26	–	26	27	26	22	27	22	24	27	24	24	25
Rhône	–	26	28	28	24	26	22	24	27	26	27	26	–	25	24	–
Beaujolais	–	–	–	–	–	–	–	–	–	–	24	–	23	27	23	28
California:																
Cab./Merlot	–	–	–	28	29	27	25	28	23	26	22	27	26	25	24	24
Pinot Noir	–	–	–	–	–	–	–	24	23	24	23	27	28	26	23	–
Zinfandel	–	–	–	–	–	–	–	–	–	–	25	23	27	22	–	–
Oregon:																
Pinot Noir	–	–	–	–	–	–	–	–	–	–	–	26	27	24	25	–
Italian:																
Tuscany	–	–	–	25	22	24	20	29	24	27	24	26	20	–	–	–
Piedmont	–	–	27	27	–	23	26	27	26	25	28	27	20	–	–	–
Spanish:																
Rioja	–	–	–	–	26	26	24	25	22	25	24	27	20	24	25	–
Ribera del Duero/Priorat	–	–	–	–	26	26	27	25	24	25	24	27	20	24	26	–
Australian:																
Shiraz/Cab.	–	–	–	–	24	26	23	26	28	24	24	27	27	25	26	–

subscribe to zagat.com